ENVIRONMENTAL POLICIES IN THE THIRD WORLD

Recent Titles in
Contributions in Political Science

ENVIRONMENTAL POLICIES IN THE THIRD WORLD

A Comparative Analysis

Edited by
O. P. Dwivedi and Dhirendra K. Vajpeyi

Contributions in Political Science,
Number 350

Greenwood Press
Westport, Connecticut

HC
59.72
E5
E623
1995

Library of Congress Cataloging-in-Publication Data

Environmental policies in the third world : a comparative analysis /
  edited by O. P. Dwivedi and Dhirendra K. Vajpeyi.
    p. cm. — (Contributions in political science, ISSN 0147–1066;
    no. 350)
    Includes bibliographical references and index.
    ISBN 0–313–29397–X (alk. paper)
    1. Environmental policy—Developing countries—Cross-cultural
  studies.   2. Developing countries—Economic policy—Cross-cultural
  studies.   3. Economic development—Environmental aspects—Cross-
  cultural studies.   I. Dwivedi, O. P.   II. Vajpeyi, Dhirendra K.
  III. Series.
  HC59.72.E5E623   1995
  333.7'09172'4—dc20   94–27948

British Library Cataloguing in Publication Data is available.

Library of Congress Catalog Card Number: 94–27948
ISBN: 0–313–29397–X
ISSN: 0147–1066

First published in 1995

Greenwood Press, 88 Post Road West, Westport, CT 06881
An imprint of Greenwood Publishing Group, Inc.

Printed in the United States of America

The paper used in this book complies with the
Permanent Paper Standard issued by the National
Information Standards Organization (Z39.48—1984).

10 9 8 7 6 5 4 3 2 1

Contents

Figures and Table

FIGURES

TABLE

Preface

It is not easy to generalize about the nature of politics and political institutions in so vast and variegated an arena as the Third World.[1] The countries in this area differ from one another in their levels of social evolution, political and economic development, technological change, and issues and problems related to environment. Common among these countries, however, are (1) low economic development, (2) the need to improve the quality of life of millions of impoverished people, and (3) environmental degradation. No discussion of sustainable economic development is complete without considering the interrelatedness of these three. They interact and impact each other and are attracting increasing attention and concern among policymakers locally, nationally, and internationally.

The rise of concern and consciousness about environmental issues in the Third World countries can be understood only in the broader context of international movement in general and the domestic impulses that drive policy formulations related to economic development in particular. These countries are faced with meeting the twin goals of economic and environmental development. They do not have the luxury to choose one over the other. The policy choices to accomplish both are not easy. Environmental decay resulting from population explosion, urban degradation, tropical deforestation, ozone depletion, and hazardous waste disposal is real, but so is the need for sustaining basic needs of day-to-day life. Their dilemma and frustration is oftentimes expressed in their policy stands taken at various international forums. Hence, there is a North–South dimension to the global environmental issues. Since the Stockholm Conference in 1972, there have persisted serious differences between the rich industrialized (North) and the poor developing (South) countries on both the nature of the issues and problems and the means and ways to tackle them. At the Earth Summit in Rio (June 1992) these differences surfaced and arrayed the countries of the South and the North in general (and the United States in particular) against one other. Who is to be blamed for the environmental mess? Who should pay for the cleanup, and how should it be cleaned up?

To narrow down these differences, the countries of both the North and the South have to eschew the politics of confrontation. The developing countries have to realize the seriousness of environmental degradation and accept their responsibilities in solving these problems. The advanced industrialized nations, on the other hand, are to provide not only moral and political leadership but also environmentally friendly technology and financial means to help clean up the global mess they have been partly responsible for creating. Both have to make hard policy choices and rise above their parochial short-term interests. It is the only way to see a new beginning for an international order as we enter the twenty-first century. A new international order cannot be hegemonic. It must accommodate all interests and concerns. At the Rio Earth Summit, it became very clear that global environmental politics has entered a new stage in which political stakes for industrialized and developing countries alike have increased.

This book presents the perspectives and concerns of the Third World nations as they prepare themselves to fight the environmental problems. Nine contributions have been especially prepared for this volume to analyze the institutional setting of the environmental policymaking process in major Third World nations with emphasis on political, administrative, and external factors influencing the decision making.

The introductory chapter, *Sustainable Development: Linking Global Environmental Change to Technology Cooperation* by Dieter Koenig discusses the paradigm shift in development theory and practice over the last decade since environment became a vital factor in determining long-term economic sustainability and the survival of humanity. The chapter analyzes conflicting policy agendas and perceptions between North and South, assesses the cross-national responses and new ways of international cooperation (in particular, the Earth Summit of 1992), and links the pursuit of sustainability to the critical issue of technology cooperation as a key element in responding to the dual challenge of underdevelopment and global environmental change.

Dhirendra K. Vajpeyi's chapter, *External Factors Influencing Environmental Policymaking: Role of Multilateral Development Aid Agencies*, analyzes the role of the major multilateral aid agencies—the World Bank, International Monetary Fund (IMF), regional banks, and the United Nations—in shaping and influencing ecological policy formulation in the Third World.

In the third chapter, *India's Environmental Policy, Programs, and Politics,* O. P. Dwivedi and Renu Khator review the emergence of environmental concern in India vis-à-vis the issue of poverty removal and development of national environmental policy strategy since 1972. The chapter also reviews the effectiveness of various environmental laws passed by the Indian Parliament, policy instruments used, and the institutional support mechanism created to give effect to federal strategy for environmental protection.

The fourth chapter, *Environmental Protection in China,* by George P. Jan, examines the policy and management of environmental protection with special emphasis on the reform period since the late 1970s under the leadership of Deng Xiaoping. The chapter deals with the environmental policy formulation process, major laws and regulations, governmental machinery, means of enforcement, an assessment of success and failures, and lessons from the Chinese experience.

In the fifth chapter, *Protecting the Environment in Indonesia: Policies and Programs,* Robert Boardman and Timothy M. Shaw explore the evolution of the national legal and regulatory framework of the environmental policy process in Indonesia and assess the progress made to date. They also discuss the character of the environmental problems faced by Indonesia, the context of economic development planning within which environmental policy goals are formulated, the scope of environmental legislation and institution building, and the achievements and constraints.

In Chapter 6, *Environmental Problems, Policies, and Prospects in Africa: A Continental Overview,* Peter J. Stoett argues that the political causes of environmental problems must be analyzed from global, continental, national, and local perspectives and that policy responses to these problems are conditioned by past political factors. The author notes that there is an immediate need for each African country to prepare its respective national environmental policy framework and provide legal mechanisms to handle environmental issues generated by the perceived need of foreign investment, industrial growth, and agribusiness. The chapter concludes that the sustainable answers to Africa's many ecological crises will be found not on the global or regional basis but at the national and local levels.

Chapter 7, *Nigeria's Environment: Crises, Consequences, and Responses,* by Pita Ogaba Agbese, is a case study of Nigeria's environmental crisis and the policies of the Nigerian government, particularly the federal government policies and responses to oil spills. The author contends that Nigeria's total dependence on foreign oil companies makes it very difficult for it to properly regulate the environmental hazards created by these companies and the ineffectiveness of government to help the victims, such as farmers and fishermen, of the reckless pollution of their environment on which their livelihood depends.

In Chapter 8, *Environmental Policy and Politics in Chile: A Latin-American Case Study,* Jorge Nef explores the basic environmental problems that have characterized Chilean development strategies, the nature of their articulation by diverse social policymakers, composition of alliance groups, and the means deployed by these groups to influence environmental policies.

Janetti-Díaz, Hernández-Quezada, and DeWaard, in Chapter 9, *National Environmental Policy and Programs in Mexico*, analyze some of the crucial elements of the Mexican national policy on environment in general and the recent policy initiatives taken by President Carlos Salinas de Gortari in particular. They also discuss the role of nongovernmental organizations (NGOs) in policy formulation, the impact of the North American Free Trade Agreement (NAFTA) on both the Mexican economy and the environment in Mexico, the United States, and Canada.

The idea for this book began to take shape when the editors were organizing sessions on behalf of the Research Committee on Technology & Development (RC35) for the XV World Congress of the International Political Science Association held in Buenos Aires, Argentina, in July 1991. Based on the support received during the World Congress, we invited scholars to join our project. Their enthusiasm and timely support, especially in meeting our various deadlines and incorporating editorial suggestions, were most gratifying. We thank them. The editors do realize that the breadth and depth of the subject matter demanded a coverage with many more nations and regions than what this volume could offer.

In our collaborative venture, several persons were helpful and deserve our heartfelt thanks: Dr. Karan Singh (Delhi, India), B. D. Dua (Lethbridge University, Canada), P. S. Tewari (Madras University, India), K. D. Trivedi (Rajasthan University, India), and V. S. Wilson (Carleton University, Canada). At the University of Northern Iowa, we thank Dr. David Walker, Associate Dean of the Graduate College, for providing funding that helped during the final stages, and Dr. Nancy Marlin, Vice President and Provost, Academic Affairs, for creating a conducive environment for research and scholarship. In addition, Kate Bielenberg and Katie Jo Niess of the Political Science Department deserve our thanks for typing the earlier drafts of the manuscript. Special thanks to Jane Hunter for many hours of last-minute editing and to Steven Havercamp for careful and uncompensated research work.

NOTE

1. In this book, the following terms have been used interchangeably: Third World, developing nations, South, and underdeveloped countries. Authors realize that with the disintegration of the Soviet Union, and the Eastern Block countries (regarded as the Second World) the term Third World has lost its relevant connotation; however, the term is still used in the absence of a better replacement.

Chapter 1

Sustainable Development: Linking Global Environmental Change to Technology Cooperation

DIETER KOENIG

REINVENTING DEVELOPMENT: CHANGING PARADIGMS

Terminology reflects our vision of the world. Over the last decade this vision has changed dramatically: A paradigm shift took place from a model called *development* to one called *sustainability*. Looking back at the main literature reveals this remarkable transformation. The Brandt Commission reports—among the most influential development studies written in the late 1970s and early 1980s—reflected the agenda of that period. These reports focused on issues ranging from mobilizing necessary funds for development to improving Third World participation in international trade to food and energy deficits. Environmental degradation in the Third World was covered only marginally and not in its global context.[1] For most of the 1980s, ecology—even though already present in some ways—was seen as an "add-on" to development rather than a "build-in."[2] Five years later worsening economic conditions in the developing world and the unbearable debt crisis confirmed the importance of most issues raised by the Brandt reports. Yet, our perspective of these issues had changed dramatically: A paperback called *Our Common Future*, published in 1987, was soon on the desk of everyone working in areas related to development.[3] Although the

United Nations secretary general had asked Gro Harlem Brundtlandt to convene the World Commission on Environment and Development as early as December 1983, it was not until the publication of its report in 1987 that environmental thinking and the notion of sustainability emerged from a marginal aspect to become *the* mainstream paradigm of 1990s' development policy. It was one of those paradigm shifts evolving underneath the surface, visible to a few researchers, insiders, and activists; when it finally reached the mainstream political agenda, it did so with an impact on our vision of the world comparable somewhat to the political revolutions sweeping all over Eastern Europe around the same time. Indeed, the ecological revolution would not have had a chance for a true and complete breakthrough on the international policy agenda without those fundamental political changes in the five years after *Our Common Future* and the decade after the first Brandt report were published. Deideologization of international relations had finally opened the doors for the kind of political, economic, and technological cooperation necessary to pursue an ecologically sound development path. The impact of the report even surprised some of its authors: Sir Shridath S. Ramphal, a member of the world commission admitted his hesitation to accepting Mrs. Brundtlandt's invitation: "If the World wasn't ready for 'Brandt' on development," he had asked himself, "would it be ready for 'Brundtland' on environment?" "Now—barely five years later such hesitation would seem strange," he wrote in 1991.[4]

The road from Brandt to Brundtland—and further to Rio's Earth Summit—marked more than the introduction and acceptance of a new catchall term such as sustainability: The terminology changed our concept of development forever in adopting a model that goes far beyond conventional economic theory. While traditionally economic trends would determine political—and ecological—developments, we were now presented with an interlocked system in which environmental issues also shaped economic and political trends.[5] A definition of sustainability was provided as "development that meets the needs of the present without compromising the ability of future generations to meet their own needs."[6]

What was new about this? The environmental degradation of the Third World had been addressed before—there had been *The Limits to Growth*, the 1972 Stockholm Conference on the Human Environment and, since the 1970s, the United Nations Environment Program (UNEP). But, while definitely not the first study to address issues of global environmental change in a comprehensive manner or in a development context, the qualitative "step-up" of the Brundtland report was its ability to convey—convincingly—the vital links between the state of our natural environment and economic achievement and to establish the fact that one could not be sustained or guaranteed without the other. The recognition of the existence of "global commons" and the need for intergenerational equity that emerged from this discussion has since received broad acceptance.[7] Moreover, the report pointed out not only how environmental degradation in one part of the world could affect all of us, but also how poverty, injustice, environmental degradation and conflict interfered with this process in complex ways.

While there is not a single, commonly accepted definition of sustainability, the one introduced by the Brundtland report is the most frequently quoted. As "to sustain" means "to keep alive," the concept of sustainability is a response to the recognition that current policies are irrevocably undermining our resource base and present biodiversity. While sustainability is not a thoroughly defined concept yet—and certainly lacks an operational definition—the new terminology aims to integrate long-term ecological considerations into economic and development strategies. In doing so, it has become as much a global concern as a local one: The new concept links rural migration and urban decline, the impact of acid rain and hazardous waste in developed countries, and deforestation and soil erosion in developing countries. It also relates to the complex relationships among all of these. Furthermore, sustainability refers to both a natural system, the earth's ecology, and a social system, the world's economy. While the former is limited, the desires of the latter are infinite. Integrating the two systems in a single model is a difficult task. Lovelock made an attempt to do so by describing the earth as a natural, self-sustaining system and introducing to us the concept of "geophysiology." This approach, also termed the "GAIA model," suggests that "we are part of a quasi-living entity that has the capacity for global homeostasis."[8] The limits of what this system may be able to bear in terms of human action and economic or resource-intensive activity have been assessed by a recently published sequel to the controversial Club of Rome study of two decades ago, *The Limits to Growth*.[9] In this new study, *Beyond the Limits*, the authors introduce a terminological refinement into the discussion of sustainability, a distinction between a status called *growth* and one called *development*. *Growth* according to this definition means "to increase in size by the assimilation or accretion of materials" while *development* is defined as "expanding or realize potentialities and bringing to a fuller, better state."[10] While our economic system is trying to achieve growth, our earth system is finite and nongrowing. We have reached a point where our economy must adapt to a pattern of development compatible with the geophysiological capacities of planet Earth. According to the study, sustainability is a concept foreign to our dominating, growth-oriented economic theory. Human society has already "overshot" its capacities and now faces the choice between "correction" and "crash."[11] Even if we do not agree with Lovelock's concept of geophysiology or the Meadows's pessimistic economic projections, both contribute to our understanding of sustainability and the potential consequences of policies that are ecologically—and eventually economically—unsustainable.

While we still lack an operational definition of the new terminology, we do have a set of indicators useful in translating the theoretical concept into concrete objectives. These include *ecological indicators* to measure the biological and physical elements (such as desertification, soil erosion, climate changes, biological diversity), *economic indicators* to assess economic development (including sustainable use of resources through new ecological accounting practice), *social indicators* (social structures likely to produce sustainable or unsustainable behavior), *demographic indicators* (such as rural–urban migration), and *political indicators* measuring policies that either encourage or prevent sustainable action.[12] These indicators are already finding their way into new operational guidelines of international agencies but are only gradually doing so in political decision making or diplomatic negotiations. Thus, the United Nations Conference for Environment and Development (UNCED) was the first comprehensive and systematic attempt to develop an international policy agenda on the basis of such a broad set of interlocked indicators in a global negotiating framework. Yet it is a long way from an emerging paradigm to a new policy. Between a model and political action there is—inevitably—social reality. The harsh reality between the paradigm of sustainability and sustainable policies is marked by the parallel existence of underdevelopment in one part of the world and resource waste in another. The conditions in the developing countries for responding to the challenge of sustainability are thus fundamentally different from those in the North.

TOWARDS A NEW POLICY AGENDA: NORTH–SOUTH PERCEPTIONS

The paradigm shift in development theory and the new vision it represents already had a visible impact on policy at the national and international levels, the most notable of which were UNCED and the agreements reached at that summit. Yet, as Rio has also shown, there are considerable differences between developed and developing countries in view of how sustainability can be translated into policy. These conflicting perceptions have their basis in the undeniable inequalities between nations. Maurice Strong, the chairman of UNCED, realized this dilemma in pointing out "the gross imbalance that has been created by the concentration of economic growth in the industrialized countries and population growth in the developing countries, [requiring] fundamental changes in both our economic behavior and our international relations. . . . Effecting these changes peacefully and cooperatively is, without doubt, the principal challenge of our time."[13]

In the negotiating process leading to UNCED, some developing countries resented a perceived attempt to interfere in their national policies through new international regimes or environment-linked aid as a one-sided conditionality. Indeed, the term *sustainability* has almost exclusively been utilized with regard to the Third World development policies and international aid programs, whereas in fact economic development and unsustainable policies of the industrialized nations have been the primary cause for the worst forms of global environmental degradation resulting in the ozone hole, an increase in greenhouse gases, and global warming. In 1988, among the top ten countries for absolute greenhouse gas emissions, six (Soviet Union, Federal Republic of Germany, Japan, the United Kingdom, Italy, and the United States) were industrialized and four (China, Brazil, India, and Indonesia) were developing, but the ten leading countries (United States, Australia, Canada, Federal Republic of Germany, the United Kingdom, The Netherlands, Italy, France, Japan, and Spain) with regard to per capita greenhouse emissions, were exclusively from the North.[14] One-sidedness in blaming developing countries for their unsustainable forest and agricultural policies has led to legitimate criticism of the new environmental morale on the part of some developing countries.

While the call for sustainability may not be divided, the causes for ecological decline differ considerably between the industrialized and the developing world: "Environmental problems of the North are the result of overdevelopment, extravagant consumption of fossil fuels, and unrestrained demands for ever-larger quantities of goods and services," says Uner Kirdar of the United Nations Development Program, while in the South environmental degradation is "a product of poverty."[15] Consequently, affluent economies and developing countries have to react to environmental change in different ways. We have, in fact, a web of environmental policy agendas evolving in this process, a "Northern agenda" to address, for example, affluent lifestyles, high energy use, and discriminatory trade patterns, and a "Southern agenda" involving new population policies, land reform, and democratization of policies relevant to the environment. A third "global agenda" leading to international regimes and cooperation would be the cross-cutting element linking the "unsustainable development" (in the North) with the "unsustainable impoverishment" (in the South).[16] In other words, a sustainable policy framework on a global level will have to address overconsumption of resources in some parts of the world and lack of resources in another.

Linking Agendas for Sustainability

	The Development Agenda	The Ecological Agenda
Northern Agenda	Preservation of wealth, affluent lifestyles, and the welfare state	Preventing catastrophe (ozone-layer depletion, impact of greenhouse effect, and global warming)
Southern Agenda	Overcoming mass poverty and achieving a higher quality of life	Sustaining local environment (stop deforestation, soil erosion, and desertification)

What linking these agendas means has been drastically described by German ecologist Ernst von Weizsaecker: "If developing countries were successful in emulating these Northern countries' lifestyles, the worldwide destruction of resources would be dramatically accelerated, leading rapidly to global ecological collapse." As a consequence, von Weizsaecker suggests transforming the Northern model "in such a way that it can be adopted by less developed countries without destroying the Earth."[17] Similarly, Maurice Strong calls for lifestyles leading to "sophisticated modesty" in the industrialized world, thus enabling people of developing countries to achieve livelihoods that "do not undermine or destroy the environment on which their future depend(s)."[18]

A major concern expressed by developing countries is indeed that the North—having grown successfully through periods of heavy pollution itself—would now be imposing restrictions on them at a time when they are just ready to industrialize. Thus, they repeatedly reaffirmed their "right to develop" in United Nations declarations. Any adoption of regimes for the protection of the global environment should "support economic growth and development of the developing countries" according to a declaration by 41 developing nations prior to UNCED. Furthermore, according to the same declaration, such regimes should not prevent them from determining their own environment and development policies without discrimination or trade barriers. They explicitly rejected "interference in the internal affairs of the developing countries" or "any forms of conditionality in aid [and accused the North of having] overexploited the world's natural resources through unsustainable economic behavior thus causing damage to the global environment at the detriment of the developing countries."[19]

In this context, the utilization of tropical forests has become a particularly sensitive and exemplary issue, its logging being perceived by the industrialized countries as a major contribution to the global warming process. Some developing countries have vehemently opposed this view, asserting sovereignty over their logging rights as one of the few development opportunities available to them. The causes being different, the required responses to global environmental change differ substantially between the North and the South, having to address wasteful lifestyles on one side and the need to overcome poverty on the other side. Beyond this general notion, differences between regions and countries exist on a much more complex basis that can only be hinted at in this context.

In Asia, for example, the Newly Industrialized Countries (NICs) of the region have developed at the expense of severe environmental decline.[20] Thus, Taiwan faces one of the most serious cases of ecological degradation following a process of rapid industrialization. Air pollution throughout the island is a major health hazard.[21] China is suffering from air pollution, too, relying heavily on coal as a major energy source. "Rushing towards the future in a haze of smog and a swirl of poisoned waters, China pays

the price of rapid and untamed economic development,"says Tin
zine in an article entitled "The Poisoned Earth."[22] In the Korean F
sulphurous haze darkens the sky of Seoul. Elsewhere in the conti
South Asia, India is feeling the effect of mounting population press\
the environment parallel to "often ill-conceived and under-regulated industrialization."[23] Japan, on the other hand, having had a dismal environmental record of its economic recovery and growth after World War II, has
developed into an ecological model for the region by successfully managing to clean up its polluted air through strict emission controls and un-
matched energy efficiency.[24] Japan's experience is often cited because it
"demonstrated that environmental improvement is fully compatible with
high rates of economic performance and can indeed make a positive contribution to performance."[25]

African countries are particularly vulnerable to the effects of global climate change. Thus, a conference on African perspectives on climate change
concluded that global warming was occurring at a time when many of
Africa's economic and life-support systems were under stress from a number of internal and external pressures: "Most of the continent has experienced poor economic performance over the last three decades. Sub-Saharan
Africa is as poor today as it was 30 years ago," concluded the Nairobi Declaration on Climate Change finding the reasons in "low agricultural growth,
declining industrial output, poor export performance, rising debt and increasing environmental degradation."[26] Deforestation, land clearing, increases in energy demand, demographic issues in connection with resource
availability, and current production patterns are also among Africa's contribution to global environmental change.[27]

In Latin America, Amazonia has become a symbol for the different and
contradictory perceptions of the global environmental crisis, the North
thinking of it as an important regulator of the global climate, while several
Latin American countries like to see it as "a resource base for national and
regional development." Latin American scientists identified several causes
behind unsustainable utilization of the tropical rain forest: urban and rural
poverty, demography, international equity, and tensions between public and
private sectors.[28] Deforestation is a problem not only in the Amazon region
but in Central America and the Caribbean. At the same time, air pollution
creates a growing health hazard in urban centers such as Mexico City,
Santiago, and Sao Paulo. Population is a major factor affecting the ecology,
Latin America having one of the highest growth rates in the world.[29]

The economies, now in transition, of Eastern Europe have already experienced ecological catastrophe with far-reaching impact on their populations, as evidenced through widespread health hazards and a shorter life
expectancy than those in the Western industrialized world. Overall there
is "a picture of intense human suffering, premature death, and economic
decline."[30] The Aral Sea is dying at a frightening pace; in the Black Sea

many species are disappearing; and radioactive leaks from power plants are frequent throughout Eastern Europe. Moreover, inefficient and wasteful energy use continues to deprive the populations of more affluent lifestyles.

The different perceptions of sustainability between North and South may not easily be overcome: They represent basic and pressing needs of people. Yet, in all parts of the world, including Asia, Africa, Latin America, and Eastern Europe, people and institutions have begun to address the issues at stake—as some of the case studies in this volume show. On the part of developing countries, in spite of harsh social realities, a gradual change in attitude away from "development first and environment later" towards pragmatic bargaining can be observed.[31] At international forums such as UNCED the developing countries increasingly link agreements on international environmental governance to technology cooperation, debt reduction, and other forms of aid that enable them to pursue sustainable development patterns. This transformation is more important since only very recently— and very reluctantly on the part of established politicians and a broader population—have environmental awareness, ethics, and lawmaking been accepted in the industrialized countries themselves. While developing and least-developed countries may not be excused for repeating mistakes made by the North, they face a much harder challenge in meeting the new environmental *morale* given poor living conditions of their populations and the immediate task to prevent further erosion of their food and energy resources. Thus, a question of lifestyle options and temporary economic strains in one part of the world may be a matter of survival in another.

Our Common Future achieved the recognition that poverty and environmental degradation were reinforcing each other and that none could be solved without the other. This requires a new quality of development. In the five years since the publication of the report, a series of concrete initiatives and changes has emerged at national and international levels to address the "development–environment" dilemma. The World Bank, for example, now has—after much pressure from negative media attention— a visible environmental department and seems to have initiated a transition from symbolic action to credible policy changes. Thus, the 1992 *World Development Report* was entirely dedicated to "Development and the Environment," while the 1991 report hardly mentioned it.[32] The signs from the bank are still contradictory, though the appointment of Mohammed T. El-Ashri, a senior researcher from the World Resources Institute, to the position of head of the bank's Environmental Department and chairman of the Global Environmental Facility could be interpreted as an indicator of policy change. On the other hand, it is no secret that the concept of sustainability and its integration into economic analysis still meets considerable resentment among the senior management. Throughout the world, the paradigm shift had an impact on governmental, nongovernmental, and private institutions.[33] Environmental issues are gradually moving to the center stage of political and public debate. The fundamental transformations under way on a global scale are forcing us to rethink the categories, models, and strategies that guide development and social change. Sustainable development will happen in an economic, political, social, and cultural environment. Poverty and environmental degradation are closely linked. So are external indebtedness and unfair terms of trade. "The recognition ... of the need for an ecologically-sustainable vision is growing very fast indeed," observes Stephen Hill. "But the sense of inequity that accompanies this vision follows closely behind."[34]

FROM TRANSFER TO COOPERATION: THE NEW ROLE OF TECHNOLOGY

In the complex relationship between development and environment, technology provides a link between human action and nature. As we face the multiple challenge of fulfilling the needs of a South that has no choice but to develop, a North that is unlikely to fundamentally cut down on its current consumption patterns, and a limited ecological resource base, a key issue in achieving sustainability will be the application of new low-resource, environmentally friendly technologies.[35] This should not suggest an "engineering solution" or "technological fix": Technological innovation is important for both environment and development, but it is not sufficient in providing adequate responses to deep-rooted social causes of the environmental catastrophe.[36] Furthermore, technology cannot compensate for shortcomings in the process of political decision making or for mismanagement. But in combination with social changes, land reforms, a more balanced and fair trade pattern between North and South, and effective, enforceable regimes for environmental protection on national and international levels, it will undoubtedly be a key factor.

We are dealing with a paradox though: Many of the environmental problems confronting us have been caused by technological progress since the Industrial Revolution. Now we need technological innovation to reverse this trend.[37] A growing world population, along with the aspirations of many people in the developing world, have created "realities that leave technological transformation as the primary strategy for avoiding environmental degradation," concluded researchers of the World Resources Institute. Technological transformation as "widespread, continuing development and adoption of ever less polluting and more resource-efficient products and services" would be able to contribute most to the expansion of wealth and productivity, holding the key to environmental sustainability as well, according to the same study.[38]

UNCED brought about a second paradigm shift in our approach to development: the substitution of the concept of "technology transfer" by the notion of "technology cooperation."[39] Behind this new terminology lies more than a rhetorical gesture. It explicitly shifts the one-sided and ill-fated concept of "transfer"—which has often been associated with the ubiquitous "development ruins" in Third World countries—to a more interactive process of exchanging technologies and resources, adapting them to local needs and capabilities or applying them in the creation of new products. Technology cooperation is a two-way street; technology transfer was not.

Many developing countries possess the natural, genetic, and biological resources needed by developed countries; thus, tropical forests with their biodiversity contain an enormous reservoir for new pharmaceuticals. Making more of these resources in exercising sovereignty over them in exchange for the provision of environmentally sound technologies will be an important asset on the part of the developing world.[40] During the negotiations leading to UNCED's biodiversity treaty, developing countries, such as Brazil, China, and India, emphasized their need for access to biotechnologies to exploit their biological resources on "preferential and non-commercial terms."[41] Biotechnology is given particular attention by developing countries because it promises not only to lead to new and improved varieties, integrated pest control, and plants resistant to difficult environmental conditions but also to promote a second green revolution.

Other new technologies offer the potential to assist in the process of economic development, to achieve environmental optimization, and to conserve the resource base. Thus, the continuing process of dematerialization—the substitution of traditional high-input materials by new low-input metal alloys, high-performance plastics, ceramics, and composites—is an important step on this way. However, dematerialization also threatens some developing countries' export prospects through product substitution. Furthermore, capacity and institution building for the assessment, choice, and management of new energy-saving and environmentally sound technologies will be among the necessary elements of technology cooperation. Most developing countries do not have the funds, manpower, or infrastructure to pursue a sustainable development path on their own. A qualitatively higher level of cooperation than traditional technology transfer through cooperative programs and projects, integration of local technologies and suppliers, and raising the engineering ability to translate both national and international research into technology application and production will be essential in this process. This may be accompanied by a variety of measures, particularly combining investments in technology, infrastructure, and new equipment that would necessarily have to be made available by the North. Improving energy efficiency on a broad scale would be another step, while a pricing and tax system reflecting the ecological costs of fossil fuels and other natural resources could stimulate the transition from waste to high-efficiency societies and lifestyles.[42]

The growing innovative capability creates a framework of choice to mankind unprecedented in history. However, sustainable development through technology cooperation will depend largely on political willingness at the international level to pursue the new environmental agenda and to cooperate in this respect beyond national concern for patents and competitiveness. First steps in developing new ways for technology cooperation have been made through the establishment, for example, of the Global Environmental Facility (GEF), located at the World Bank in Washington, and through UNEP's International Environmental Technology Center in Osaka and Shiga, Japan. The former is giving priorities to projects related to greenhouse warming, namely, technologies likely to reduce emissions at the lowest cost—both promising but unproven technologies and proven technologies with potential for widespread use. Priority for support was given to projects on end-use efficiency, reduction in emissions, intensity of energy production, non–carbon dioxide emissions reductions, and generic areas such as the slowing of deforestation.[43] The latter is currently being established to provide training and consulting services, to carry out research, and to disseminate related information to developing countries and the economies in transition of Eastern Europe. A particular focus will be technologies serving environmental protection measures for urban areas and fresh water resources.[44] In addition, the United Nations Development Program (UNDP) announced another pilot project, Capacity 21, to support capacity building of developing countries in environmental management. While the GEF gives priorities to projects benefiting the global environment and covered by global conventions, Capacity 21 aims at building local abilities and supporting programs not covered under conventions. Both the GEF and Capacity 21 will have considerable funding abilities and will be addressing broader agendas; the UNEP initiative will operate on a more modest basis and serve specialized needs. Technology cooperation will be a key element of the GEF and UNEP programs, while Capacity 21 will relate to its framework in developing countries' abilities.

Technology cooperation cannot be understood narrowly; it covers a broad range of products, services, and communication, including education and training for technologists specialized in environmentally sound technologies and processes and familiarity with and consideration for local conditions and cultures.[45] The "Agenda 21" presented at the Rio summit reflects the complex relationships within the triangle of environment, development, and technology by incorporating a variety of factors: access to and transfer of environmentally sound technologies; capacity building for technology management (including policy); human resource development; the role of data and information; technology assessment, acquisition, dissemination, and generation; and necessary research requirements and needs. However, technology cooperation faces a number of constraints that remained unresolved at UNCED. The refusal of a major member of the United Nations to sign the biodiversity treaty agreed upon by the conference was symptomatic of one of these difficulties—the concern for property rights and the adequate protection of patents. While the environment is predominantly a public, and increasingly an international public-sector affair, technology is basically a private-sector commodity. Thus, the complexity of technology cooperation is not easily overcome by simple policy formula or agreements between governments. As a consequence, technology too frequently proved to be, as Mikoto Usui noted, "a non-issue, or at best, too fragmented a problem for meaningful negotiations."[46] Other constraints are found at the opposite end of commercial relations in the form of trade barriers blocking developing countries from markets needed to finance a sustainable path to national development.

UNCED's Business Council for Sustainable Development, itself consisting of industrial leaders from throughout the world, stressed a strong involvement of the private sector in creating partnerships and strategic alliances for the widespread dissemination of environmentally sound technology. The frequent failure of government-guided technology transfers in the past through central organizations such as development aid organizations is based—according to the Council—on the fact that governments have to serve a multitude of conflicting interests all at the same time, leading to the neglect of needs and conditions of people in developing countries. Private technology cooperation based on the business principle of achieving mutual benefits for all parties involved would—on the other hand—be more flexible and more likely to be concerned with real needs.[47] While this belief will certainly find its critics too, the fact that business leaders of the world do seriously look for new ways of technology cooperation with developing countries in the interest of global environmental security is in itself a major step forward.

A new model of collaboration is already being tried through the Vienna Convention and Montreal protocol to protect the ozone layer, in particular, its amendments with concrete provisions for cooperation in providing clean technologies. In assisting developing countries in the process of acquiring, introducing, and adapting technologies replacing chlorofluorocarbons (CFCs), the agreement sets an example for other areas of cooperation as a critical "test case for the much broader issues of technology cooperation" according to the World Resources Institute. "If the sharply focused problem of affordable CFC alternatives for the developing world cannot be solved," the Institute concludes in a study, "there may be little hope of resolving the much thornier problems of providing energy-efficient technology to developing countries to minimize future carbon emissions."[48] So far 70 nations—representing over 90 percent of global CFC production and consumption—have signed the CFC convention, among them 30 developing countries, with others remaining skeptical about it. In responding to developing countries' concerns, a special fund, financed by the largest CFC users, was established to compensate them for increased costs needed to acquire the CFC substitutes. Proprietary rights continue to be a problem in the CFC area; and confronted with international chemical manufacturers reluctant to dispose of rights and patents that have required high research and development (R&D) expenses, the multilateral fund may be used to purchase those rights and to pay royalties.

In the meantime, other initiatives have emerged to share the burden of cleaning up and preserving the environment: Five Nordic countries established the Nordic Environment Finance Corporation to raise risk capital for environmentally sustainable investments in central and eastern Europe, largely because these regions are the source of acid rain from which Scandinavia is suffering. In Japan, similar initiatives are targeting coal-burning power plants in China.[49] Many environmentally sound technology alternatives, not only in the CFC area, are already available. Their introduction into the marketplace, both in the North and in the South, requires a political will that is only gradually emerging, as well as strategic alliances between governments, scientists, and the private sector. Von Weizsaecker observes in this context that "the distance to resource-efficient technology and culture may be much shorter for developing countries than for industrialized countries that are handicapped by wasteful habits and clumsy infrastructures."[50] Water, energy, and land use, for example, are less wasteful in India and Egypt than in the United States.

A comprehensive and interesting initiative—including new approaches to technology cooperation—has been proposed by American Vice President Al Gore who calls for a new plan requiring the wealthy nations to allocate funds for transferring environmentally sound technologies to the Third World in order to help impoverished nations achieve sustainable economic progress.[51] A particular function would be given to the United Nations through a new Stewardship Council with a role similar to the one carried out by the Security Council in matters of peace. Gore's proposal provides a catalog of concrete steps and measurements, including the strategic goal of achieving a rapid creation and development of environmentally appropriate technologies in the fields of energy, transportation, agriculture, building construction, and manufacturing to substitute for ecologically destructive technologies currently in place. Not without irony he proposes a Strategic Environment Initiative (SEI) borrowing from the terminology of a heavily funded arms development program of the 1980s, the Strategic Defense Initiative. The SEI, aiming at developing and disseminating a new generation of sophisticated and environmentally sound substitutes for older, inappropriate technologies, would involve a series of steps and measurements, including tax incentives, R&D funding, government purchasing programs, the establishment of training centers, export controls, law revisions, and new patent and copyright protection. Specific problems covered by this initiative include new technologies in agriculture (such as refinements in irrigation technology, new techniques for low-input crop technologies, advances in plant genetics, crop rotation, new discoveries in agricultural and fishing

techniques, and more sophisticated techniques of food production); forestry (for example, planting trees on a large scale); energy (reducing carbon dioxide); and building technology (better designs for reducing energy
consumption), as well as waste reduction and recycling. Beyond the issue
of environmentally sound technologies, the proposal covers population, new
ways of ecological accounting in the economy, new international agreements,
education and training, and the need to establish social and political conditions most conducive to the emergence of sustainable societies. In terms of
technology cooperation and policy, these proposals go beyond the agreements
achieved at UNCED and provide some of the missing concrete targets that
UNCED could not agree upon.

The dynamics of technological change should be such that there will not
be one technology for the developed world and one for the developing,
but global technologies coexisting with traditional ones in many parts of
the world. In the area of environmentally sound technologies, international
cooperation will be necessary on a much larger scale than ever before. This
will have to include strengthening the capacities of developing countries
to assess and choose technologies on the basis of their own needs and to
adapt them to specific local conditions. The new role of technology will be
an essential factor in the path towards sustainability.

UNCED: BREAKTHROUGH
OR POLITICS AS SYMBOLIC ACTION?

"No single meeting can change the world," wrote Fred Pearce in the
New Scientist a week before the Earth Summit was to start.[52] Nevertheless,
UNCED did change the world, if only our vision of it. Contrary to the
initial reaction it received, UNCED was a success. True, it neither met all
the demands—let alone needs—of the developing world, nor did it achieve
agreement on the concrete targets some countries and nongovernmental
organizations had hoped and lobbied for. But it did represent an irreversible transformation of the world that would have been unthinkable only
half a decade earlier. The negotiating process toward the conference and at
the summit itself reflected the differences between North and South and
their respective agendas. There were frustrations, there was anger, a threat
by individual governments to boycott the conference altogether; but in the
end there was the most comprehensive international agenda ever passed
for both development and environment. The shortcomings of this agenda
and of the treaties negotiated in Rio are obvious, but they have "hidden
teeth that will develop in the right circumstances" as one observer put it.[53]
The twelve-day event was the largest gathering ever of heads of states,
delegates from over 170 nations, nongovernmental organizations, representatives of indigenous people, and the media. "No conference has ever
faced the need to make such an important range of decisions," Maurice

Strong had written a year earlier, "decisions that will virtually determine the face of the earth."[54] After two weeks of negotiations, the summit adopted five major documents: the "Rio Declaration on Environment and Development," which contains 27 principles pertaining to the integrative relationship of environment and development; Agenda 21, which is commonly referred to as a "blueprint" in the area of sustainable development and which constitutes the specific program of action for the implementation of the principles enunciated in the "Rio Declaration" (covering 40 topics and over 100 programs); "The Framework Convention on Climate Change," aiming at combating the greenhouse effect and global warming; "The Convention on Biological Diversity," concerned with the conservation of the Earth's species; and "A Statement of Principles on Forests," focusing on both the environmental and economic aspects of forests.[55]

These agreements represent an attempt to consolidate contrasting positions held by developing and developed nations, the former emphasizing their "right to development" and the latter aiming at imposing equal obligations regarding the global environment on all nations. The five principal documents emerging from the Earth Summit had to reconcile these conflicting positions: Thus, the "Rio Declaration" is a nonbinding statement of broad principles to guide environmental policy, vaguely committing its signatories not to damage the environment of other nations by activities within their borders and to acknowledge environmental protection as an integral part of development. To carry out the pledge of the declaration, an 800-page, nonbinding action program, Agenda 21, was adopted. The agenda includes several provisions for technology cooperation in access to and transfer of environmentally sound technology, R&D in this area, and capacity building for technology management. This issue is also covered by the declaration itself in calling for cooperation among states in strengthening endogenous capacity building for sustainable development through exchange of scientific and technological knowledge, as well as adaptation, diffusion, and transfer of technologies.

The "Global Warming Convention," by contrast, is a legally binding treaty recommending the curbing of emissions of carbon dioxide, methane, and other greenhouse gases likely to increase global warming. However, as a result of opposition from major countries, it lacks concrete targets. The treaty calls for the setup of mechanisms to assist developing countries in minimizing their greenhouse gas emissions. The "Biodiversity Convention" is likewise a legally binding treaty requiring signatories to protect plants and wildlife within their borders. It also requests the establishment of mechanisms to assist developing countries in this respect. A major point of conflict that prevented the United States from signing this treaty was its obligation for countries using the genetic resources of any nation to share the research, profits, and technology resulting from the original material with that nation.

The"Statement on Forest Principles" is a nonbinding, seventeen-point document aiming at forest protection and international cooperation in this respect. A legally binding convention is to follow at a later stage.

Some observers and nongovernmental organizations left Rio with the conviction that these agreements were completely insufficient as a response to global environmental change. But only half a decade earlier the idea of global leaders agreeing to anything close to the steps listed here would have seemed completely unrealistic. Therefore, the summit succeeded not only in focusing the attention of the world on global environmental change and its causes but in initiating the first steps of a global effort to combat the earth's ecological destruction. The results of UNCED will stay with us, and we will not be able to ignore them.

Where will UNCED lead us? I imagine two possible scenarios: The first one, based on past experience, I call the "Vienna scenario." In August 1979, the United Nations convened the "Conference on Science and Technology for Development" (UNCSTD) in Vienna. Like UNCED, UNCSTD was held upon a decision by its General Assembly and was attended by high-level delegations. It involved several years of preparation, lengthy and tiresome preparatory committee sessions, a forum of nongovernmental organizations, and the participation of the business community. The developing countries had very specific ideas about their needs in a new scientific and technological world order, and the developed countries felt very strongly about their opposition to some of these proposals. Still, a compromise was found, funds were pledged, and institutional arrangements were made within the United Nations system, both for financing purposes and for policy measures. In the end, most of the pledges and promises made by the industrialized countries never materialized; and the conference and its ambitious "Vienna Program of Action" were quickly forgotten outside the small community of United Nations and development aid professionals directly concerned with its implementation.[56] The U.N. mechanisms established for the purpose of implementing the program struggled hard over the years to carry out their mandate in the absence of both funds and political willingness on the part of major industrialized countries. In the end, they were simply abolished as independent offices, and the Vienna Programme of Action remained largely unfulfilled.

UNCSTD was the last of the megaconferences held by the United Nations in the 1970s to address issues of a new economic world order. Science and technology and the Third World's equal access to them was considered an essential prerequisite for development. Like the Earth Summit, the Vienna Conference received considerable public attention and raised high hopes on the part of developing countries. Eventually it achieved nothing more than symbolic action on the part of the industrialized countries, which had rather grudgingly agreed to a compromise with the developing nations but never did much to see the program of action implemented. After the slashed hopes of Vienna, there never was to be a similar event again—so we thought.

Thirteen years later, though, the world was ready for another attempt, more ambitious than UNCSTD ever dared to be—UNCED. At first sight, the Rio Summit's similarities with UNCSTD are striking, if not frightening. Moreover, ironically, one of the key issues at Rio was taken from the unresolved agenda of Vienna: technology cooperation and the access of developing countries to the industrialized world's advanced technology. In spite of these similarities—including the frustrations many observers felt during and right after both conferences—I dare to conclude that my second scenario, which I will call the "Rio scenario," is different. Vienna was founded on the demands of the developing nations which the industrialized countries were neither prepared nor willing to meet. While they felt morally compelled to agree to its program of action, their lack of enthusiasm about it resulted in a lack of political and financial support.

Rio, on the other hand, had its roots in the concerns of the developed countries themselves, driven by the awareness that global environmental change would not come to a halt at the borderline between North and South. For a long time, people in the industrialized world were able to ignore the problems of the developing nations because they seemed irrelevant to their lives. This false notion of security no longer exists: Underdevelopment anywhere in the world will result—one way or another—in global climate change, and eventually everyone will be affected. This leads me to believe that sustainability is more than just the new buzzword of development theory and practice. The agenda of UNCED will succeed if we maintain the momentum of political will. The geopolitical situation has provided us with greater freedom of action on the international level than ever in the last fifty years. The East–West conflict, which had prevented global solutions to the challenges—from development to environment—for "too long," no longer exists. This allowed UNCED to happen; in the long run, it will increase the political leverage of the South.[57] Ecological interdependence has created a situation in which "even the most wealthy and powerful countries cannot shelter themselves from the consequences of change."[58] Thus, a world that was not ready for the Vienna Program of Action or for the consequences of the Brandt Commission reports a decade ago, may at last be ready for the Rio agreements.

Within the United Nations system, the impact of Rio goes far beyond that of Vienna. After Vienna, new small entities were established within the United Nations to implement its program of action. Rio led to programmatic and institutional changes throughout the system, affecting nearly every aspect of its work in one way or another. The new Commission for Sustainable Development within the U.N. Secretariat, Capacity 21, the Global Environmental Facility, and the initiatives by the United

Nations Environment Program are only the most visible and immediate reactions to a new paradigm that transcends the system and the world community as a whole. We have no time to lose. There are the long-term demands, such as the ozone hole and global warming; but there are also critical environmental zones and hot spots that require immediate action: the Aral Sea, which has been reduced by two-thirds of its size in only thirty years leading to climatic and environmental disaster around it; or Ethiopia, which is losing one billion tons of topsoil every year in a part of the world already plagued by hunger. Altogether 160 million acres of land south of the Sahara have been an object of decertification over the past fifty years. The heavy pollution of Silesia, Poland, affects peoples' life expectancies, while the deforestation in the Himalayas contributes to disastrous floods in Bangladesh.

While the developing countries undoubtedly possess most of those regions that need our immediate attention and are most severely affected by global environmental change, their role in the international community is likely to become stronger. Jim MacNeill, one of the principal authors of the Brundtland report, argues that previously economic interdependence represented dependence of the South on the North, while ecological interdependence will represent the reverse direction, thus altering power relations among nations.[59] This interdependence, combined with political will (usually "the scarcest resource"),[60] will remain the essential asset of Rio. Rio was not the last step, it was only the first political result of the paradigm shift from development to sustainability. Global environmental change will not go away. Eventually, both North and South will have to meet with reality: The North will have to face up to some redistribution of resources and wealth and the South to the need for population stability.[61] "The road from Rio will be longer and more challenging than the road to Rio," said Maurice Strong after everything was over, "we cannot afford to be complacent."[62]

NOTES

1. The Brandt Commission, *North–South: A Programme for Survival* (London: Pan Books, 1980); see also the Brandt Commission, *Common Crisis North–South: Cooperation for World Recovery* (London: Pan Books, 1983).

2. Jim MacNeill, Pieter Winsemius, and Taizo Yakushiji, *Beyond Interdependence* (New York: Oxford University Press, 1991), p. 29.

3. The World Commission on Environment and Development, *Our Common Future* (New York: Oxford University Press, 1987).

4. Sir Shridath S. Ramphal, "Endangered Earth," in *Sustaining Earth*, ed. David J. R. Angell (New York: St. Martin's Press, 1991), p. 3.

5. MacNeill et al., *Beyond Interdependence*, p. 52.

6. World Commission, *Our Common Future*, p. 43.

7. *In Fairness to Future Generations: International Law, Common Patrimony and*

Intergenerational Equity, ed. Edith Brown Weiss (New York: Transnational Publishers, 1988); see also *Global Environmental Change: New Dimensions in International Law and Institutions,* ed. E. Brown Weiss (Tokyo: United Nations University Press, 1993).

8. James Lovelock, "Geophysiology: A New Look at Earth Science," *The Geophysiology of Amazonia—Vegetation and Climate Interactions,* ed. Robert E. Dickinson (New York: John Wiley and Sons, 1987), p. 19.

9. Donella H. Meadows et al., *The Limits to Growth* (New York: Universe Books, 1972).

10. Donella H. Meadows, Dennis L. Meadows, and Jorgen Randers, *Beyond the Limits* (Post Mills, Vt.: Chelsea Green, 1992), p. xix.

11. Meadows et al., *Beyond the Limits,* pp. 1–13.

12. For a detailed analysis of these indicators see Peter Bartelmus, "Sustainable Development—A Conceptual Framework," Working Paper No. 13 (New York: United Nations Department of International Economic and Social Affairs, 1989); comparable criteria were introduced by Ignacy Sachs in several publications, for example: I. Sachs and Donna Silk, *Food and Energy—Strategies for Sustainable Development* (Tokyo: United Nations University Press, 1990).

13. Maurice F. Strong, statement, "The Background to and the Prospects for the 1992 Earth Summit," EcoAsia Conference, Tokyo, 1991.

14. World Resources Institute, *Environmental Almanac* (Boston: Houghton Mifflin Co., 1992), p. 276.

15. *Ecological Change: Environment, Development and Poverty Linkages,* ed. Uner Kirdar (New York: United Nations Publications, 1992), p. 5.

16. G. Gallopin, P. Gutman, and H. Maletta, "The Rich Get Richer," *Work in Progress* 12.1 (1989): 6.

17. Ernst Ulrich von Weizsaecker, "Sustainability: A Task for the North," *Journal of International Affairs* 44.2 (1991): 421–422.

18. Strong, *Background,* p. 9.

19. United Nations General Assembly, "Ministerial Declaration on Environment and Development," Document A/46/293 (adopted by the Ministers from 41 Developing Countries in Beijing, 1991).

20. World Resources Institute, *World Resources 1992–1993* (New York: Oxford University Press, 1992), p. 42.

21. *Far Eastern Economic Review* 19 Sept. 1991, p. 12.

22. Ibid., p. 13; "China—The Poisoned Earth," *Time* 29 April 1991, p. 27.

23. Ibid., p. 14.

24. Ministry of Foreign Affairs, *Economic Development and the Environment: The Japanese Experience* (Tokyo: 1992); cf. *Industrial Pollution in Japan,* ed. Jun Ui (Tokyo: United Nations University Press, 1992).

25. Maurice Strong, "Required Global Change: Close Linkages between Environment and Development," in *Ecological Change,* pp. 18–19.

26. African Centre for Technology Studies, "The Nairobi Declaration on Climate Change," International Conference on Global Warming and Climatic Change: African Perspectives, Nairobi, 2–4 May 1990.

27. *Francophone African Workshop on the Human Dimensions of Global Change* (Ottawa: Human Dimensions of Global Change Programme, 1990).

28. *A Common Understanding for a Common Future: Latin American Perspectives on Global Environmental Change,* Report of a Workshop, Caracas, Venezuela, Sept. 26–28, 1989 (Ottawa: Human Dimensions of Global Change Programme, 1989).

29. Enrique V. Iglesias, "The Delicate Balance between Environment and Development: The Latin American Experience," in *Ecological Change*, pp. 41–42.

30. MacNeill et al., *Beyond Interdependence*, p. 55.

31. Ibid., p. 30.

32. The World Bank, *World Development Report 1992: Development and the Environment* (New York: Oxford University Press, 1992); cf. The World Bank, *World Development Report 1991: The Challenge of Development* (New York: Oxford University Press, 1991).

33. Linda Starke, *Signs of Hope—Working towards Our Common Future* (New York: Oxford University Press, 1990).

34. Stephen Hill, "Visions of the 1990s—New Perspectives on Global Science and Technology Policy," 3rd International Conference on Science and Technology Policy Research, Oiso, Japan, 9–11 March 1992.

35. Guenter Kroeber, "Environmentally Sound Technology Assessment in the Context of Sustainable Development," in *Environmentally Sound Technology for Sustainable Development*, ed. Dirk Pilari (New York: United Nations Publications, ATAS Bulletin No. 7, 1992).

36. O. P. Dwivedi, "Political Science and the Environment," *International Social Science Journal* 109 (1986): 379.

37. Paul E. Gray, "The Paradox of Technological Development," in *Technology and Environment*, ed. Jesse H. Ausubel and Hedy E. Sladovic (Washington: National Academy Press, 1989).

38. George Heaton, Robert Repetto, and Rodney Sobin, *Transforming Technology: An Agenda for Environmentally Sound Technology in the 21st Century* (Washington: World Resources Institute, 1991), p. ix.

39. Stephan Schmidheiny, *Kurswechsel: Globale Unternehmerische Perspektiven fuer Entwicklung und Umwelt* (Munich: Artemis & Winkler, 1992).

40. Fred Pearson, "The Hidden Cost of Technology Transfer," *New Scientist* 9 May 1992, p. 27.

41. MacNeill et al., *Beyond Interdependence*, p. 62.

42. von Weizsaecker, "Sustainability," p. 422.

43. The World Bank, p. 176.

44. *The Earth Times*, Nov. 2–6, 1992.

45. *The Global Partnership for Environment and Development—A Guide to Agenda 21* (New York: United Nations Publications, 1992), pp. 112–113.

46. Mikoto Usui, "Creative Approaches to International Cooperation in Research and Technology Transfer," in *Environmentally Sound Technology*, pp. 236–237.

47. Schmidheiny, *Kurswechsel*, p. 168.

48. World Resources Institute, *World Resources 1992–1993—A Guide to the Global Environment* (Oxford: Oxford University Press, 1992), p. 152.

49. Schmidheiny, *Kurswechsel*, p. 173.

50. Ernst U. von Weizsaecker, "Environmental Policy and Taxation as Instruments of Technology Policy," in *Environmentally Sound Technology*, p. 261.

51. Al Gore, *Earth in the Balance—Ecology and the Human Spirit* (Boston: Houghton Mifflin, 1992), p. 295.

52. "Who Pays for the Earth?" *New Scientist* 30 May 1992, p. 13.

53. William K. Stevens, *Asahi Evening News* 16 June 1992.

54. Maurice Strong, Introduction, in MacNeill et al., *Beyond Interdependence*, pp. v–vi.

55. For all documents, see United Nations, "Report of the United Nations Conference on Environment and Development," United Nations Conference on Environment and Development (United Nations Document A/CONF.151/26, Preliminary version, five volumes, 1992).

56. United Nations, "The Vienna Programme of Action," Conference on Science and Technology for Development (New York: United Nations Document DSEI.E.73, 1979).

57. MacNeill et al., *Beyond Interdependence*, pp. 52–73.

58. Ibid., p. 72.

59. Ibid., pp. 72–73.

60. R. Goodland, H. Daly, and S. El Serafy, "The Urgent Need for Environmental Assessment and Environmental Accounting for Sustainability," 12th Annual Meeting of International Association for Impact Assessment, IAIA, Washington, D.C., 19–22 August 1992.

61. Ibid.

62. Maurice Strong, *Earth Summit Times* 7 July 1992, p. 13.

Chapter 2

External Factors Influencing Environmental Policymaking: Role of Multilateral Development Aid Agencies

DHIRENDRA K. VAJPEYI

> What good is a house if you don't have a decent planet to put it on.
> —Henry D. Thoreau

Under relentless economic and political pressures, the policymakers in the Third World are often in conflict with the ever-increasing demands to satisfy basic human needs—clean air, water, adequate food, shelter, education—and to safeguard the environmental quality. Given the scarce economic and technical resources at their disposal, most of these policymakers have ignored long-range environmental concerns and opted for short-range economic and political gains. Quite often they were influenced by domestic and external constraints. Frequently development projects undertaken to improve economic and natural resources were "the direct or indirect causes of environmental damage."[1] Smog-covered cities, acid rain, and thousands of tons of hazardous industrial waste in industrialized countries have become painful reminders of potential ecological and environmental apocalypse. It took almost two decades, Stockholm (1972) to Rio

(1992), of conscience-raising efforts by national and international policymakers to accept that the price of development has been unnecessarily high and that the payment has been made in the wrong way—through destructive exploitation of the natural and social environment."[2] By the late 1980s, major international actors—U.S. Agency for International Development (USAID), IMF, the World Bank, other regional banks, the Organization for Economic Cooperation and Development (OECD), the United Nations, and the national governments both in the industrialized West and the Third World gradually started to reevaluate their past policies and approaches related to environmental and economic development. This shift was partly due to domestic and international public opinion pressure and partly due to the realization that economic development, mainly measured in per capita income growth, without ecological development, does not contribute to the overall improvement of the quality of life and oftentimes results in imbalanced distribution and control of economic wealth. The following discussion analyzes the historic role of these aid-giving agencies in shaping and influencing ecological policy formulation in the Third World.

INTERNATIONAL AID INSTITUTIONS AND ENVIRONMENTAL ISSUES

As discussed in the introductory chapter of the book, today the concept of "sustainable development" is widely accepted as the mainstream of development policy objectives. Two types of economic actors or decision makers have played an increasingly important role in this process, regardless of their ideological and administrative perspectives. The first is the United Nations, and the second consists of the World Bank, the IMF, USAID, OECD, and regional banks such as the Inter-American Development Bank, Asian Development Bank, and African Development Bank.

The World Bank

The sheer size of the World Bank's commitment to economic growth of the less developed countries makes it one of the most dominant players in the global development process. Its performance on the environmental front has been both praised and criticized. Stein and Johnson's study of nine multilateral development agencies found that "the World Bank has the most advanced environmental policy and practices of any aid organization . . . and undoubtedly exerts intellectual leadership on environmental matters in the entire international development community."[3] However, others have not been as charitable. Reviewing its role, Richard Falk observed that

Despite the publicity attached to McNamara's inspirational annual reports with their exhoratory appeals for a common effort to reduce mass misery in the non-western world, the operational policies of the Bank were quite a different matter. It became clear over the last decade that the Bank, together with IMF, was policing the development process often in a manner that directly opposed the mandates of a supposed ideology of empathy. . . . Increasingly, it became clear that the real impact and function of the Bank was to integrate Third World economies into the world capitalist trading and investment systems for the sake of the First World.[4]

There is no doubt that the World Bank was, in its early years, influenced by the stage theory of economic growth. Environmental concerns were not serious issues, not only for the World Bank but even for the United Nations; but since 1970 the bank's activities and mission have been somewhat refocused and redirected. McNamara set up the Office of Environmental Adviser in 1970 to assess the World Bank's role and policy objectives in the environmental sphere. "The question is not whether there should be continued economic growth. There must be. Nor is the question whether the impact on the environment must be respected. It has to be. Nor—least of all—is it a question of whether these two considerations are interlocked. They are. The solution of the dilemma revolves clearly not about whether, but about how."[5] Several documents and position papers were prepared by the bank staff on environmental problems in developing countries. It adopted the concept of "additionality," requiring the bank to provide funds to cover additional costs directly attributable to its environmental standards.[6] However, the bank's definition of environment has been very broad, and there is always enough room to dodge the real issues related to environment and ecology.

It seems that despite the environmental commitment of the World Bank, there still remain many practical hurdles in implementing these policies—especially at the stages of project preparation and project appraisal. "Environmental issues are inevitably mixed into economic and technical studies, and thus often get overlooked. This problem is compounded by the fact that the Bank generally does not gather environmental information and hence has no easy basis for taking environmental change into account."[7] Environmental evaluation becomes a subsidiary element of technical evaluation. Another major gap in "expression of Bank policy is the lack of any clear and specific official linkage between lending policies to benefit the poorest, and lending to prevent the erosion or further destruction of the environments on which the poorest are so dependent but which their desperate search for a living so often threatens."[8] Deforestation is one such issue.

The International Monetary Fund (IMF)

The International Monetary Fund was established in the post–World War II era to stabilize monetary conditions prevailing among the major industrialized countries by providing "short term financing to member countries to enable them to correct temporary payment difficulties without resorting to measures destructive of national or international prosperity."[9] Under Article I of the fund's *Articles of Agreement*, its other activities are

To facilitate the expansion and balanced growth of international trade, and to contribute thereby to the promotion and maintenance of high levels of employment and real income and to the development of the productive resources of all members as primary objectives of economic policy, to promote exchange stability, to maintain orderly exchange arrangements among members, and to avoid competitive exchange depreciation, and to assist in the establishment of a multilateral system of payments in respect of current transactions between members and in the elimination of foreign exchange restrictions which hamper the growth of world trade.[10]

During the 1970s and 1980s, however, the scope and nature of the fund underwent change. Since then, most of its advice and all of its credit has gone to the Third World countries. Critics of these changes have pointed out that the fund has become "a debt collector for creditor governments and banks because it would not disburse Fund credit to any member that was not up to date in its interest payments. Finally, the Fund began to be part of the solution as it started to draw net resources away from the debtor countries instead of making more money available to them."[11]

One of the new major responsibilities entrusted to the IMF by the U.S. Congress was in the area of the environment. The U.S. executive director of the fund was asked to play a more assertive role in persuading other members to "carry out a systematic review of the impact of its policies on the environment and the sustainable management of natural resources and to encourage the Fund to eliminate or reduce potentially adverse impacts of Fund programs on the environment."[12] It was strongly recommended that the fund should incorporate environmental aims in its conditionality.[13] This new demand led to the internal and external debate about the very mission of the fund. The critics argued that (1) environmental issues can be more efficiently and effectively handled by the World Bank—the mission of the fund, according to these critics was not to stimulate development in the Third World; and (2) the very structure of the fund poses problems for it to play a constructive role in the environmental sphere. "The IMF should make sure that its own programs do not exacerbate these problems, and should help interested governments deal with adverse social consequences of stabilization programs; but it lacks the instruments for coping with these issues directly. To load such functions onto the Fund would threaten its central monetary activities without ensuring a commensurate impact on poverty or the environment."[14] Hence the role of the IMF in environmental issue has been minimal.

USAID

In the thick of the Cold War in 1950, the U.S. Congress passed the Act for International Development (AID) to "aid the efforts of the peoples of economically underdeveloped areas to develop their resources and improve their working and living conditions by encouraging the exchange of technical knowledge and skills and the flow of investment capital to countries which provide conditions under which such technical and capital help can effectively and constructively contribute to raising the standards of living, creating new sources of wealth, increasing productivity and expanding purchasing power." USAID was primarily intended to be the financial arm of U.S. foreign policy. USAID policy was based on two pillars—one was the economic growth model that measured economic development in the increase of gross national product (GNP). Export-oriented or import-substitution industries were favored. Developing nations were encouraged to borrow large amounts of money to build on their strength in low-wage manufacturing and in raw materials exporting technologies. The second pillar was that strong emphasis was placed on political modernization and institution building (Westernization).

USAID funds were primarily allocated to less developed countries that were willing to accept these models by modernizing their agriculture and transportation and by instituting administrative and political reforms. Some funds were also allocated to improve health, education, and community development projects. But despite good intentions and billions of dollars spent, the U.S. foreign aid program was in serious political trouble by the 1960s. Inefficiency, waste, poor management, and increasing amounts of economic and military aid to South Vietnam had tarnished its image. Congressional criticism of the foreign assistance program continued throughout the early 1970s. "Political criticism of foreign aid was reinforced by increasing criticism of the economic growth theory. The criticism arose from mounting evidence that poverty in developing nations was becoming more widespread and serious, and the growing realization that problems in developing countries differed drastically from those faced by industrialized countries during their periods of economic development."[15] It was argued that "somehow our assistance does not seem to have reached the heart of the problem—unemployment, the exploding population, the growing wretchedness of the urban slums, illiteracy, malnutrition, and disease."[16] As a result of these realities, the Foreign Assistance Act of 1973 stated that in the future the aid policy must "reflect" the new realities. It recognized that "economic growth alone does not necessarily lead to social advancement by the poor. Thus our policies and programs must be aimed directly at the poor majority's most pervasive problems."[17]

In response to the "new directions" and concerns, USAID strategies and approaches to development started gradually to shift their focus to rural areas. The primary target groups of U.S. assistance were redefined to be "subsistence farm families, small scale commercial farmers, landless farm laborers, pastorialists, unemployed laborers in market towns, and small scale non-farm entrepreneurs."[18] Until 1982, environmental issues and concerns were hardly discussed and debated. With the increasing environmental degradation and the acceptance of the concept of sustainable development, USAID's focus has shifted, and there is commitment to ecological issues such as water and air pollution, population, deforestation, energy, and social justice. Environment is no longer a nonissue. USAID now provides financial assistance to more than 80 countries in Asia, Africa, Latin America, the Middle East, and the Caribbean.

The Regional Banks

The regional banks, reflecting the differing priorities of their regions, vary in size, resources, and styles of management. Most of them have patterned their operational organizations on the World Bank model and demonstrate interest and concern for ecological matters. Following is a brief discussion of prominent regional banks.

The Inter-American Development Bank. The Inter-American Development Bank (IDB) was established in 1961; and since 1972 it has financed projects in the poorest countries of the region. In contrast to the World Bank's "productive" lending toward "social improvement" to meet the needs of the poor, the IDB has not taken a strong stand to meet the "basic needs" of the poor. It has loaned heavily to help build infrastructure and mining. Its record on environment, at best, is uneven. This is partly due to the Latin American governments' lack of concern about environmental issues. "These governments, with a few notable exceptions, until quite recently, have been extremely wary of environmental issues. In some governmental quarters, environmentalism and increasing concentration of lending on basic need projects is still associated with a neocolonialist strategy that will slow the pace of Latin American development."[19] However, there is an increasing awareness of environmental issues especially among the younger staff. New environmental guidelines, it is recognized, are necessary in certain sectors—electric power, irrigation, fisheries, agricultural development, urbanization, forestry, water and sewage—yet the environmental concerns are still largely a function of personal interests.

The Asian Development Bank. The Asian Development Bank (ADB), which started its operations in 1966, provides financial support to development projects in the poorer countries within the region. The bank also provides technical assistance in project preparation, sectoral studies, policy formulations, development planning, and institution building. It has been sensitive to the environmental impact of projects, given the immense ecological fragility of the region in general and the population problems in particular. The borrower governments, however, are considered responsible for the environmental assessments. Assurances from governments of project modifications to prevent environmental damage are achieved generally by covenants or agreements to "side letters."[20] By and large, the bank's overall record on environmental issues has been lackluster. Until 1979 it had no "formal constitutional commitment to environmental protection, and no specific procedures or checklists for ensuring that various aspects of environmental impacts are considered in the loan process."[21] However, recent activities of the ADB show that there is a definite shift in the attitudes of bank officers and a greater awareness and concern toward environment. Specific environmental problems are identified during the planning and coordination of development projects. "At the ADB the approach has been more evolutionary, but there has been a significant strengthening of the Environmental unit—from two staff through the mid 1980s to six staff currently—plus upgrading to divisional status in 1989, and the creation of an Environmental Office in 1990. Projections call for staff numbers to grow to 12 in 1991 and 20 by the end of 1992."[22] In recent years, the ADB has become quite active in environmental planning and management and in "promoting 'sustainable development' through country policy studies for Indonesia, Korea, Malaysia, Nepal, Pakistan, the Philippines and Sri Lanka."[23]

The African Development Bank. The African Development Bank was established in 1964 as a purely regional institution with hardly any external financial support. On environmental issues, the bank does not have a very strong record. Its consultants carry out feasibility studies of projects. Environmental and economic factors are identified, but usually the environmental concerns are ignored. An unnamed official from a Western aid agency was quoted as saying, "In a sense, we're talking about a kind of recolonization—about sending smart white boys in to tell them how to run their countries."[24]

If sustainability as a criterion for sound development is given only token acceptance, even by many World Bank officials and staff, it has received much less attention in other multi-lateral aid institutions. . . . The regional banks have officially said very little about the relationship between poverty, development, and environmental degradation. This may indicate a lack of perception of, or concern with, the long term future more often than outright opposition. But outright opposition exists, too, among those who argue that modernization can continue to rely on the latest technological innovation to outstrip resource depletion and to abate pollution. Such views face, however, an unresolved dilemma between ever greater dependence on more sophisticated technologies and the external dependence which such reliance may perpetuate.[25]

However, the trend is towards more careful analysis of development projects' impact on Africa's environment. Droughts, famines, and the fast-increasing urban population are forcing even the most reluctant officials of the bank and of African countries to give greater attention and importance to the environmental issues of deforestation, energy, population, and agriculture. It has created a new division for the environment.

The above discussion points out that one of the most significant changes since the mid-1980s has been the shift in attitudes, in both the industrialized and less developed countries, towards the concept of economic development and its relationship with the quality of environment. Earlier environmental problems were seen as "something that can be addressed only in the aftermath of successful economic development. There is now more and more realization that successful development will be achieved only by protecting the global environment and by balancing population and resources."[26] Economic development without ecodevelopment is inconceivable.

ENVIRONMENTAL ISSUES

As mentioned earlier, until very recently ecological and environmental issues were considered peripheral to economic development policy formulation. But massive oil spills, the CO_2 greenhouse global warming, unseasonable rains and floods, disintegration of the stratospheric ozone, acid rain, and the Chernobyl and Bhopal tragedies have all started to weigh heavily on public consciousness despite the reluctance to total commitment by some industrialized countries which believe that "up to two decades of intensive research on global climate change is required before major policy decisions can be made."[27] Most of the countries of both the South and the North, under the leadership of the United Nations nevertheless feel that time is running out and that the wait-and-see (laissez-faire) approach will further worsen the global environment. The Brundtland Commission has specifically outlined and identified these problems under the "Alternative Agenda" (see Chapter 1).

The second part of my discussion takes up two major issues which have attracted much attention in environmental debates both at Rio and elsewhere. They are (1) deforestation and (2) energy production and consumption.

Deforestation

Forests provide the largest natural habitat for wildlife and precious plant life, and they exert a tremendous influence on global ecological well-being. Forests absorb carbon dioxide from the air, store it in their systems, and thus regulate the supply and flow of fresh air. Increasing population; poverty; and demand for new land, fuel, and raw materials are destroying the earth's rain forests. Large-scale deforestation will complicate the greenhouse gas situation in the atmosphere, adversely affect "genetic and evolutionary diversity, contribute to the loss in the restorative and reproductive capabilities of those areas that can be reforested, and further impoverishment of the people who can no longer derive even the basic necessities from the area."[28] Tropical forests, harboring some of the richest biodiversity, are under severe pressure the world over. In 1990, satellite imagery indicated that the deforestation rate may have been as high as five million hectares per year in the past decade. Among the major causes is commercial logging, followed by shifting cultivation and fuelwood consumption for domestic energy. Biologist E. O. Wilson estimates that chopping down tropical forests leads to the extinction of at least 50,000 invertebrate species every year—about 140 every day. The tropical rain forests of Africa, Southeast Asia, and Central and South America are falling under the chain saws of the "rainforest executioner." An area the size of Ireland disappears every year. According to the World Bank estimates, these rain forests will disappear within sixty years (see Figures 2.1 and 2.2).

Aggressive efforts of the International Council for Research in Agroforestry (ICRAF), United Nations Environmental Programs (UNEP) Ecosystem Task Force, U.N. Food and Agriculture Organization (FAO), and others are having some effects on the wholesale destruction of forests; but it is not enough. Most aid organizations "are still doing very little [and] have shown little interest in undertaking forestry projects, which they tend to regard as complicated and financially unrewarding."[29] To quote an In-

Figure 2.1
Area of Forests Cleared Annually (Millions of Hectares)

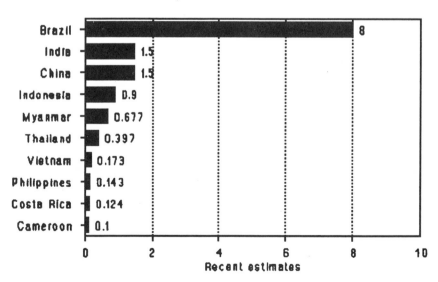

Source: The Economist, Aug. 1991, p. 36.

Figure 2.2
Percentage of Forests Cleared Annually

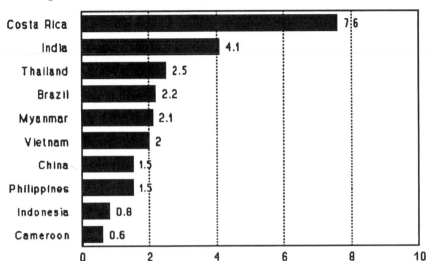

Source: The Economist, Aug. 1991, p. 36.

ter-American Development official, "Deforestation is being financed with our money, but is very much against our philosophy."[30]

Deforestation in Amazonia. According to a UNESCO study (1978), Amazon forests are among the most ecologically complex vegetation formulations on the planet. Amazonia encompasses the largest reserve of tropical moist forest, as well as seasonal forest. The number of plant species in the Amazon is estimated to be roughly 250,000.[31] The development of the Amazon basin has been hailed by some as a solution to the problem of inequitable land distribution and underemployment in other areas of the countries involved. However, there is very little evidence that the Amazonian frontier has provided much relief from these social and demographic pressures,[32] and there is growing evidence that following the initial pioneering period, Brazilian frontiers have tended to lose population as land becomes increasingly concentrated in the hands of more successful operators and the original pioneer population either moves on or returns to its places of origin.[33] Other effects of deforestation on human population and environment include

1. Native peoples throughout the Amazon are being displaced from their lands, resulting in serious tensions and conflicts between natives and the colonists.[34]

2. The current rate of deforestation may lead not only to desiccation of adjacent forests and disruptions in the world's hydrologic cycle but also to a major drop in the productivity of Amazonian fisheries. Dam construction blocks fish migrations, and destruction of flooded forest to convert the area to intensive agri-

culture will very likely destroy the productive potential of this little-understood food chain that carries the burden of providing protein for Amazonian populations and that has begun to play a role in exports as well.[35]

3. New diseases alien to the native population have created serious environmental, health-related problems. Epidemics of smallpox, measles, the common cold, onchocerciasis (African river blindness), influenza, and other contagious diseases have contributed to serious health hazards in the area. Environmental pollution from the growing use of pesticides and herbicides, frequent oil spills in the Aguarico River Basin, garbage, trash, and sewage dumped downstream from frontier towns is causing health problems, stillbirths, miscarriages, infant deformations, and adult kidney ailments.[36]

"Amazonian development efforts serve to highlight the dilemmas presented by development everywhere; how to achieve equity and growth; how to work for conservation and development; how to modernize the agricultural sector when improved agronomic practices for the humid tropics have yet to be developed; whether to favor extensive (pastures) or intensive (crops) forms of land use; whether to guarantee native rights to land or the claims of peasants and corporations that invade those areas. None of these dilemmas can be easily resolved. Each dilemma is the product of structural and functional relations within nation-states and between nations. The choice to give priority to one aspect of a dilemma over another reflects local, national, and international demands."[37] The role of international organizations is crucial and critical in arresting the senseless deforestation projects that affect the quality and the very existence of future generations. Since the effects of these policies are felt worldwide, responsibilities should also be shared internationally. While the World Bank, under tremendous pressure from several quarters—academics, grassroots nongovernment organizations (NGOs), U.S. environmental pressure groups, and the U.S. Congress—has adopted new conservation standards for its projects and promised the creation of a global database on environmental conditions in developing countries (e.g., it froze $255 million in funds to the Brazilian Polonoreste region 1,000-mile road). Brazil has been blamed for its policy, which involved clear cutting of the rain forest, but the policy was developed in close cooperation with the bank and other aid agencies.[38]

In an article "The Month Amazonia Burns,"[39] indictment for supporting environmentally damaging policies was placed not only on the government of Brazil for reckless "development" of the Amazonia region, but also on the donors (i.e., the World Bank and the IDB) which loaned $82 billion in the 1980s to develop and build 166 hydropower dams.[40] "Some of the indignation directed against Brazil has been deeply hypocritical. No government can say, hand on heart, that it has not encouraged a bit of environment thuggery in its time. The roads into the Amazon . . . have generally been built with the help of first-world donors; the timber taken out has found its way into first-world sitting rooms."[41]

Panama. In Panama the process of deforestation is being encouraged and financed by "institutions with the word 'Development' in their titles."[42] Both the Inter-American Development Bank and the World Bank have been financing Panama to improve its cattle-ranching industry. Both banks claim that their combined investment of $19 million was intended not only to increase the production of beef but also to improve pastures, re-plant trees in deforested areas, and encourage sensible use of the land. Instead, the money was loaned to farmers (*arreras*) to cut and burn the forest to make pastures. Forest is viewed as an enemy of the ranchers. In the 1960s, the former Panamanian strongman, General Omar Torrijos, launched "La Conquista del Atlánticó (The Conquest of the Atlantic)" to clear the forests on the Atlantic slopes of the continental divide. The pas-ture-raised cattle are slaughtered for cheap hamburger to be exported to rich Northerners. No restrictions on deforestation were imposed by the Banco de Desarrollo Agropecuario (BDA).[43] The Panamanian project to improve livestock was devised by cost-benefit analysts, bankers, and rich ranchers to develop Panama. The program seems to make good financial sense; but it did not take into consideration the high price of the defores-tation, erosion, and desertification.

Africa. Uncontrolled, unregulated deforestation in Africa has reached a critical point. Africa is losing between three and five million hectares of tropical forest each year, an area greater than Togo and larger than several Western European countries. At this rate the tropical forests in Africa will be gone within sixty years. They have already almost disappeared in Ni-geria, Benin, Togo, Ghana, and Côte d'Ivoire.[44] Many reasons contribute to deforestation in Africa:

1. The growing population of land-hungry peasants cuts the forests for agricultural land.

2. There is increasing demand for timber for export to Japan and other rich countries.

3. Most rural Africans use firewood as fuel.

4. Overgrazing of the forests also contributes to deforestation.

5. The problem of pollution of tropical forests is an ever-growing concern.

Pollution is mainly caused by acid rains. The contaminated zone extends from the basin of the Congo river to the West African coast. In studies conducted by Crutsen and by Lacko, scientists have found exceptionally high levels of contamination. One of the main reasons for this high acid contamination and hence the consequent damage to ozone is the fires in the African Savannahs.[45]

As discussed in the context of Amazonia development, tropical forestry projects have been a small part of the World Bank's and regional banks' lending programs in general. Sub-Saharan Africa was no exception. Mount-ing criticism of these policies and general concern about deforestation and its impact on global ecology, however, have brought about a shift in the policies and attitudes of these aid agencies. At least on paper, "Today every single project financed by the World Bank is subjected to careful environmental assessment including forestry projects."[46] In November 1990, the vice president for the Africa Region of the World Bank told the board of executive directors, "On the question of forestry lending, the policy of the Africa Region is not to finance any forestry project unless it can be demonstrated that it is environmentally sustainable."[47] However, these policies are still in the process of being formulated and are frequently ignored in the name of improving forestry management and agriculture. As recent as October 1991, forestry projects were being financed in West Africa by the World Bank. Korinna Honta, a staff economist of the Washington-based Environmental Defense Fund observed "you have further degradation of the environment, further impoverishment of some of the poorest people on earth, and all this is being touted as a model environmental project."[48]

Asia and the Pacific. In Asia, the rate of deforestation is alarming. In the Malayasian state of Sarawak, one of the largest, oldest, and richest rain forests in the world is being logged at such a rate that most of it could be gone within five years.[49] Political expediency, personal greed, and bureaucratic corruption have played havoc on these forests. According to several accounts, "Timber concessions totaling 3 million acres (1.2 million hectares) and worth $22.5 billion were given to relatives and friends of the Chief Minister of Sarawak, and the minister of the Environment is the owner of more than 750,000 acres (300,000 hectares) of timber concessions."[50] In Nepal, most of the country's tree cover has been slashed. Throughout Nepal, storms wash away exposed soil, creating avalanches of mud that clog rivers and bury villages.[51] In the Philippines, severe deforestation has reached crisis proportions; and by 2000, no virgin forests will be left. Thailand lost 45 percent of its forest from 1961 to 1965, and its forest cover fell from 29 percent in 1985 to 19 percent in 1988.[52] In China, despite a variety of measures including aerial sowing of adaptable grasses and wind-breaking forestry, the soil erosion continues and in some areas has increased by 30 percent since 1950, mainly because of heavy deforestation. It is estimated that China's forested area decreases by 1.5 million hectares annually.[53] The nationwide construction boom, the increasing demand for paper, and the rapidly growing requirements of domestic and export packaging have combined to accelerate the demise of China's remaining natural forests. Between 1979 and 1988 forest areas shrank by over 23 percent.[54] China is the third highest emitter of the greenhouse gases, producing 9.1 percent of the world total (see Figure 2.3). South Asia, India, Sri Lanka, and Bangladesh have lost almost all their primary rain forest. In India the rate of deforestation is alarmingly high, and the country is losing 1.3 million hectares of forest each year.[55] India is the fifth highest emitter of greenhouse gases in the world (see Figure 2.3). In 1980, India adopted the social forestry pro-

Figure 2.3
Greenhouse Gas Emissions (Billion Tons of Carbon)

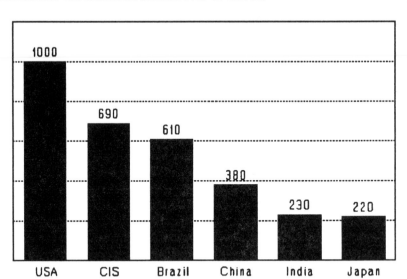

Source: India Today, June 19, 1992, p. 19.

gram to balance the people's need for fuel and fodder and the need to maintain forests. More than 50 percent of the cost of several social forestry programs was funded by major international donor agencies such as the World Bank, Overseas Development Administration (ODA), IMF, USAID, and Swedish International Development Authority (SIDA).[56]

Summary. The overall performance record of the World Bank over the last 15 years or so has been mixed. While in its position papers it has repeatedly committed itself to a vigorous policy of refusing to support those projects that contributed to deforestation, until 1979 it had approved only five industrial afforestation and reforestation projects. The Inter-American Bank supported a $17-million project through the Argentine Banco de la Nacion for afforestation and reforestation to stop erosion in the mountainous Andean areas, to replace degraded tropical forests in arid Patagonia, and to replant areas cleared for agricultural and cattle development in the subtropical Missiones area. The World Bank's loans for industrial tree plantation have been few and small. In Zambia and Kenya, the bank approved only $5.3-million and $2.6-million loans respectively. The 1970 Kenyan loan was particularly interesting because it was not only the first countrywide forestry program but also in many ways the herald of the "social forestry projects" to come. It was designed to establish 100,000 hectares of industrial tree plantation (soil-enriching wattle to provide charcoal for Kenya's cement industry and pulpwood and saw logs from pine and cypress) and to devise a means of producing this wood under the "taungya" system (an established method for interplanting trees and food crops), and thereby, it was hoped, to improve the standard of living of some eight thousand families. Despite some initial difficulties, the project went into its second phase in 1976, with both the Kenyans and the World Bank learning a great deal in the process, and later was successfully completed.[57]

Energy

Our constant quest for a more leisurely life and our conspicuous consumption of natural resources have forced us to devise new ways and means to harness and exploit these resources. It seems that the environmental price for gas-guzzling automobiles, air conditioners, refrigerators, and personal computers in every home has been quite high. However, the use and depletion of natural resources is uneven. An average American consumes more food and energy than the global average. The United States, with 4.8 percent of the world's population, uses 25 percent of the world's commercial energy. At the other extreme, India, with about 16 percent of the world's population, uses only about 1.5 percent of the world's commercial energy. In 1990, the 251 million Americans used more energy for air conditioning than 1.1 billion Chinese used for all purposes (see Figures 2.4 and 2.5). If past trends are any indication, then the global demand for energy will double by the year 2025. The excessive use of electricity and biomass for energy degrades the earth's environment and damages ozone and thereby exposes human life to various diseases and imbalance in nature's cycle. Chlorine from human-made chlorofluorocarbons (CFCs)—DuPont trade-

Figure 2.4
Industrial Carbon Dioxide Emission, 1985, by Region

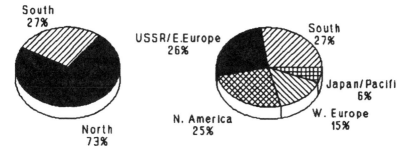

Source: Compiled from World Resources Institute, *World Resources 1988–89* (Washington, D.C.: 1991).

Note: Industrial carbon dioxide emission is defined as carbon dioxide released by fossil fuel combustion and industrial processes.

Figure 2.5
Greenhouse Gas Contributions to Global Warming

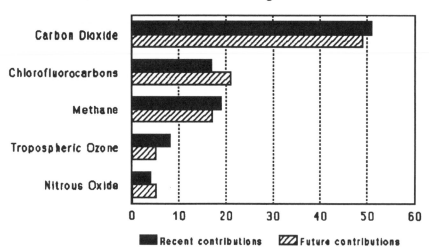

Source: World Bank, *Striking a Balance* (Washington, D.C.: The Bank, 1989), p. 32.

mark freons—used in refrigerators, cleaning computer chips, and hospital sterilization, as well as solvents, dry cleaning, and other aerosols damages the ozone.

Since 1945 the use of CFCs has increased substantially. Industrial countries account for 84 percent of CFC production. The United States uses 29 percent of the global output of CFCs. An American uses six times more CFCs than the global average. In 1986, the U.S. Environmental Protection Agency projected 800,000 additional cancer deaths in the United States alone over the next 88 years because of ozone destruction.[58] In the 1980s, researchers found that up to 50 percent of the ozone in the upper stratosphere over the Antarctic is destroyed each September and October during the Antarctic spring. During these two months in 1987 and 1989 this Antarctic hole was larger in area than the continental United States.[59] Depletion of ozone will cause the following:

1. squamous-cell skin cancer,
2. melanoma (another form of skin cancer),
3. increase in eye cataracts,
4. suppression of the human immune system,
5. decrease in important food crop (corn, rice, soybean, wheat) production,
6. rise in the sea level, and
7. overall global warming.

Despite differences among the scientific community on the extent of the global warming, there is a widespread consensus that the effects of global warming will be detrimental to the earth's climate and human growth. "Current models indicate that the Northern Hemisphere will warm more and faster than the Southern Hemisphere, mostly because there is so much more ocean in the south and water takes longer to warm than land. The earth's average atmospheric temperature will rise 1.5° C to 5.5° C (2.7° F to 9.9° F) over the next fifty years (by 2040) if greenhouse gasses continue to rise at the current rate"[60] (see Figure 2.6).[61] Its impact on low-lying areas such as Bangladesh could be catastrophic. Overall consequences of greenhouse, global warming, and depletion of ozone caused by excessive and reckless energy emissions on the earth's environment could be, in the long run, rivaled only by a devastating total war.

Role of the Development Aid Agencies. One of the most often heard criticisms of the international aid agencies in the energy area has been their insensitivity to the needs of poor people in less developed countries. Most of the poor live in the rural areas, and almost 70 percent of them rely on biomass as their primary fuel for cooking and heating. About half of this comes from burning wood or charcoal produced from wood, 33 percent from crop residues, and 17 percent from dung.[62] FAO projects that by 2000, three billion people in 77 less developed countries will experience a fuelwood crisis, thus further compounding the problems of deforestation and uneven policies of energy use (Figure 2.1). The aid agencies have financed projects that have mainly benefited the urban middle class and industrial entrepreneurs. Industry accounts

Figure 2.6
Rises in Concentration of Atmospheric Carbon Dioxide

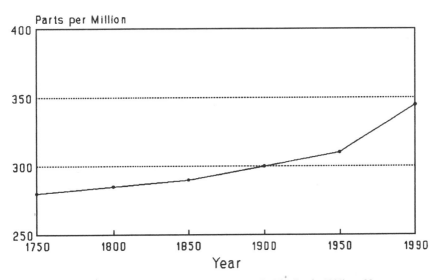

Source: World Bank, *Striking a Balance* (Washington, D.C.: The Bank, 1989), p. 32.

for about two-thirds of the Third World commercial energy consumption. Large-scale energy projects, no doubt, provide much needed power and reduce Third World dependency on importation of oil. These projects, however, especially large hydroelectric dams and oil or gas-fired power stations, are not always environmentally sound investments.

In the past, the World Bank has given 20 percent of its total aid to these projects, as has the Inter-American Development Bank (20 percent). The Asian Development Bank's investment has been about 23 percent, closely followed by the African Development Bank. Electric grid-based energy planning and lending has been popular with these agencies. Rural people and interests have been ignored in the past. Some encouraging developments, however, are taking place. The World Bank and the Inter-American Development Bank are shifting their policies and giving more attention to rural electrification programs and environmental factors. The Arenal Hydroelectric project in Costa Rica was modified because of observations made by the Smithsonian Institute concerning the potential volcanic eruption of Arenal near the projected dam. Another project that World Bank officials brag about to point out their commitment to the environment is the geothermal project in El Salvador where "extensive steps were taken to protect the Rio Paz and its riparian inhabitants from high levels of arsenic and boron."[63] In the recent past, the Asian Development Bank, like the World Bank, had no consistent policy on energy-related lending. It gave "some consideration" to the environmental effects of the project (e.g., in the case of the Mindanao Power Projects in the Philippines, the bank expressed an interest in the environmental impact of the project).

As a result of political, social, and economic pressures and the changing mood about the environment, these aid agencies are shifting their lending practices. Since the oil embargo in the 1970s and the economic crisis it created, the shortage of firewood, and increasing global demands for energy, the World Bank and the regional banks are moving towards more flexible development policies to help the rural poor. In 1975 the World Bank's study *India: The Energy Sector* observed that "with respect to these dominant forms of fuel consumption in rural areas, there has so far been relatively little study planning or concerted development."[64] In 1977 at the Tenth World Energy Conference held in Istanbul, the World Bank issued its new policy regarding the energy lending. The following main types of activities were suggested: (1) study of the rural energy demand and supply to formulate an effective energy policy, (2) investigation of applicability of rural energy technologies in the rural development.[65]

The energy policies of the Inter-American Development Bank have been heavily tilted towards urban interests. The IDB argues that the overwhelming urban problems in Latin America take precedence over the less urgent problems in rural areas. Long-range IDB policies were expressed in *Energy for Rural Development* that "a decade or two must pass before any of what are now regarded as promising unconventional energy sources will assume a significant role in the energy supply picture . . . promising sources do not match well with the demands of energy users in developing nations."[66]

While considering the role of the aid agencies' policies, one could only hope that they will reconsider their energy lending policies in the light of environmental needs. So far the World Bank and the regional banks have not done enough. At best their policies have been inconsistent and opportunistic.

CONCLUSION

The Earth Summit at Rio turned out to be as much a conference on environment as on economic behavior. One of the key issues for developing countries was financing the environmental mess the industrialized countries have created. Serious and quite often contentious debate took place not only as to who should pay for the cleanup of environmental pollution but also as to how these funds, if any, should be distributed. In Rio the North–South division dominated these debates.[67] Several proposals were floated to settle the "financial impasse": The European Community pledged a $4.5-billion fund to jump-start the environmental cleanup; Canadian Prime Minister Brian Mulroney promised to swap $145 million of its official debt from Latin American Countries, including Cuba, for sustainable development projects. Canada also promised to contribute $16.6 million to a rain forest project in Brazil and $10 million to model forest projects in three developing countries; [68] Italian Minister for Environment Giorgio Ruffalo proposed an energy tax of $1 a barrel of oil to be levied on the 24 members of the Organization for Economic Cooperation and Development. The estimated $25 billion raised annually through this tax, which would also serve to limit emissions of carbon dioxide, would largely be for the development aid; Japan, it is expected, would contribute 20 to 25 percent of the developed world's share of new financial aid;[69] the Group of 77 committed itself to collectively raise about 80 percent of the $600 billion needed to implement Agenda 21;[70] and the United States pledged $50 million to the GEF, which is administered by the World Bank.

The developing countries came away from the Earth Summit with many pledges and proposals from the rich nations but no firm commitment to finance environmentally friendly technologies and trade concessions. So far most of the pledges made at Rio have not materialized. Another contentious issue related to finance was the role of multilateral aid agencies as to who should control the distribution of these funds. The Americans, the Japanese, and the Europeans were opposed to creating any new institutions to administer such aid. They preferred the existing institutions such as GEF. The developing countries, on the other hand, felt that the current world economic order was unjust and hegemonic; and despite the useful services of multilateral aid agencies in past, they remain political arms of the donor countries. "The era of sustainable development must not create new conditionalities for developing countries. They must not be denied the right to choose their own growth strategies."[71] It was also felt that issues such as human rights should not be linked with environmental issues. The developing countries see the GEF as an instrument of rich countries of the North and strongly oppose the disbursement of the "Environment Fund" by these countries. The South proposed the establishment of a "green fund" that would be much more broadly administered.[72] Donor countries, however, felt at least as strongly that setting up a huge new fund that countries could draw upon almost as they pleased was self-evidently a poor idea.[73] The impasse continues, and "as with money and technology transfer the gaps that came out in Rio were not bridged, and the upshot seems to be: Advantage North, Disadvantage Earth."[74]

As noted earlier, despite opposition to environmentally damaging projects, the multilateral aid agencies have cleared projects. The discussion also shows that there are encouraging policy trends being debated and adopted by these groups and agencies—the World Bank, regional banks, the United Nations, the Third World, and industrialized countries. The long and arduous task of making the earth economically prosperous and at the same time qualitatively and environmentally livable has just begun. The destruction of the environment can no longer be regarded as the sole business of short-sighted, stage-theory economists, opportunistic political leaders, and the bureaucrats of the multilateral aid agencies. Environment is not a problem of the South or of the North. It is a global problem that must be tackled internationally, nationally, and locally. The need is to adopt an ecological ethic in making decisions to avoid the "tragedy of the commons."

NOTES

1. Lynton K. Caldwell, *International Environment Policy* (Durham, N.C.: Duke Press Policy Studies, 1984), p. 172.

2. Ibid., p. 173.

3. Robert Stein and Brian Johnson, *Banking on the Biosphere? Environmental Procedures and Practices of Nine Multi-lateral Development Agencies* (Toronto: Lexington Books, 1979), p. 11.

4. Richard Falk, Foreword to *Development Debacle: The World Bank in the Philippines*, by Walden Bellow, David Kinley, and Elaine Elinson (San Francisco, Calif.: Institute for Food and Development Policy, 1982), p. x.

5. Robert McNamara, "U.N. Conference on the Human Environment," quoted in Stein and Johnson, *Banking*, p. 12.

6. Ibid., p. 12.

7. Ibid., p. 19.

8. Ibid., p. 22.

9. Richard E. Feinberg and Catherine Gwin, "Reforming the Fund," in *The International Monetary Fund in a Multipolar World: Pulling Together*, ed. Catherine Gwin and Richard E. Feinberg (New Brunswick, N.J.: Transaction Books, 1989), p. 5.

10. Foreign Assistance Act 1953 (Washington, D.C.: U.S. Government Printing Office, 1953), p. 6.

11. Gwin and Feinberg, *International Monetary Fund*, p. 70.

12. Jacques Polak, *The Changing Nature of IMP Conditionality* (Princeton, N.J.: Princeton University Press, 1991), p. 27.

13. Ibid., p. 28.

14. Gwin and Feinberg, *International Monetary Fund*, p. 4.

15. Dennis A. Rondinelli, *Development Projects as Policy Experiments: An Adaptive Approach to Development Administration* (New York: Methuen and Co., 1983), p. 71.

16. Owens Edgar and Robert d'A Shaw, *Development Reconsidered* (Lexington, Mass.: D. C. Heath, 1972), p. 2.

17. Ibid.

18. Dennis A. Rondinelli, *Development Administration and U.S. Foreign Aid Policy* (Boulder, Colo.: Lynne Reinner Publishers, 1987), p. 74.

19. Stein and Johnson, *Banking*, p. 26.

20. Ibid., p. 34.

21. Ibid., p. 36.

22. David Turnham, "Multilateral Development Banks and Environmental Management," *Public Administration and Development* July-August 1991: 368.

23. Turnham, "Development Banks," p. 373.

24. *Financial Times*, 3 April 1985: 36.

25. Stein and Johnson, *Banking*, p. 7.

26. Robert J. Berg and David F. Gordon, eds., *Cooperation for International Development: The United States and the Third World in the 1990s* (Boulder, Colo.: Lynne Reinner, 1989), p. 9.

27. C. Boyden Gray and David B. Rivkin, Jr., "'No Regrets' Environmental Policy," *Foreign Policy* Summer 1991: 55.

28. Caldwell, *Environment Policy*, pp. 193–194.

29. Stein and Johnson, *Banking*, p. 116; *The New York Times* 15 Oct. 1991.

30. Lloyd Timberlake, "From Washington to Panama: Buying Destruction," in *Only One Earth: Living for the Future* (New York: Sterling Publishing, 1987), p. 23.

31. T. Lovejoy and H. O. R. Schubart, "The Ecology of Amazonian Development," in *Land, People, and Planning in Contemporary Amazonian*, ed. F. Barbira-Scazzocchio (Cambridge: Cambridge University Center for Latin American Studies Occasional Publications, 1980), p. 3.

32. Emilio F. Moran, *The Dilemma of Amazonian Development* (Boulder, Colo.: Westview, 1983), p. 12.

33. Luc Mougeot, "Alternate Migration Targets in Latin American Countries and Brazilian Amazonias' Closing Frontier," East Lansing, Mich.: Latin American Studies Center, 1981, mimeo.

34. Shelton H. Davis, *Victims of the Miracle: Development and the Indians of Brazil* (New York: Cambridge University Press, 1977); Charles Wagley, *Welcome of Tears: The Tapirape Indians of Central Brazil* (New York: Oxford University Press, 1977).

35. Moran, *Dilemma*, p. 11.

36. James Yost, "Twenty Years of Contact: The Mechanisms of Change in Wao

("Auca") Culture," in *Cultural Transformations and Ethnicity in Modern Ecuador*, ed. N. E. Whitten, Jr. (Urbana: University of Illinois Press, 1981), p. 201.

37. Moran, *Dilemma*, p. 3.

38. Rodney R. White, "Environmental Management and National Sovereignty: Some Issues from Senegal," *International Journal* Winter 1989–90: 120.

39. "The Month Amazonia Burns," *Economist* 9 Sept. 1989: 15–16.

40. G. Tyler Miller, *Environmental Science, Sustaining the Earth* (Belmont, Calif.: Wadsworth, 1991), p. 333.

41. "Month Amazonia Burns," pp. 15–16.

42. Timberlake, "Washington to Panama," p. 32.

43. Ibid., p. 29.

44. "Sub-Saharan Africa: Environmental Indicators," *World Bank Report* (Washington, D.C.: 1989).

45. Tamara A. Alikhanova, "Ecological Impact on Economic Activities in West Africa," Moscow: Institute for African Studies, Academy of Sciences of the USSR, 1990, mimeo.

46. Ismail Serageldin, closing address "Saving Africa's Rainforests," Conference on Conservation of West and Central Africa Rainforest, sponsored by the African Development Bank, the International Union for the Conservation of Nature (IUCN), and the World Bank, Côte d'Ivoire, 5–9 Nov. 1990.

47. Ibid., p. 28.

48. Korinna Honta, "Environmental Dilemma and Development," *The New York Times* 15 Oct. 1991: A7.

49. Stan Lesser, "A Reporter at Large, Logging the Rain Forest," *The New Yorker* 27 May 1991: 43.

50. *Utusan Konsumer Penang* October 1987, March 1988; *The Guardian*, London: 4 Feb. 1988. Quoted in Gareth Porter and Janet Brown, *Global Environmental Politics* (Boulder, Colo.: Westview, 1991), p. 40.

51. Don Hinrichsen, *International Wild Life* May-June 1992: 23.

52. *Newsweek* 1 June 1992: 23.

53. Baruch Boxer, "China's Environmental Prospects," *Asian Survey* July 1989: 669–673.

54. Smil Vaclav, "China's Environmental Morass," *Current History* Sept. 1989: 279.

55. O. P. Dwivedi and Renu Khator, "India's Environmental Policy, Programs, and Politics," in this volume.

56. Renu Khator, *Environment, Development and Politics in India* (Lanham, Md.: University Press of America, 1991), pp. 141–142.

57. Stein and Johnson, *Banking*, p. 119.

58. Mark Crawford, "United States Floats Proposal to Help Prevent Global Ozone Depletion," *Science* November 1986: 927–929.

59. Miller, *Environmental Science*, p. 224.

60. Ibid., p. 214.

61. William Chandler, "Development and Global Environmental Change," in *Cooperation for International Development: The United States and the Third World in the 1990s*, ed. Robert J. Berg and David F. Gordon (Boulder, Colo.: Lynne Reinner), p. 51.

62. Miller, *Environmental Science*, p. 335.

63. *Energy for Rural Environment* (Washington, D.C.: World Bank, 1976), p. 9.

64. *India: The Energy Sector* (Washington, D.C.: World Bank, 1976), p. 11.

65. Stein and Johnson, *Banking,* p. 85.

66. Ibid.

67. *India Today* 19 June 1992: 12.

68. *The Globe and Mail,* 9 June 1992: A8.

69. John Newhouse, "The Diplomatic Round: Earth Summit," *The New Yorker* 25 May 1992: 76–77.

70. *India Today* 19 June 1992: 8.

71. Ibid.

72. Newhouse, "Diplomatic Round," pp. 76–77.

73. Ibid., p. 70.

74. Johan Halmberg, Director of British-based International Institute of Environment and Development, quoted in *India Today* 19 June 1992: 12.

India's Environmental Policy, Programs, and Politics

O. P. DWIVEDI AND RENU KHATOR

Mahatma Gandhi once said: The earth has enough for everyone's need but not enough for everyone's greed. This wise counsel has been proven right, especially during the post-Gandhian era, except that when Gandhi gave this counsel, the population of India, as well as the world, was not increasing with the same alarming proportion as has happened after his death. In the case of India, its environmental problems are a factor of its continuing poverty and ever-growing urban population, coupled with the rise in industrial activity.

In June 1972, Mrs. Indira Gandhi emphasized at the first U.N.-sponsored conference on environment that poverty was the worst form of pollution, and consequently, it was a most urgent issue facing the international community. During the next two decades, her prophetic words were not heeded, while poverty continued to engulf the Third World. This issue was then again highlighted by the World Commission on Environment and Development Report, *Our Common Future*. At the Earth Summit in Rio de Janeiro, the removal of poverty as an integral part of the world strategy for environment and development became a truism, although still lacking commitment from most of the industrialized nations.

Between the period from the United Nations Human Environment Conference in Sweden in 1972 to the Earth Summit in Brazil 1992, India took various steps to control pollution and conserve resources. It also kept reminding the industrialized world that so long as poverty remains the main stumbling block in its road to development, its efforts to protect the environment and conserve resources would not bear the necessary fruits. India's sentiments have been echoed by other Third World nations. For India, as for other nations of the South, removal of poverty and environmental protection are the two sides of the same coin, sustainable development.

During the two environmental decades (1972–1992), the major issue before the government of India has been how to strike a balance between the urgent need to secure food sufficiency, health, drinking water, and shelter and the desire to protect the environment. Although various institutional and legal mechanisms were initiated, the pressures of the growing population and an ineffective system of environmental law enforcement, along with the scarcity of funding, have added to the misery of the nation. The government of India was forced to acknowledge through its "Policy Statement for Abatement of Pollution" that "the state of the environment continues to deteriorate."[1] India's response to environmental problems is being watched by nations the world over—because if India is able to prevent the deterioration of the environment and provide for the removal of poverty, it will be an example for others in the Third World to follow. In this chapter, the authors have attempted to examine the challenges and responses to the environmental problems faced by India.

EMERGENCE OF ENVIRONMENTAL CONCERN
AND DEVELOPMENT OF NATIONAL POLICY

The major environmental concerns of India today are the result of continuing poverty, coupled with growing population and the side effects of enhanced industrial activities (including human settlements and movements). Conditions of poverty affect the meager natural resources which the nation wishes to protect and conserve. They also create problems with respect to the fulfillment of basic human needs for a large section of India's population. At the same time, India's people are impatient when it comes to making attempts to improve their living conditions. Towards that they would not hesitate to put more demands on the environment if the short-term gains could ensure basic daily needs. Population has become a major source of environmental degradation because it now exceeds the threshold limits of the life-support system within the country's boundary. The population of 844 million in 1991 is increasing at the rate of 2.11 percent annually, adding about 17 million people. In addition, India has probably the largest cattle population on earth, about 500 million head, but only 13 million hectares for grazing. The multiplying population of both the human beings and animals is putting a tremendous pressure on the environment. In the race for survival, both animals and human beings suffer. For example, over 250 million children, women, and men suffer from under-nutrition. The prospects for the future are alarming indeed.

In addition to the distressing situation arising out of population pressures brought by human beings and animals, India faces immense challenges from the side effects of industrial development and human settlements; some of these are highlighted here:

1. Dwindling forest cover caused by overgrazing, harvesting of trees for commercial and domestic fuel purposes, and illegal encroachments. During 1987–88, the actual forest cover in the country was 64.07 million hectares.[2] Most of the loss has occurred since independence. This has not only resulted in the extinction of rare plant, animal, and microbial species but also contributed to soil erosion, floods, and groundwater depletion.

2. Polluting industries: There are about 4,000 water-polluting large industries, with only half of them having any pollution abatement plants installed. There are over one million medium-sized industrial plants that do not have any pollution-abating units. These industries have polluted the river basins and groundwater to such an extent that in the case of the holy River Ganga, the government of India had to establish a special authority to monitor the water pollution–causing industries and to require them to install abatement units, as well as to require the local municipal authorities to install sewage treatment plants.

3. Air pollution: In many cities, industries are located too close to the residential areas. Emissions from these industries are causing many respiratory diseases, aggravated by auto emissions and population congestion. The severity of the Bhopal disaster could have been less had it not been for the proximity of the Union Carbide Plant to the city population.

4. Unplanned and encroaching urbanization is yet another environmental pollutant. India is actually facing a classic urban nightmare. In 1981, there were only 12 cities with populations over one million. By 1991, the number had climbed to 23. In 1951, India's urban population was 62 million; by 1981, it had grown to 158 million; and by 1991, it reached about 227 million; among these, over 30 percent of the population live in slums.[3] When such a large number of people is concentrated in small, unplanned spaces, they suffer not only from the shortage of drinking water and sewer facilities but also from a host of other diseases.

5. Environmental refugees: India has undertaken to build a large number of megaprojects related to dams and to mining and mineral exploration activities. These projects have caused a much less talked about environmental refugee problem. A study reveals that about 14.5 million people have been displaced, and among these only 3.9 million have been rehabilitated.[4] Plights of these people have attracted worldwide attention; one example is the reversal of the decision in 1992 by the World Bank not to finance the Narmada River Project.

6. Pesticides and agriculture: India is the largest producer and consumer of pesticides in South Asia. The most productive agricultural regions of the nation show a severe pesticide pollution problem (including the use of insecticides, herbicides, and fungicides in the country). "More than 665 people died in 1989–90 because of pesticide poisoning, and thousands of cases of crippling resulting

from pesticides have been recorded in the country."[5] In addition to problems arising out of the indiscriminate use of pesticides, another worrisome problem is the fertilizer pollution resulting from the intensive farming methods used in various parts of the country. Synthetic inorganic nutrients generally escape to river basins, dams, and coastal waters causing algae growth, oxygen depletion, and related problems.

The year 1972 marks the watershed in the history of environmental policy development in India.[6] Prior to 1972, environmental concerns, such as sewage disposal, sanitation, and public health, were dealt with by different ministries of the government; and each pursued its objectives without any integral coordination either within the federal structure or between the federal and state governments. Prior to the convening of the World Conference on the Human Environment in Sweden in 1968, the U.N. General Assembly requested each country to prepare a report on the state of its environment. India established a National Committee on Environmental Planning and Coordination (NCEPC) in February 1972. The committee not only prepared the country report, which was presented by Prime Minister Indira Gandhi at the Swedish conference in June 1972, but also started establishing linkages with the Planning Commission and other federal ministries, as well as state governments. An Office of Environmental Planning and Coordination was established to assist the committee with the federal Department of Science and Technology. This office became the precursor of the federal Department of Environment and eventually the Ministry of Environment and Forests.

Between 1972 and 1980, NCEPC tried to establish its functional relationship with other power ministries within the government but faced problems mostly because "different departments started viewing this committee as a competitor rather than planner and coordinator."[7] Despite these two problems, the efforts of NCEPC paid off. The Fifth Five-Year Plan incorporated environmental aspects into the planning and development process. A constitutional amendment in 1976 obligated the nation to protect the environment. Article 48A of the Constitution Amendment declared that the state shall endeavor to protect and improve the environment and to safeguard the forests and wildlife of the country.

This constitutional commitment was the major step taken by any nation on earth as India became the first country to change its constitution to protect its environment. However, between 1977 and 1979, not much happened in the field of environmental protection, partly because Mrs. Gandhi was defeated in the 1977 general election. For the Janata party, environmental protection was not a priority item; but the January 1980 general election brought Mrs. Gandhi back into power. She appointed a committee under the chairmanship of N. D. Tiwari to recommend legislative measures and appropriate machinery for environmental protection at the federal level. At the recommendation of this committee, a separate Department of Environment was established on November 1, 1980. It was hoped that state governments and Union Territories would also establish such mechanisms.

The Sixth Five-Year Plan (1980–85), devoted an entire chapter on environment and development, emphasizing sound environmental and ecological principles in land-use planning, agriculture, forestry management, wildlife preservation, water and air pollution control, marine and coastal zone protection, fisheries, renewable resources and energy, and human settlements. The plan also provided guidance on environmental concerns to the federal and state administrators; and further, it allocated financial resources for environmental conservation and protection efforts.

Various changes also took place in the institutional setup at the federal level. Being the focal point for environmental policy planning and management, it assumed responsibility for environmental planning, coordination (not only among various federal government ministries but also between the center and state governments), environmental awareness and promotion, preparation of environmental policy guidelines for various sectors, environmental appraisal of development projects, promotion of environmental research and education, and international cooperation. In order to accomplish these activities, the department brought together a multidisciplinary team of scientific, technical, and administrative professionals in its secretariat. Several scientific agencies, such as the Zoological Survey of India, the Botanical Survey of India, and the National Museum of Natural History, were brought under the authority of the department. In January 1985, the government created a Ministry of Environment and Forests so that the various aspects related to natural resources (under the legislative control of the federal government) could be brought under one administrative setup and an appropriate coordination could be achieved. Thus, upgrading the status of the department provided added clout for the agency to press for pollution control and environmental conservation activities. At the end of the 1980s, the status of this ministry was upgraded. In addition to a minister of state, a senior minister with the rank of cabinet minister was appointed. The passage of the Environmental Protection Act of 1986 enhanced the policy and institutional base of the ministry.

Since its inception, the ministry has undertaken a massive pollution-control program. In February 1985, it established the Central Ganga Authority (CGA) to improve Ganga River quality by reducing the pollution load, establishing a series of sewage treatment plants along the main urban centers, renovating all the existing sewage pumping and treatment plants, providing waste-water sub-pumping stations at the outfall points of open drains not yet connected to the existing sewage system, extending the sewage treatment system to cover the unsewered areas, and constructing an electric crematorium. By 1992, 261 schemes were sanctioned by the Central Ganga Authority; and of these, 173 had been completed.[8] Seven new sewage treatment plants, out of a total of thirty-five to be established, have become operational. The authority has also identified 68 industries along the river basin that are grossly polluting the river. Using the provisions of the Environment Protection Act of 1986 and the Water Pollution Prevention Act of 1974, the authority has been able to get 43 of these industries to install their effluent treatment plants. Eight of the remaining 15 are constructing these units. Ten industries have been legally closed, while negotiations are under way with 7 of the industries which do not have the effluent treatment plants.

Other major initiatives undertaken by the ministry during the decade 1980–1990 are survey of natural resources (including intensive floral survey, faunal studies and survey, forest survey), passage of the Wildlife Protection Amendment Act 1991, establishment of tiger reserves and biosphere reserves, creation of guidelines for environmental impact assessment for major thermal and hydroelectric power projects, formulation of a national river action plan to undertake works (akin to the Ganga action plan) in other grossly polluted stretches of major rivers of the nation, establishment of the National Wastelands Development Board to promote afforestation and wastelands development, funding for various research studies (dealing with wetlands, mangroves, biosphere reserves, forestry, wildlife, and items relating to the Ganga action plan), environmental education and forestry-officers' training programs, wildlife education and training program, provision of cooperation to international programs, and participation in the formulation of international conventions and treaties, such as the Global Convention on Conservation of Biodiversity and the Montreal Protocol.

In order to accomplish these activities, the size and budget of the ministry have grown. In 1982, the Department of Environment had 250 (including technical and administrative) personnel with five divisions. By 1992, the number had grown to 1,023, with 23 divisions and various directorates and boards, such as the Ganga Project Directorate and National Wastelands Development Board, thirteen autonomous agencies (such as the Central Pollution Board in New Delhi, Center for Mining Environment), sixteen associated units (such as Forest Survey of India, Zoological Survey of India, Botanical Survey of India, Wildlife regional offices, and National Museum of Natural History), and one public-sector undertaking, Andaman & Nicobar Island Forests & Planning Development Corporation Ltd. During this period, the budget has increased from Rupees 138,643,000 to Rupees 2,664,400,000.[9]

Policy Instruments Used. The government of India, through its water pollution prevention and air pollution legislation has favored the policy of regulation and enforcement rather than the effluent charge strategy. The first mechanism requires the following four steps to be undertaken by the government:

1. The necessary national standards for the abatement of pollution must be established, which would then be implemented and enforced by the cen-

tral and state pollution control boards. The regulatory mechanism also includes the introduction of an "environmental audit" program for industries, as well as government public enterprises and local government undertakings, so that the operations and activities affecting the environment, particularly with the compliance with standards relating to effluent and emission control, can be measured and evaluated.[10] The Policy Statement for Abatement of Pollution issued by the government of India in February 1992 mentions the need for such an audit statement to be issued by industrial concerns and public undertakings. The government plans to change the existing standards, which are based on the level of concentration of pollutants in effluents and in emissions; instead, standards will be source-related to encourage the minimization of waste and promote recycling and reuse of materials.

2. The government needs to establish a set of penalties for noncompliance with the standards and regulations. For example, the Water (Prevention and Control of Pollution) Act of 1974 provides for imprisonment for up to three months or a fine of up to Rupees 5,000 or both; in the case of continuing violations, an additional fine of Rupees 1,000 per day can be levied. Under the Air (Prevention and Control of Pollution) Act of 1981, imprisonment up to three months and a fine of up to Rupees 10,000 or both can be handed down; in case of repetition, a fine of Rupees 100 per day can be levied; under the Environmental Protection Act of 1986, imprisonment of up to five months, a fine as high as Rupees 100,000, or both could be given; and in case of continuing offenses, a fine of Rupees 5,000 per day can be levied.

3. The third step involves a continuous process of monitoring and surveillance of the targeted industries to detect noncompliance with standards.

4. The fourth step requires that the enforcing agency take immediate steps, after warnings and recommendations have remained unheeded, using the judicial process to impose sanctions and penalties.

LEGAL MECHANISMS

More than two dozen laws protect India's environment. They cover all aspects of the environment—from pollution to conservation, from deforestation to nuclear waste. Some of these laws existed even before the environmental movement arrived on the world scene: Forestry Act of 1927, Orissa River Pollution Act of 1953, Punjab State Tubewell Act of 1954, West Bengal Control of Water Pollution Act of 1957, Jammu and Kashmir State Canal and Drainage Act of 1963, and the Maharashtra Water Pollution Prevention Act of 1969 are just a few examples. Despite these laws, by 1970 India was faced with an environmental crisis. Immediate and drastic actions were needed to cope with the magnitude of this crisis.

In the following section, five major environmental laws passed since 1970 are identified.[11] These laws are significant for two reasons. First, they help us understand the evolutionary process. Each major enactment points to a different set of political calculations and a different interpretation of costs and benefits. Second, the five laws form the nexus of all environmental activities in the nation. Despite being specific in nature, these laws together have built a common context for all environmental policy actions. Vogel calls this context "national style" and claims that different styles are the result of different underlying political processes and can lead to varying degrees of performance.[12]

The Water Act of 1974

The Water Act was passed in 1974 for the prevention and control of water pollution. The inclusion of "water pollution" as an agenda item came in 1962. The first response came from the Ministry of Health which appointed an expert committee to study the problem and prepare draft legislation to regulate the quality of water. It was realized that the issue could no longer be handled by state governments, which, according to the Indian Constitution, are responsible for regulating water quality. The committee recommended a shift in jurisdiction from state governments to the federal government. In 1965, a proposal was sent to all state governments to relinquish their jurisdiction in this area and to authorize the federal government to legislate. The response was apathetic. After much persuasion, six states granted their consent in 1969, and draft legislation was introduced in Rajya Sabha, the upper house of the parliament, in the same year. However, the parliament failed to show much enthusiasm.[13] The future of the issue remained ambivalent until after Indira Gandhi's return from the 1972 United Nations Conference on Human Environment. Mrs. Gandhi criticized the idea of channeling resources for the protection of the environment when nearly half of the Third World's population was hungry. However, upon her return, she assumed a crusading role in the promotion of the environmental issue, and the Water Act was finally passed overwhelmingly in 1974.

The Water Act covered all major sources of pollution by defining water pollution as "such contamination of water . . . or such discharge of any sewage or trade effluent or of any other liquid, gaseous or solid substance into water as may, or is likely to create a nuisance or render such water harmful or injurious to public health or safety, or to domestic, commercial, industrial, agricultural or other legitimate uses, or to the life and health of the animals or plants or of aquatic organisms."[14]

Under the legislation, a separate bureaucratic network was created—one central board, one state board in each consenting state, and some joint boards of two or more states to ensure abatement of interstate water pollution. The central water board was granted the right of advisement, execution, consultation, and coordination. State boards were granted the same rights within their territorial jurisdictions. Boards' powers were backed by several judicial provisions. Failure to comply was punishable by a term of three months in prison and a fine of Rupees 5,000. Repeated offenses could lead to a fine of Rupees 1,000 (U.S. $100) a day and a prison term of up to six years.

In later years, the provisions of the Water Act were strengthened twice. In 1977 the Water Cess Act was passed, and in 1988 the Water Act itself was amended. Under the Water Cess Act, each industry and local body was required to pay a nominal cess (tax) on water consumption. This cess was refundable up to 70 percent if the discharge of water did not exceed the permissible limits. Under the 1988 amendments to the Water Act, all industries—new or old—were required to obtain environmental clearance. In addition, penalties were doubled, and powers of the boards were more specifically defined.

While the Water Act provided comprehensive coverage of the issue of water pollution, it left many grey areas difficult to administer. First, the scope of the act was inadequately and restrictively defined. It failed to cover some critical sources of water pollution, such as groundwater contamination. Second, it allowed government agencies an undue flexibility. Municipalities, which should be primarily responsible for treating residential waste, remained free from direct liability. The head of any agency was not punishable "if he proves that the offense was committed without his knowledge or that he exercised all due diligence to prevent it."[15]

Third, the act failed to establish an independent revenue base for the boards. The Water Cess Act was an attempt in this direction; nonetheless, the amount of the fee was too small to make any dent.[16] Fourth, the act did not allow victims the right of prosecution. Charges could be brought to the courts only by boards. However, boards were overburdened and underfunded to such an extent that only 5 percent of public complaints could be processed by them.[17] Fifth, the penalties established by the act were also unrealistic. The cost of defiance for polluting industries was lower than the cost of compliance. Consequently, industries found it cheaper to pay fines than to adhere to pollution control guidelines. Last, the act provided no mechanism to prevent board "capture." In fact, during the last decade water boards have faced pressures from two sources: first by regulated interests; second by political bosses.

On the whole, the performance of the Water Act remains dismal. The level of pollution has not declined, although it is difficult to guess what would have been the level of pollution, had there been no legislation. According to the National Engineering and Research Institute (NEERI), 70 percent of the available water is polluted, and an estimated 73 million workdays are being lost every year, costing society 60 million Rupees 6 crores, because of pollution-related health problems. In addition, only 3 percent of the total population has access to the sewage treatment system and only 27 percent of the large and medium-sized industries have full or partial treatment facilities.[18]

The Air Act of 1981

The problem of air pollution is as severe as the problem of water pollution. According to a survey, the level of air pollution in major cities has nearly tripled in the last fifteen years. In 1984, 31 out of 48 thermal plants had no pollution-control measures. Over 40 percent of the vehicles in Delhi did not comply with emission standards.[19] According to the 1991 World Resource Institute, India ranks as the fifth largest climate polluter in the world, ranking after only the United States, the Soviet Union, Brazil, and China. Motor vehicles provide half the pollution in major cities. The countryside is not spared pollution either. Rural air pollution is caused primarily by wood-burning stoves. It is estimated that in the three hours of cooking time, women inhale as much carcinogenic benzopyrene as is contained in a pack of twenty cigarettes.

To control air pollution, the Air (Prevention and Control of Pollution) Act was enacted in 1981. The legislation defined air pollution as the presence of any "solid, liquid, or gaseous substance in such concentration as may be or tends to be injurious to human beings or other living creatures or plants or property or environment."[20] Like the Water Act, the Air Act specified penalties and prosecution guidelines. Also, no new industrial outlets could be built without the prior consent of air boards.

The Air Act suffered from the same shortcomings as the Water Act. Its language was not all-inclusive, penalties were minimal, time limits were not set, public input was not sought, and third-party rights were nonexistent. In addition, administrative support for the act was also questionable. Although the legislation provided for the creation of a separate enforcing network, the enforcement was placed under the jurisdiction of the water boards.[21] However, water boards were already resource starved and, in reality, could not cope with the burden of new responsibilities.

The Environment Protection Act of 1986

A small gas leak from Union Carbide's plant in Bhopal caused a major environmental disaster in 1984. The incident was labeled an accident, and blame was placed squarely on Union Carbide. Nonetheless, the incident shook both the world and the Indian policymakers. It was realized that despite fifty pieces of legislation, thirty of them on pollution alone, society was not safe from environmental disasters. This realization led to the enactment of the Environmental Protection Act (EPA) in 1986. The act has three major objectives: (1) to be supplementary rather than a new law, (2) to provide a clear focus of authority, and (3) to "plug loopholes" in existing laws.[22] The act provided the first official definition of "environment" and emphasized the interrelationship between people and their environment: "'Environment' includes water, air and land and the interrelationship which exists among and between water, air and land, and human beings, other living creatures, plants, micro-organism and property."[23]

The Environmental Protection Act allowed the central government to delegate authority and to use existing resources to implement the act. The act was similar to the Water Act in tone, words, and emphasis. Nonetheless, there were some added features. The act covered the entire nation and was not limited to the consenting states—a feature of the Water Act. Penalties were doubled. In addition, the third-party right to prosecute was granted, even though to a very limited extent. The act stated that any person, after giving a notice of sixty days to the central government, may take an offending party to the court.[24] The act fell short of environmentalists' expectations because it barred civil courts from entertaining environmental complaints, it freed agency heads from assuming full responsibility, and it denied citizens the right to sue the government for ignoring its duties. According to Ranbir Singh, "This act has been likened to a cobra that is seemingly fierce. It raises its hood and hisses menacingly but if you pry its jaws open, you will discover it has no venom in its fangs."[25]

The Forest (Conservation) Act of 1980 and National Forest Policy of 1988

Forests in India received special consideration from the British. They were used for export purposes, and their protection was considered crucial to the British interests. In 1878, a special ordinance passed by the British classified Indian forests into three categories: restricted forests, which were restricted from the people; protected forests, which were accessible to the people although certain restrictions applied; and village forests, which were open to the public. This classification, for the first time, defined forests as commercial goods and placed them directly under the government's domain.[26]

In 1927, the British passed the Indian Forestry Act and took complete control of the forests. Since then, the management of forests has been directly under the control of the government. The government of free India accepted this responsibility and passed the Forest Policy Act in 1952. At the time of the policy's inception, 22 percent of the nation was under tree cover. One of the goals of the policy was to increase this cover to 33 percent. However, several reports in the late 1970s indicated that instead of increasing, the tree cover had, in fact, been further reduced. Consequently, the government of India issued a guideline to all state governments against the use of forest land for any nonforestry purpose. Unfortunately, the guideline proved ineffective. Within the next 25 years, tree cover was reduced to only 14 percent of total area.[27] Consequently, the government passed the Forest (Conservation) Act in 1980. The passage of the act was primarily based on the truth that the forests are being destroyed very fast in the country, especially in the Himalayas and other hill areas. The continued process of ruthless destruction of forests is not only leading to heavy erosion of soil, erratic rainfall, and frequent floods but also causing acute shortage of fodder, industrial wood, and firewood. More significant is the loss of productivity due to degraded and eroded lands.[28]

According to the Forest (Conservation) Act, a prior approval of the central government was required for any diversion of forest land by anyone, including government agencies. The definition of "non-forest purposes" included developmental projects, transportation projects, and cash crops, such as tea, coffee, spices, rubber, medicinal plants, and horticultural plants. The unique feature of the act was that it placed liability on public officials and in cases of negligence allowed their imprisonment for up to fifteen days. In 1989, nearly 4,000 requests were submitted, of which nearly 50 percent were approved.[29]

The performance of the forestry laws left much to be desired. According to a report by the Forest Survey of India released in 1987, 1.5 million hectares of forests were still being lost each year; and 12,000 million tons of soil were being lost to erosion each year. Among other consequences, this assault on forests doubled the vulnerability of the surrounding land to floods and droughts in just one decade, from 1970 to 1980.[30] Needless to say, environmentalists were beginning to question not just the design of the policy but also its underlying assumptions. Consequently, in 1988, revised version of the 1952 National Forest Policy came into existence. The revised policy declared seven basic objectives of forest management: (1) maintenance of environmental stability and conservation of the country's natural heritage; (2) checking soil erosion and sand dunes; (3) increasing the forest cover through social forestry; (4) meeting the rural people's needs for fuelwood, fodder, and timber; (5) increasing the productivity of forests to meet the nation's increasing needs; (6) efficient use of forest produce; and (7) creating mass awareness.

The newly stated objectives clearly indicated a more regulatory direction in the management of the forests. Increasing forest productivity, motivating people to develop forest areas, providing fodder and fuel through "conveniently located depots" at reasonable prices, and approving land-use proposals all were to be the responsibility of the government. Even though the policy was applauded for recognizing the dependency of the people—rural and urban—on forests, it was also vehemently criticized for ignoring the need of decentralization and deregulation of the process. It was reported in a newspaper that "nothing has been proposed about the forest department, land laws, judiciary, panchayats and so on. If supplementary changes in socioeconomic and administrative legal system are not required, why a new policy at all?"[31]

During the last two decades, the government of India has made significant progress in providing legal protection to the environment, yet several loopholes exist. For instance, noise pollution is not covered by any law, though several laws, including the Air Act, the Factories Act, and the Motor Vehicle Act, put certain restrictions on polluters. The use of pesticides is another overlooked area. According to a report, out of 22,000 deaths worldwide due to pesticide poisoning, about one-third take place in India.[32] BHC, DDT, and endosulfane are the primary causes of pesticide pollution.

In addition, nuclear waste continues to pose significant problems. This waste is controlled under the Atomic Energy Act of 1962. Under the act, the federal government has full jurisdiction over the management of nuclear waste. The activities of the Department of Atomic Energy, which is the primary agency responsible for nuclear waste management, are not open to public scrutiny for national security reasons. This nonaccountability keeps this policy area away from the active environmental agenda.

INSTITUTIONAL SUPPORT

Institutional support for the environmental issue began with the creation of the NCEPC in 1972.[33] The move was a direct response to the call by the United Nations to prepare a status report on the nation's environment. NCEPC was an advisory body, and its scope was extremely limited. Nonetheless, it served an important function by initiating a forum for political debate on the issue. Water boards created by the Water Act of 1974 were the second major providers of institutional support. However, they too were ineffective. The trivial nature of the institutional support base changed in 1980 with the creation of the Department of Environment (DOE). The body was created in response to the recommendations made by an investigative committee (known as the Tiwari Committee) appointed by Indira Gandhi (Department of Science and Technology, 1980). Like its counterpart of the same name in the United Kingdom, the DOE was formed by amalgamating components from different departments and independent agencies. In its watchdog capacity, the department was to carry out several environmental functions, such as appraisal of developmental projects, protection of wildlife, monitoring of water and air quality, promotion of research, and international cooperation.[34] The DOE faced harsh criticism right from its cradle. It had no political or financial base; therefore it failed to perform as a regulatory agency. It was ineffective partly because of its advisory capacity and partly because of its fragmented structure.

The Ministry of Environment and Forests

With the rise of Rajiv Gandhi as "the new age leader" in 1985, the issue of environment received some serious attention. Environmental laws were tightened, new programs were initiated, and the enforcing network was significantly strengthened. The major step taken by the Gandhi govern-ment was to raise the status of the Department of Environment to a minis-terial agency. The Ministry of Environment and Forests (MEF) came into existence in 1985. Several organizations were brought under its fold, and several new components were created to give it a unified status.

The ministry today is headed by a union minister of environment, who is assisted by a minister of state for environment and a full-ranked secretary. It consists of eighteen divisions, eleven autonomous agencies, and six associ-ated units. Since its inception, the MEF has continued to grow in size and specialization. Forest conservation was added as a division in 1987, and haz-ardous substances management and forestry international cooperation in 1988. In 1991, the ministry had a total technical and clerical staff of 1,023 in its head-quarters in New Delhi. This number indeed is minuscule when compared to the staffing strength of 15,000 in the U.S. Environmental Protection Agency; nonetheless, it is a significant increase from the figure of 250 in 1982.

The ministry performs two types of functions: custodial and regulatory. Under the custodial functions, it assumes full responsibility over certain as-pects of environmental management. These include pollution monitoring, ecogeneration, assessment of flora and fauna, forest resource development, wildlife protection, and wetland management. Under the regulatory func-tions, the ministry sets standards, conducts environmental impact assessments, and controls industrialization. One of its major regulatory programs is the Ganga action plan. Initiated in 1985, the plan is being implemented by the CGA, and aims to restore the quality of the Ganges.[35] With a budget of U.S. $180 million, the plan consists of 262 schemes in the three states housing the river. As of 1990, 179 schemes were either complete or near completion.[36]

The MEF is also entrusted with the right to conduct Environmental Impact Assessments (EIA). The objective of EIA is "to achieve sustained develop-ment with minimal environmental degradation and prevention of long term adverse effects on environment by incorporating suitable preventive and con-trol measures."[37] However, EIA, like many other regulatory tools, is proving ineffective. To begin with, the ministry is not properly equipped to carry out this major function. Lack of information and scarcity of basic resources have limited its ability to such an extent that the function itself has turned into a political burden. The MEF is criticized for delaying approvals beyond a toler-able time. Today, the ministry draws criticism not only from developmentalists and industrialists but also from its own constituents, which include social activists, pubic and elected officials, and state governments.

Ironically, the environment assessment function has created major conflicts even within the ministry itself. One side is claimed by technical experts who favor a purely technical assessment of projects, while the other side is sup-ported by bureaucrats who prefer a more balanced look at them. In addition, the practice of EIA has also added to corruption because there is ample room for the use of administrative discretion at every level.

In addition, the ministry also serves as the primary source of data collection. The Environmental Information System (ENVIS) Network is housed in the ministry, with ten regional branches. The objective of ENVIS is to collect, store, retrieve, and disseminate environmental information to all concerned.

Institutional Support in a Federal System

One of the challenges of the environmental crisis is its complexity, which asks for global planning yet demands local action. Since all layers of government are involved in one way or another, environmental programs often turn into political turf battles. The Indian federal system is no exception. State water boards were the first exclusively environmental institutions to emerge. For a long time, they suffered from political malnutrition and economic disability. Kerala Water Board, for instance, claimed five years after its inception that "the board is still in its infancy and is working under severe handicaps of non-availability of funds to the extent required and consequent lack of manpower and infrastructure." It further presented its plight by saying that "the plan outlay under the retention and control of water pollution is fixed at Rs. 50 lakhs [approximately US $500,000] in the Sixth Five-Year Plan against the proposed outlay of Rs. 3 crores [$3 million] spread over a period of five years. . . . But unfortunately the government has very recently suggested that even this meager plan outlay of Rs. 50 lakhs should be reduced to Rs. 30 lakhs."[38]

In fact, the funding support of state-level environmental agencies remains a major source of discontent. In the budgeting process, a preferential treatment is given to the central government. In fact, the majority of the budget is at the disposal of the central government. Ironically, in the environmental field, while state governments are the primary implementers of environmental policies, they are not the primary receivers of environmental monies. The ratio of budget outlay for the Seventh Five-Year Plan (1985–1990) was 7 to 1 in favor of the central government.[39] In addition to the water boards, 19 departments of environment also exist in the states. These departments are entrusted with the responsibility of providing assistance to their state governments and to implement policies of the Ministry of Environment and Forests. Constant appeals are made by the central government to strengthen the power base of these departments, but most still remain without adequate power bases. Their effectiveness varies from state to state depending on the states' commitments and their levels of public awareness.

In brief, the distribution of responsibilities—where the central government is responsible for making decisions and state governments for implementing them—has failed to work. The arrangement puts the state-level environmental agencies under the authority of two masters—the state governments and the MEF. Consequently, they face conflicting pressures—those set by the state governments and those set by the MEF. Often, the conflict emerges over difference in the calculations of costs and benefits. A state government may view a project as necessary for its economic sustainability and therefore may pressure the state environmental agency to be "reasonable" in its judgment. At the same time, however, the MEF may view the project from a national standpoint and pressure the state environmental agency to apply universal standards. State-level agencies are thus forced to please and represent two separate masters without having the resource bases to serve even one of them.

FROM RAJIV TO MANEKA AND BEYOND

While the issue of environment received attention during the Rajiv Gandhi years, this attention was secondary to Gandhi's overall emphasis on "technologization of India." After Gandhi's government failed to secure a majority in the 1989 elections, the nation came under the rule of a loosely assembled confederation of opposition parties led by V. P. Singh. From its inception, the Singh government was marred by disagreements among party members. The environmental cause remained untouched by this political warfare, however, primarily because of Maneka Gandhi. Singh appointed Maneka Gandhi, an administratively inexperienced yet environmentally committed leader, to head the Ministry of Environment and Forests. Maneka was aggressive and outspoken; her brash style of administration offered new opportunities to consider the environmental issue. She made it political simply by making it controversial. Her outspokenness annoyed public officials and businessmen alike and attracted media attention. Maneka Gandhi's strategy dealt with substantive issues. In brief, it combined the following items: (1) establishment of environmental courts to empower rural and urban people who thus far had no redress for environmental crimes committed against them, (2) comprehensive review of all environmental laws, (3) immediate crackdown on factory and vehicular pollution and implementation of the Motor Vehicle Act of 1989, (4) amendment of the Environmental Protection Act to make it mandatory for all projects to go through environmental impact assessment, (5) replacement of harmful chemical pesticides with biological pesticides, (6) introduction of the concept of environment-friendly products, (7) establishment of the National Waste Management Council, (8) revamping of Project Tiger, and (9) regular televising of environmental news.[40]

One of the most controversial policy moves was the idea of establishing environmental courts to speed up the process of environmental decision making and make it more costly for polluters to pay the penalty than to comply. However, the proposal to establish environmental courts failed to win governmental support. By 1989, the Maneka agenda was beginning to become a political burden for the government. Her enthusiasm was unpalatable to a government that was growing politically unstable, as well as economically bankrupt. Consequently, a barrier was created in the person of Nilmani Routray, a 77-year-old political veteran. Routray was assigned to the newly created position of union minister, a position higher in authority than

Maneka's position as minister of state. Maneka was left with symbolic powers, which some newspapers referred to as nothing more than "the management of Delhi Zoo."[41] Routray was given the ultimate responsibility to oversee the Ministry of Environment and Forests.

In 1991, Rajiv Gandhi's assassination changed the political equilibrium for the environmental issue again. Not only did the Congress(I) party lose its leader, it also had to survive on the support of other parties as it formed a minority government after the 1991 general election when neither Congress(I) nor any other party emerged as a clearcut winner. Consequently, a coalition government led by Congress(I) and headed by P. V. Narsimha Rao was formed. The Ministry of Environment and Forests was assigned to Kamal Nath. Kamal Nath led the India delegation to the Rio Earth Summit in June 1992. He reiterated Rajiv Gandhi's proposal that a Planet Protection Fund should be established by the rich North to assist the developing nations in their struggle for environmental protection and sustainable development. In the foreword to the national report prepared for the UNCED Conference in Rio de Janeiro, Kamal Nath stated: "It is clear that action for environment and development can be effective only if the various levels of government work in close harmony with NGO and concerned citizens."[42] The ministry also issued a policy document in June 1992, the National Conservation Strategy and Policy Statement on Environment and Development.[43]

While it is quite early to comment on the performance of the Nath ministry, some observations can be made. Overall, the support base for the environmental issue does not seem promising. Several factors account for this pessimism. First, a coalition government is hardly likely to take bold steps to shake up the existing equilibrium, particularly if public dissatisfaction is not threatening. Second, the troubled economy of the nation is unlikely to leave any room on the agenda for environmental issues. With the inflation rate in double digits and foreign debt nearing US $50 billion, the agenda is full of structural adjustments and economic recovery issues.[44] Two issues are of particular importance—liberalization of the economy and streamlining of the public sector—both initiated in mid-1991 and both expected to have a lasting impact on the nation's priorities.[45]

ENVIRONMENTAL POLICY AND MANAGEMENT: DANGERS LURKING?

Throughout the world, the feelings of desperation and failure are prevalent in the environmental policy area, partly because of the magnitude of the problem itself and partly because of an ever-increasing gap between policy goals and policy performance. Researchers offer several explanations for the environmental deficit. Most of these explanations can be clustered into two broad categories: policy related and administration related. Policy-related explanations point to the existence of a policy trap—or the absence of an adequate legal mandate to resolve the issue. On the other hand, administration-related explanations indicate the existence of an administrative trap—a situation where policies are ineffective because their administration is nonexistent or largely inadequate. According to Randall Baker, the administrative trap exists because "there is considerable dysfunction between the nature of ecological problems and the problem-solving structures within the public arena."[46]

In India's case, the "policy-trap" argument can hardly be substantiated. Indeed, several areas of environmental protection fall in this category. Hazardous waste, nuclear waste, acid rain, and the ozone layer are clearly in need of more regulation. Yet there are sufficient environmental regulations to cover the environmental issue to a reasonable extent. The question is certainly not of numbers but of design. It is not the absence of a policy, but the inadequacy of its design that is at the core of the discussion because faulty policy designs lead to administrative traps which, in turn, lead to policy failure. The argument of administrative trap or administrative failure has already found wide support in the literature.[47] These and related issues are discussed in the following sections.

Inadequate Foundational Support

While over two dozen environmental laws exist, they collectively fail to establish a solid, forceful, and comprehensive administrative network. More often than not, administrative guidelines are established without an effort to follow them up. The water and air acts are prime examples of this paradox. The administrative network created for the enforcement of the two pollution control laws fails on several accounts. It fails to establish any clearcut lines of accountability. Overcentralization of legislative power cripples legislative innovativeness. Ironically, under the Indian federal system, only the responsibility for the environment is delegated, the authority to manage it is not.

Although the legal foundation for the environmental issue in India is a hybrid of the American and the British foundations, the mix is not properly balanced to suit the indigenous context of efficient management. In line with American policy, Indian environmental policy emphasizes adherence to standards, establishment of universal standards, and a centralized process, but it leaves the bureaucracy unaccountable. It does not create any mechanism to "watch the watchdog"—a function largely performed by the public and the media in the United States. Similarly, the Indian policy is an imitation of the British environmental policy when it comes to administrative flexibility and the use of discretion. Unlike the British policy, this flexibility does not properly reach to the local levels. This hybrid arrangement has produced an administrative authority that is inherently weak and enjoys little or no public support.

The Environment Protection Act of 1986 realized the need for an integrated policy approach, but even this act failed to create an integrated administrative network. Consequently, while the act filled policy gaps, it failed to fill the gaps in the administrative system.

Over the years, the environmental administrative machinery has successfully evolved from a showpiece agency into a viable force—from an advisory Department of Environment into a full-fledged Ministry of Environment and Forests. Nonetheless, it must still learn to use its force.

Lack of Administrative Rationality

The administrative network is embedded in a culture that does not foster compliance.[48] Polluters and offenders find the cost of compliance greater than the cost of defiance. Low penalties and lengthy prosecution procedures make it easier for polluters to pay fines than for them to install pollution control measures. Only the sunrise industries, particularly the ones that enjoy the government's protection, can afford to install pollution control devices. For others, the competition to survive is so intense that it prevents them from making any new capital investments. In addition, even though the Ministry of Environment and Forests is developing a research base to provide technical assistance to the users of natural resources, the help is far less than the demand. At present, industries are burdened to find their own solutions. The cost of research adds another excuse for resistance. Several countries, notably Hong Kong, provide some form of institutionalized research support to polluters. The Hong Kong Productivity Council, for instance, helps industries by designing their individualized technological solutions. No such technological cooperation is available in India.

For regulators, the cost of enforcement is higher than the cost of nonenforcement. Public officials lack a political constituency. In India, they also lack public credibility. In addition to suffering from the lack of political support and public credibility, environmental regulators also suffer from interdepartmental rivalry. Relatively speaking, the MEF is a newcomer, entrusted with a role that infringes upon the traditional jurisdictions of other agencies, particularly of transportation, industrial development, rural development, and agriculture. Paradoxically, the MEF's power base does not match its complex set of responsibilities.

The politicization of the MEF further adds to the burden of regulating. Top positions in the MEF remain dependent on political loyalty rather than on environmental commitment—a phenomenon made clear by the appointment of Routray over Maneka Gandhi in 1990. Moreover, lower-level bureaucrats are not free from political and social pressures either. They are often undercut by powerful social interests. For example, it is a common practice for an industry to approach a higher-up "connection" if lower-level bureaucrats fail to adhere to their whims and fancies.[49]

Lack of Grassroots Support

Even though significant social support for the environmental issue exists, opportunities to transform it into political support are minimal. Political parties prefer to rally around those issues that are politically attractive. Environment, despite its appeal, has a drawback: It has a countergrowth dimension. As long as political parties support the principles of environmental protection, they remain in the safety zone. When they start to pinpoint strategies, such as industry closure or restrictions on forest contractors, however, they run the risk of being perceived as antipublic. Thus, political parties, in general, shy away from microlevel campaigning on the issue.

Interest groups also fail to provide political opportunities. Under the Indian parliamentary system, groups are forced to identify with political parties. Since voting in the parliament is on party lines, groups find it worthless to lobby individual legislators. Their interests are best served by keeping in touch with party bosses and with high-level civil servants. This situation forces groups to be captivated by political parties. Dependent on the mercy of the party bosses, the groups often turn to individual civil servants. Civil servants, thus, become the targets of "politicking."

India and the Earth Summit in Rio (1992)

The Indian delegation to the Earth Summit in Rio de Janeiro consisted of the Union Environment and Forest Minister Kamal Nath and nine ministers of environment from state governments. This delegation was preceded by a group of senior officials of the federal and provincial governments. The Indian delegation proposed a "Planet Protection Fund" to buy environmentally friendly technology and make it available gratis to any nation. This concept was first advanced by the Indian Prime Minister Rajiv Gandhi in 1989. The summit considered six treaties dealing with toxic and nuclear waste, foreign debt, forests, agriculture, plant and animal diversity, and a clearing house to share information on advances in environmental technology. In the summit, some nations were critical of the stand taken by the industrial nations. For example, the governor of the Brazilian State of Amazonia stated that the ecology movement was a First World plot to keep the Third World poor. The biodiversity treaty was signed by 98 countries, including Canada, India, and others, but U.S. President George Bush declined to sign it.

Concluding Observations

The two decades since the U.N.-sponsored Human Environment Conference in 1972 have seen a steady and growing awareness among the elites in India about the ecological challenges facing their nation. This has been followed by an impressive growth of institutions established to deal with the problems of pollution and environmental conservation at both the national and the provincial level. At the same time, the mounting pressures of population, expanding urbanization, and the growing base of poverty have led to the ecologically unsustainable exploitation of natural resources which is threatening the fragile balance between ecology and humanity in India. Although India is not alone in this challenge, its problems will have to be tackled by its own people. The real challenge before India is how to preserve its environment, meet the basic needs of its growing population on an overburdened land, fulfil the necessary energy requirements of the people, and yet leave a legacy for future generations so that they may also enjoy the bounty of nature which the present generation is recklessly exploiting. The task is no doubt stupendous, for the hitherto unimaginative developmental strategies and largely imitative developmental schemes would have to be replaced by environmentally sound and sustainable development. The nation will have to search for ways to usher in *sarvodaya* in the least wasteful ways compared to the present system; for this, the country would do well to derive from its rich cultural heritage and the traditional conservation ethos a way to look ahead in harmony with environmental imperatives of the land.

NOTES

1. India, Ministry of Environment and Forests, "Policy Statement for Abatement of Pollution," New Delhi, Government of India, 1992, p. 3.

2. India, Ministry of Environment and Forests, "National Conservation Strategy and Policy Statement on Environment and Development," New Delhi, Government of India, 1992, p. 3.

3. India, Ministry of Environment and Forests, "Traditions, Concerns and Efforts in India," report prepared for the UNCED Conference in Rio de Janeiro, June 1992, Ahmedabad, Centre for Environmental Education, 1992, p. 13.

4. Saad Ali, "Environmental Refugees: Multi-dimensional Problem," *Survey of the Environment, 1991* (Madras: The Hindu, 1991), p. 34.

5. G. Venkataramani, "Pesticides: Harm Far Outweighs Use," *Survey of the Environment, 1992* (Madras: The Hindu, 1992), p. 129.

6. O. P. Dwivedi, "India: Pollution Control Policy and Programs," *International Review of Administrative Sciences* 43.2 (1977): 123–133.

7. O. P. Dwivedi, "Environmental Regulations in India," *The Environmental Professional* 7 (1985): 101.

8. India, Ministry of Environment and Forests, "Annual Report, 1991–92," New Delhi, Government of India, 1992, p. 54.

9. India, Department of Environment, "Annual Report, 1982–83," New Delhi, Government of India, 1983, p. 74; India, Ministry of Environment and Forests, "Annual Report, 1991–92," pp. 96–99.

10. India, Ministry of Environment and Forests, "Abatement of Pollution," p. 11.

11. Dwivedi, "Environmental Regulations," pp. 121–127.

12. D. Vogel, *National Styles of Regulation: Environmental Policy in Great Britain*

and the United States (Ithaca: Cornell University Press, 1986).

13. *Lok Sabha Debates* (New Delhi: Government of India, 1974), p. 240.

14. "Water (Prevention and Control of Pollution) Act," New Delhi, Proceedings of Government of India, 1974.

15. "The Water Act," section 48.

16. M. R. Garg and N. S. Tiwana, "The Water Cess Act, 1977: Problems and Suggestions," *Environment Management in India*, ed. R. K. Sapru (New Delhi: Ashish, 1987).

17. R. Khator, *Environment, Development and Politics in India* (Lanham, Md.: University Press of America, 1991).

18. A. Aggrawal and S. Narain, *The State of India's Environment, 1984–85: The Second Citizens' Report* (New Delhi: Centre for Science and Technology, 1985).

19. Ibid.

20. "Air (Prevention and Control of Pollution) Act," New Delhi, Government of India, 1981.

21. Ibid., section 3.

22. India, Ministry of Environment and Forests, "Annual Report, 1986–87," New Delhi, Government of India, 1987, p. 10.

23. "Environment (Protection) Act, 1986," New Delhi, Government of India, 1986.

24. Ibid., section 19b.

25. Ranbir Singh, "Noise Pollution: Some Legal Perspective," *Environment Management in India*, ed. R. K. Sapru (New Delhi: Ashish, 1987), p. 132.

26. S. Kulkarni, "The Forest Policy and the Forest Bill: A Critique and Suggestions for Change," *Towards a New Forest Policy: People's Rights and Environmental Needs*, ed. W. Fernandes and S. Kulkarni (New Delhi: Indian Social Institute, 1983), p. 87.

27. "Forest Cover Depleting Fast in India," *The Hindu* 9 June 1990.

28. India, Ministry of Environment and Forests, "Annual Report, 1989–90," New Delhi, Government of India, 1990), p. 23.

29. Ibid., p. 24.

30. India, Department of Forests, "Forest Survey of India, 1987," New Delhi, 1987.

31. V. Pandey, "Forest Policy: Cosmetic Changes," *The Hindu* 3 June 1990.

32. D. Hathi, "Safe to Wash, Peel & Boil," *Deccan Herald* 9 June 1990.

33. Dwivedi, "Environmental Regulations," pp. 121-127.

34. India, "Report of the Committee for Recommending Legislative Measures and Administrative Machinery for Ensuring Environmental Protection," New Delhi, Department of Science and Technology, 1980, p. 2.

35. India, Ministry of Environment and Forests, "An Action Plan for Prevention of Pollution of the Ganga," New Delhi, Government of India, 1985.

36. India, Ministry of Environment and Forests, "Annual Report, 1989–90," p. 46.

37. India, Ministry of Environment and Forests, "Annual Report, 1986–87," p. 28.

38. Kerala, State Pollution Control Board, "Annual Report," Trivendram, Government of Kerala, India, 1983, p. 6.

39. Khator, *Environment, Development and Politics*, p. 113.

40. R. Kane, "The Good Green Work Undone," *The Independent* 21 June 1990; B. Sahgal, "What if Maneka Has a Yuppie Accent?" *The Times of India* 8 June 1990.

41. "Routray, Maneka Rift Comes to the Fore," *Indian Express* 2 June 1990.

42. India, Ministry of Environment and Forests, "Traditions, Concerns and Efforts in India," report to UNCED, June 1992, Ahmedabad, Centre for Environment Education, 20 May 1992.

43. India, Ministry of Environment and Forests, "National Conservation Strategy."

44. S. Chakravarti, Z. Agha, and S. A. Aiyar, "The Economy: Bold Gamble," *India Today* 31 July 1991: 11.

45. H. Sanotra, "Reshuffling the Raj," *India Today* 15 August 1991: 18–19.

46. Randall Baker, "Institutional Innovation, Development, and Environmental Management: An Administrative Trap?" *Public Administration and Development* 9 (1990): 29–47.

47. J. Bandopadhyay, N. D. Jayal, U. Schoettli, and C. Singh, *India's Environment: Crises and Responses* (Dehradun: Natraj, 1985); *Environment Management in India*, ed. R. K. Sapru (New Delhi: Ashish, 1987).

48. Khator, *Environment, Development and Politics.*

49. O. P. Dwivedi and R. B. Jain, *India's Administrative State* (New Delhi: Gitanjali, 1985).

Environmental Protection in China

GEORGE P. JAN

All developing countries are confronted with the conflict between development and environment. Economic development requires rapid industrial expansion at minimal cost; but this often leads to detrimental effects on the environment, such as liquid, gaseous, and solid waste pollution. How to reconcile this contradiction is a great challenge to the developing countries. China is no exception.

In many respects, China's environmental problem is more severe because of the imbalance between its enormous population and its limited resources, especially arable land. The per capita acreage of farmland in China is much smaller than that of most countries of the world.[1] The rapid economic expansion since the early 1980s reduced the size of farmland, and the loosened control of population growth in the past several years in the countryside further accentuated the shortage of farmland per capita.

Historically, there was a close linkage between population and political stability in China. Whenever there was a serious imbalance between farmland and population, there was political instability, often in the form of domestic rebellion. For example, the fall of the Ming dynasty in 1644 and the Taiping Rebellion from 1850 to 1863 were caused in part by the imbalance between farmland and population.

With no possibility of substantial land reclamation, the only alternative for China to solve the problem of overpopulation is to develop the nonagricultural sector. But industrialization without adequate environmental protection will cause degradation of the Chinese ecosystem. This will adversely affect China's economic development. Adequate environmental protection will require additional capital and modern technology, both of which are in short supply. How to resolve this problem is a great challenge to the Chinese government.

The main purpose of this chapter is to investigate environmental protection in China since the late 1970s when China launched its reforms. Special attention is placed on China's environmental policy, laws and regulations, government agencies, and the present conditions of environmental protection resulting from the enforcement of the environmental protection policies and laws. The scientific and technical aspects of environmental protection are outside the scope of this inquiry. It is also hoped that this chapter can shed some new light on environmental management in the developing countries.

THE CHINESE ENVIRONMENT

China is a Third World country and has many of the same developmental problems as other developing countries. But China has some unique conditions that need special consideration. The first is the large population. With more than 1.1 billion people in 1990, China is the most populous country in the world, representing one-fifth of the human race. Another special condition is the scarcity of arable land per capita. The arable land in the early 1980s included 99.3 million hectares, only 10.4 percent of the total land area. Even the unofficial estimate was only 139.3 million hectares, constituting 14.6 percent of the total land area.[2] A source in Taiwan indicated that in 1978 China had 1,490,840,000 mus (1 acre equals 6 mus) of arable land and 962,590,000 people. The per capita arable land was 1.55 mus (0.26 acre). By 1988, China had 1,435,830,000 mus of land and 1,096,140,000 people, a loss of 55,010,000 mus to industrial expansion and other nonfarming use. The per capita arable land was 1.31 mus (0.22 acre).[3]

Official Chinese sources indicate that in 1991 the per capita arable land was less than 1.5 mus (0.25 acre). Every year China loses 5 million mus of farmland to industrial and other construction use. The quality of land has been deteriorating because of soil erosion and pollution. China has insufficient aquatic resources. The per capita aquatic resource is 2,700 cubic meters, only one-fourth of the world average. Because of insufficient mineral energy, forests were destroyed for fuel. The rate of forest coverage is only 12.9 percent.[4] China has 23 percent of the world's population and 5 percent of the world's arable land. The per capita water, land, and other resources are very low compared to those of other countries.[5]

Because of the destruction of forests and water resources and in the wake of industrial pollution, the climate in some regions has changed. This in turn increased the frequency and intensity of natural disasters, such as floods and droughts. In the 1960s, natural disasters occurred once every three to five years. In the 1970s, once every three years, and in the 1980s, the area affected by natural disasters has increased by 58 percent from the 1960s.[6]

Because of the deterioration of the ecosystem and the pollution caused by agricultural chemicals, the insect problem became more serious. Now all agricultural production must use chemicals. This has increased the cost of agricultural chemicals and accelerated the decline of agricultural production in some years because of natural disasters.[7]

The main sources of pollution today are industrial liquid, solid, and gaseous wastes. The treatment and recycling rate is only 20 percent. This means that about 80 percent of the industrial wastes eventually enter the ecosystem. In 1981, 60 million mus of farmland were directly polluted by industrial wastes. Economic loss was more than 10 million Renminbi. The number of pollution incidents causing economic loss of 1,000.00 Renminbi or more increased from 2,573 in 1983 to 2,753 in 1985. It reached 3,699 in 1986. In 1988, the fines for pollution amounted to 82,630,000 Renminbi.[8]

In 1991, 30 million mus of farmland and 10 million mus of grassland were polluted. Acid rain has seriously affected the ecosystem in south China.[9]

According to an investigation of 55,000 kilometers of the rivers in China from 1982 to 1983, 85.9 percent of them were unfit to drink or use for fishing, 23.7 percent were unfit for irrigation, and 4.3 percent of them were so seriously polluted that the fish had disappeared. Pollution of the waters results every year on the average in 1,000 incidents of fish death. The fishery industry loses 50,000 tons of fish and shrimp and 100,000 tons of natural marine products, with a total loss of 300 million Renminbi.[10]

Rural industries are another source of pollution that caused damage to agriculture. According to official Chinese statistics, in 1988, the value of production by rural enterprises was 474,309,000,000 Renminbi. They increased 33.9 percent over the previous year. Of the total value, industrial production was 324,350,000,000 Renminbi, representing 25 percent of China's total industrial production. It increased 34.5 over the previous year. In 1988, the value of rural industrial production equaled the value of the total industrial production of China in 1975.[11]

The expansion of rural industries increased pollution in rural areas. In 1984, the discharge of industrial waste water, air, and solids was 10.69 percent, 9.34 percent, and 11.10 percent of the national total respectively. Eleven percent of rural industries were polluting. The overall pollution caused by rural industries was about 10 percent of the national total. It was estimated that by 1991 it represented 20 percent.[12]

Although China attempts to control pollution in the rural areas, the rapid expansion of rural industries has made the situation worse than before, especially in the more industrialized rural areas in the coastal regions in south and southeast China. In these regions, all the small rivers in rural areas have been polluted. In many places a small factory polluted a whole small river. The condition continues to deteriorate.[13]

Pollution in the cities is also serious. In 1991, city residents annually produced 10 billion tons of waste water, 73 billion tons of trash, 60 billion tons of human waste, and 2.5 million tons of sulphur dioxide from burning 150 million tons of coal. This constituted one-sixth of the total sulphur dioxide discharge.[14] Trash from cities occupied 300,000 mus of land.[15]

Agricultural development also created ecological problems for China. The reclamation of land without environmental design caused desertification. In recent years, China experienced the increase of desert area by 20 million mus a year. The drought and desert area in China reached 1,090,000 square kilometers. For instance, in Inner Mongolia, the desert area increased from 340 million mus in 1960 to 450 million mus in 1980.[16]

The area of soil erosion increased from 1,160,000 square kilometers in 1949 to 1,500,000 square kilometers in 1991. As a result of soil erosion, one-fourth of the capacity of the 86,000 water reservoirs built since 1949 has been silted up. The reclamation of farmland around the lakes in south China adversely affected their capacity to absorb excess water from rivers during the flood season. The fishery industry has also declined as a result.[17]

It was estimated that in 1988 China's economic loss to pollution and degradation was from about 100 to 160 billion Renminbi, representing 7 to 12 percent of China's GNP in that year.[18]

In summary, China is now facing a serious problem of environmental pollution and degradation. All major indicators of environmental change point to worsening conditions in the future. These include population, arable land, wood reserves, water needs, waste water, energy use, and SO_2 emissions.[19] The Chinese government is fully aware of the need to improve environmental management. Some progress has been made in certain areas, but the overall situation continues to worsen.

Another factor is that China is a communist country with a planned economy. Before the early 1950s, its economic developmental strategy was influenced by the Soviet model of emphasizing the development of heavy industries. As a communist system, China confronts the perennial conflict between economic incentive and equitable distribution.

ENVIRONMENTAL PROTECTION POLICY

Although the Chinese communist government, established in 1949, was aware of the importance of environmental protection in its national economic development, China did not pay serious attention to this problem until the 1970s. A beginning was made in 1972 when China attended the Stockholm Conference on Human Environment. After this conference, China began to develop rudimentary government structures and adopted some regulations designed to protect the environment. In 1973, China held its first national conference on environmental protection where many problems were discussed. In 1974 the State Council, roughly the cabinet of the Chinese government, set up the Leading Group of Environmental Protection which was responsible for formulating environmental policies. In 1979, the Law for Environmental Protection was promulgated, the most comprehensive environmental protection law ever adopted in China. A series of government decrees was also promulgated later.

The Chinese government adopted some basic policies designed to reconcile the conflict between industrial growth and environmental protection. One is the policy of controlling the growth of large urban areas and the distribution of industries in rural areas by constructing or expanding small cities and towns. Another policy is to control pollution through law. Another is to encourage industries to manage pollution control and recycling through tax incentives. Another is to impose fines on polluting industries. The fines generally cost polluting industries more than pollution control. Thus, it is hoped that there will be an incentive for industries to control pollution rather than to be fined.[20]

The Chinese government began to take environmental protection work more seriously in the 1980s after the Second National Environmental Protection Conference in December 1983. Premier Li Peng, in his speech to this conference, pointed out that in addition to grasping industrial and agricultural production, national defense, and science and technology, China also must properly solve two pressing problems: population and environment. He pointed out that while the population problem had received heavy emphasis, the environmental protection problem had yet to generate sufficient concern. He stated that China must handle the relationship between economic construction and environmental protection in the course of achieving the Four Modernization.[21]

Despite the official policy statement from Li Peng and other officials emphasizing the importance of environmental protection, the actual implementation of this policy was very limited. For instance, from 1982 to 1985, the total investment in environmental protection was only 36.9 billion Renminbi. Of this amount, 25.4 billion Renminbi went for industrial pollution control and 11.5 billion Renminbi for urban environmental protection.[22] Environmental protection was included in the five-year plans as a separate chapter for the first time in the Sixth Five-Year Plan, adopted in 1982.[23]

During the Seventh Five-Year Plan period, from 1986 to 1990, environmental protection work was carried out more effectively. In new or expanded construction, an environmental impact study was required. In building a new industry, pollution prevention, the construction project, and the operation of the industry must be designed simultaneously. This is the so-called "three simultaneous" policy.[24] According to official Chinese statistics, by 1991, 95 percent of major construction and 80 percent of medium and small construction complied with the three simultaneous policy. In 1989, the Chinese government for the first time evaluated the performance of environmental protection work in 32 large and medium-sized cities. Now the policy is to require industries that polluted the environment to clean it up, and organizations that develop industries must protect the environment. In 1979, the Chinese government issued the first list of items to be cleaned up with a time limit. The list contained 120,000 items, including the items required by local governments. These were to be cleaned up in the 1980s. In 1990, the Chinese government issued the second list of items to be cleaned up with a time limit. The government imposed a fee on industries that exceeded the pollution standards. From 1982 to 1991, the government collected 7.6 billion Renminbi in such fees.[25]

According to official statistics, the targets of environmental protection for the Seventh Five-Year Plan period were basically met. The rate of industrial wastewater treatment increased from 36 percent in 1986 to 55.6 percent in 1989. The solid waste from urban industries with a production value of 10,000 Renminbi was reduced from 5.79 tons in 1986 to 3.35 tons in 1989. From 1985 to 1987, China established more than 400 standard noise-control districts. However, the official sources also indicated that environmental protection in China was far behind the needs. Insufficient investment, backward science and technology, poor quality, and inefficiency were some of the major problems.[26]

During the Eighth Five-Year Plan period, from 1991 to 1995, China intends to further improve its environmental protection work on the basis of what it has accomplished. The advantageous aspects include the controlled condition of the most seriously polluting industries, greater awareness of environmental problems by the people, the incorporation of environmental protection into national policy, the promotion of environmental work at the international level, which influenced China's environmental protection work. The disadvantages include the increase of population and rapid economic development worsening the environment, insufficient government investment in environment protection, and the backwardness of China's development of science and technology.[27]

During the Eighth Five-Year Plan period, the goals are to control the worsening of environmental pollution, improve the environment of some cities and areas, and check the further deterioration of the ecosystem.[28]

In order to realize the goals of the Eighth Five-Year Plan, China will implement the following measures:

1. Include environmental protection work in national and local economic and social development plans and set up targets for environmental protection work to increase investment in this field.

2. Increase supervisory and service work to control the development of seriously

polluting industries and promote environmental protection industries.

3. Strengthen the legal system of environmental protection and environmental protection organizations and improve environmental protection standards.

4. Develop science and technology related to environmental protection.

5. Guarantee the level of investment, strengthen investment management, and improve investment efficiency.

The investment for environmental protection during the Eighth Five-Year Plan period should be at least 0.85 percent of GNP.[29]

The present official environmental policy can be summarized by Premier Li Peng's statement in 1992 at an international conference on environmental protection held in Beijing. Li stated at this meeting that the policy of China was to ensure a well-protected environment in the process of economic development.[30] This ambitious goal cannot be achieved easily.

As a communist country, China relies on central planning and regulation to manage its environment. China's basic strategy in the implementation of its environmental protection policy is campaign exhortation and the bureaucratic, authoritative approach. This is supplemented by the limited use of the market-exchange approach.[31]

ENVIRONMENTAL PROTECTION ORGANIZATIONS

In order to enforce the environmental laws, decrees, and policies, the government has set up agencies to oversee their implementation. At the national level, the Environmental Protection Commission under the State Council is the highest agency directly responsible for environmental protection. This commission is headed by a vice premier. Its executive organ is the National Environmental Protection Agency. Environmental protection offices were also set up in many ministries whose operations might cause environmental problems and in all provincial governments, autonomous region governments, and municipal governments under direct central administration (i.e., Beijing, Shanghai, and Tianjin), as well as most of the prefectures, cities, and counties. The organizations at the national level were responsible for formulating principles, policies, decrees, and standards. Lower-level organizations and offices carry them out. Up to 1982, there were no clearly defined functions for the central and lower organs. Environmental management lacked coordination.[32] Environmental offices were also set up in enterprises and industries. By 1991, China had about 60,000 people working on environmental protection.[33] The national peoples' congresses at all levels have the power to supervise the environmental protection work in areas under their jurisdiction. By 1982, China had over 80 research institutes, staffed by 3,500 people, to study environmental protection problems. In addition, China had more than 200 monitoring stations employing over 4,400 people. The total number of people involved in environmental protection research work amounted to 15,000.[34]

ENVIRONMENTAL LAWS AND REGULATIONS

In order to implement the environmental protection policies, China enacted laws and regulations to achieve its goals. As early as 1956, China promulgated the Sanitary Standards for Designing Industrial Enterprises. In 1959, it adopted the Sanitary Regulations for Drinking Water. In 1972, the principle of "three simultaneous" was adopted. As noted earlier, this is to guarantee that the pollution abatement equipment will be developed and constructed simultaneously with the development and construction of a new industrial facility during the three stages of (1) projection, (2) construction, and (3) operation.[35]

In 1973, the document, "Some Regulations Concerning Environmental Protection and Improvement," was adopted. This was the first legal document with comprehensive regulations for environmental protection. In the same year, a number of other environmental protection regulations were adopted, such as the Regulations for Natural Conservation Enclaves; the Regulations for the Protection of Rare Wild Animals; the Standards for the Discharge of Industrial Waste Solids, Liquids, and Gases; and the revised Sanitary Standards for Designing of Industrial Enterprises. In 1975, the Sanitary Standards for Foodstuffs were promulgated. Most important of all, the 1978 Constitution of the People's Republic of China incorporated the policy on environmental protection. Article 11 of this constitution stipulates that "the state protects the environment and natural resources, and prevents or eliminates pollution and other hazards harmful to the public."[36]

In 1979, the Standing Committee of the Fifth National People's Congress (NPC) approved the Environmental Protection Law of the People's Republic of China (for trial implementation). In 1989, this law became the official Environmental Protection Law of China. The NPC also adopted a series of environmental protection regulations, such as the Ocean Protection Law, Water Pollution Prevention Law, Atmosphere Pollution Prevention Law, the Forestry Law, the Regulations for Protection of Aquatic Resources, the Standards for Quality of Water for Farmland Irrigation, the Standards for Quality of Water for Fisheries, and the Standards for Safety in Using Insecticides.[37] More than 20 regulations have been adopted by the NPC. Local governments also adopted many regulations for environmental protection. Thus, the legal framework for environmental protection has been established from the national level to the local level.[38]

In addition to domestic laws and regulations, China has joined international organizations and subscribed to international conventions concerning the protection of environment. China has joined the International Convention for Civil Responsibilities for Oil Pollution and Damages and the Convention on International Trade in Endangered Species of Wild Fauna and Flora.[39] China has also joined the Convention for the Prevention of

Dumping Waste and Other Polluting Materials into the Ocean, the Convention for the Protection of Natural Relics and Artificial Relics, and other international environmental protection conventions.[40]

China inaugurated the "China Council for International Co-operation on Environment and Development (CCICED)" at a meeting in April 1992 to expand international cooperation in this field. The council is supported by the Canadian International Development Agency (CIDA).[41]

At the United Nations Conference on Environment and Development in June 1992, Dr. Song Jian, State Council member and minister in charge of the State Science and Technology Commission and chairman of the Environmental Protection Commission of the State Council of China, took the position that environmental protection must be carried out in coordination with economic and social development. He linked environmental protection with world peace and stability. The Chinese official suggested that the "new global partnership" should take into account the improvement of the economic condition of the people and the different conditions in each country. Each country should be allowed to choose its own ways of economic development and environmental protection that best suit its own national conditions. The developed countries should help the developing countries with environmental management by providing funds and technology transfer. The developing countries must actively participate in this "new global partnership." Dr. Song claimed that China had actively and seriously participated and assumed its share of obligation in international cooperation in the field of environment and development.[42]

China's insistence that each country be allowed to decide on its own environmental protection policy suited to its national condition makes it impossible, however, to establish international standards for worldwide environmental protection efforts.

SCIENTIFIC RESEARCH

Because environmental protection is a new endeavor in China, the country lacks the knowledge, technology, experience, and qualified personnel to do the job. Environmental research involves many scientific disciplines. China had, as of 1987, 3,500 technicians engaged in scientific research on environmental protection. They come from seven areas, namely, the Chinese Academy of Sciences, the Chinese Academy of Social Sciences, the research institutes under the State Council, universities and colleges, research institutions in the provinces, municipalities and autonomous regions, research personnel in various industries, and research personnel in the environmental protection departments. These people study a variety of subjects related to environmental protection ranging from basic research on environmental chemistry, biology, ecology, geography, atmosphere, and desert control to environmental economics, laws, and management.[43]

China has achieved some results in its scientific research, such as recovery and utilization of highly concentrated sulphur dioxide, electroplating without the use of cyanide, the treatment of wastewater from the electroplating process, ammonium sulfite pulping of straw pulp at paper mills, dehairing of hides with enzymes, the treatment of mercury pollution, the purification of wastewater from oil refining, the injection of polluted water into oil fields, the treatment of organic waste through lagoons, the control of surface subsidence, the composting of city garbage, biological control of insect pests in farming and forestry, biological nitrogen fixation, desert control, and the use of bio-gas as an energy source. But the Chinese admit that scientific research on environmental protection is far behind advanced world standards.[44]

PROBLEMS AND PROSPECTS

Despite some progress made since the late 1970s, environmental protection in China is still far from sufficient in controlling pollution. The overall environment continues to deteriorate at an alarming rate. This is readily admitted by the Chinese official sources. According to the Chinese Ministry of Agriculture, pollution was widespread throughout China and it became very serious in some areas. It was estimated that in 1991, 100 million mus of farmland were polluted, causing a reduction in grain production. Among the 50,000 kilometers of rivers investigated, 47 percent were unfit to drink and 4.3 percent were devoid of fish.[45]

The dwindling farmland and the increase of population is another problem of the Chinese ecosystem. Net increase of population was more than ten million a year, further reducing the per capita farmland. At present, China's per capita farmland and water resources are only one-third and one-fifth of the world average respectively.[46] Because of the lag in forestation and improper use of natural resources, soil erosion in China reached 3 billion mus, representing one-fifth of the total land area of China. The desert area in China doubled from the 1950s to the 1970s. Now 59 million mus of farmland are seriously threatened by desertification. The desertification of grassland is also very serious. On the average, annual desertification of grassland reached 5.5 million mus; 770 million mus of grassland have become desert or deteriorated, representing 14.4 percent of the total grassland of China.[47]

Excessive cutting of trees, about 100 million cubic meters annually in recent years, has seriously depleted the forestry resource. The area affected annually by natural disaster increased 68 percent, causing serious loss in agricultural production and the lives and property of the people.[48]

In 1990, the Chinese government conducted a survey of pollution by rural industries in 29 provinces, autonomous regions, and the three municipalities under direct national government jurisdiction. The survey included 573,000 rural industries with a total production value of 1,858 billion Renminbi. Among the industries in the survey, only 14.8 percent met the standard for wastewater treatment. Only 22.7 percent implemented the policy of environmental assessment, 14.4 percent implemented the policy of "three simultaneous," and 5.8 percent were forced to close down because of pollution. Among the industrial boilers, only 37.9 percent met the standard of pollution control.[49]

The Ministry of Agriculture believes that during the Eighth Five-Year Plan period, from 1991 to 1995, agricultural environment will continue to worsen. Agricultural environmental pollution will become more serious for several reasons:

1. The rapid development of industry and transportation in the cities and the countryside, the rapid growth of the population, the difficulty in controlling the loss of farmland, and the more serious problem of limited agricultural natural resources per capita all are major problems.

2. The rapid development of industry greatly increases wastes. The state has only limited capital, and it cannot allocate sufficient capital for pollution control. Industrial pollution will be the main threat to agricultural environment.

3. The rapid development of industries in the rural areas, the modernization of animal husbandry industries in the urban areas, and the increased use of chemical fertilizer and agricultural plastics will lead to increased pollution from the agricultural sector itself.[50]

The targets for agricultural environmental protection by 1995, the end of the Eighth Five-Year Plan are

1. The use of water by agricultural commercial bases and the irrigation of agricultural developmental areas and the quality of atmosphere in the countryside are expected to reach 95 percent or higher of required standards.

2. The implementation of the "three simultaneous" policy in rural industries will reach 90 percent or higher.

3. The treatment of wastewater will reach 20 percent or higher.

4. Twenty model environmental protection industries will be established.

5. The implementation of the three simultaneous policy by state industries in the agricultural sector is expected to reach 100 percent.

6. Gaseous waste and water waste control will reach 50 percent.

7. Agricultural chemicals in agricultural products will be reduced to less than 1 percent.

8. Fifty model areas for agricultural ecosystem with an area of 150,000,000 mus to produce 20 billion jin (catty) of grain will be established.

9. Eighteen natural preserve grassland areas with 50 million hectares, representing 0.8 percent of the total grassland area of China will be established.

10. Thirty protection areas for rare wild animals will be created.[51]

Western observers are not very optimistic about environmental protection in China. For instance, Christopher Flavin, a climate specialist at the World Watch Institute, an environmental research group in Washington, D.C., predicts that China will probably become the No. 2 emitter of greenhouse gases in the world within the next ten years. This will come about because China's major source of energy is coal, and burning coal produces carbon dioxide, the most significant greenhouse gas. China produces one billion metric tons of coal a year, more than any other country in the world. It will produce 1.4 billion metric tons by the end of this century. By 2020, China could produce 2 billion metric tons of coal a year.[52]

Chinese officials and researchers have clearly indicated that China cannot stop using coal. To do so would adversely affect China's economic development and the living standard of the Chinese people. China will not sacrifice economic development for the protection of the environment.[53] Most Chinese people do not care about the environment, especially in the townships and village enterprises.[54]

CONCLUSION

More than most other developing countries, China is facing a serious challenge in its struggle for environmental protection, the result of China's enormous population and the relative scarcity of nature resources. This, combined with China's ambition to rapidly develop its economy to improve the living standard of the Chinese people, makes it more difficult to have effective environmental protection. The lack of capital and technology is another problem.

In addition, politically China cannot afford to slow its economic growth or invest a large share of its limited resources in environmental protection. In the conflict between economic development and environmental protection, China apparently has chosen the former, despite its official policy of economic development with environmental protection. For these reasons, there is no hope that environmental degradation in China will be substantially improved in the near future. It may get worse if the central government cannot effectively implement its current environmental policies.

This dilemma is found in most developing countries to one degree or another. In part, the solution to the environmental problem in the developing countries must include significant assistance from the advanced countries in the form of capital and technology. But the advanced countries are reluctant to help the developing countries on a large scale to improve their environment. The reluctance of the United States to sign the treaties worked out at the Earth Summit in 1992 in Rio de Janeiro is an example.

Environmental protection in China and in other countries, especially in developing countries, must be achieved through joint efforts by the international community. Advanced countries must be willing to sacrifice their own economic well-being to help improve the environment of the poor, developing countries. Failing to do this will lead to irreparable damage to our global environment. Environmental protection is no longer the affair of any one country. It has become an urgent global issue. Environmental pollution recognizes no national boundaries. No country, especially a poor country, can solve this problem alone.

NOTES

1. Vaclav Smil, "Environmental Change as a Source of Conflict and Economic Losses in China," occasional paper, Toronto, Joint Project on Environmental Change and Acute Conflict of the University of Toronto and the American Academy of Arts and Sciences, 1992, pp. 6–7.

2. Dirk Betke and Johannes Kuchler, "Shortage of Land Resources as a Factor in Development: The Example of the People's Republic of China," in *Learning from China? Development and Environment in Third World Countries*, ed. Bernhard Glaeser (London: Allen & Unwin, 1987), p. 95.

3. *Zhonggong Nianbao* (Yearbook on Chinese Communism) (Taipei, Taiwan: Zhonggong Yanjiu Zazhi She [Institute for the Study of Chinese Communist Problems], 1991) 1: 32, 1: 62.

4. "The Present Environmental Condition, Developmental Trend and Protection Policy of Chinese Agriculture," background report prepared by the Ministry of Agriculture, People's Republic of China, 1991, pp. 1–2.

5. Baruch Boxer, "China's Environmental Prospects," *Asian Survey* 29.7 (1989): 672.

6. "Present Environmental Condition," pp. 2–3.

7. Ibid., p. 3.

8. Ibid., p. 4. (Renminbi is the official Chinese currency. In 1991, the official exchange rate was U.S. $1.00 to Renminbi 5.20. In 1988, it was 3.70 Renminbi to U.S. $1.00. The rate fluctuates daily.)

9. Ibid.

10. Ibid., p. 5.

11. Ibid., p. 6.

12. Ibid., p. 7.

13. Ibid., pp. 7–8.

14. Ibid., p. 8.

15. Ibid., p. 9.

16. Ibid., p. 15.

17. Ibid., p. 16.

18. Smil, "Environmental Change," pp. 29–30.

19. Ibid., p. 32.

20. Wu Zijin, "The Origins of Environmental Management in China," in *Learning from China? Development and Environment in Third World Countries*, ed. Bernhard Glaeser (London: Allen & Unwin, 1987), pp. 113–114.

21. Lester Ross and Mitchell A. Silk, *Environmental Law and Policy in the People's Republic of China* (New York: Quorum Books, 1987), pp. 36–37.

22. Qu Geping, "A Basic Assessment of the Seventh Five-Year Plan and the Tasks of the Eighth Five-Year Plan," *Zhongguo Huanjing Guanli* (Environmental Management in China) April 1991: 2.

23. Yan Zheng, "The Environmental Protection System of China," *Huanjing Baohu* (Environmental Protection) March 1991: 5.

24. Ibid.

25. Ibid.

26. Geping, "Basic Assessment," p. 2.

27. Ibid., p. 3.

28. Ibid.

29. Ibid.

30. *Beijing Review*, 35.18 (1992): 10.

31. For a more detailed discussion of pollution control in China, see Lester Ross, *Environmental Policy in China* (Bloomington: Indiana University Press, 1988), pp. 131–175.

32. Zijin, "Origins of Environmental Management," p. 112.

33. Zheng, "Environmental Protection System," p. 6.

34. Zijin, "Origins of Environmental Management," p. 112.

35. Ibid., pp. 115, 119.

36. Ibid., p. 115.

37. Ibid., pp. 115–116.

38. Zheng, "Environmental Protection System," p. 6.

39. Zijin, "Origins of Environmental Management," p. 116.

40. Zheng, "Environmental Protection System," p. 6.

41. *Beijing Review* 35.18 (1992): 10.

42. *Beijing Review* 35.24 (1992): 12–15.

43. Zijin, "Origins of Environmental Management," pp. 116–117.

44. Ibid., p. 117.

45. "Agricultural Environmental Protection, the Eighth Five-Year Plan," draft for comments prepared by Energy Dept., Ministry of Agriculture, People's Republic of China, August 1989, p. 7.

46. Ibid., p. 8.

47. Ibid.

48. Ibid.

49. "Survey Bulletin on the Basic Condition of the Sources of Pollution by the Rural Industries of China (Quanguo Xiang Zhen Gongye Wuran yuan Diaocha Jiben Qingkuang Gongbao)," December 11, 1991. The final draft of the bulletin was prepared by the Environmental Protection Agency of the State Council, the Ministry of Agriculture, and the State Statistical Bureau, 1991, pp. 1–3.

50. "Agricultural Environmental Protection," pp. 8–9.

51. Ibid., p. 10.

52. *The New York Times*, 25 May 1992: 5.

53. Ibid.

54. Ibid.

Chapter 5

Protecting the Environment in Indonesia: Policies and Programs

ROBERT BOARDMAN AND TIMOTHY M. SHAW

Indonesia's ambitious modernization and industrialization strategies, combined with its large natural resources, particularly of hardwood forests, oil, and gas, make it an intriguing target for environmental study: an ambitious "near-NIC" sensitive to "green" issues in a vibrant region. A large population—fourth in the world—has put increasing pressure on the country to find the most appropriate strategies for utilization of its resources, especially in light of the costs to the Indonesian economy of the collapse of world oil prices since the late 1980s. Since the early 1970s, Indonesia has embarked on a path of steadily expanding environmental regulation of its resource exploitation and industrialization activities.

THE RISE OF ENVIRONMENTAL CONCERNS IN INDONESIA

An analysis of environmental problems in Indonesia and an appraisal of the current state of environmental law and policy in that country has to begin with a definition of terms. The term *environment* in the social, political, and economic context of Indonesia takes in a wide range of potential subjects. These include, among others, questions of pollution, especially air and water; atmospheric change; protection of natural areas; environmental regulation of industries and communities; environmental impact assessment (EIA); sectoral analyses of the ecological consequences of mining, agriculture, tourism, and fishing; environmental education and coalitions; and the role and effectiveness of government institutions and legal frameworks. In most Western countries, environmental issues came to prominence in the 1960s in the form of pollution problems associated with industrialization, in part as a consequence of catastrophic oil tanker spills or chronic pollution of urban air and waterways. The scope and focus of environmental laws and policies have expanded considerably since then. Underlying philosophical approaches have also shifted. Far greater attention is paid in the 1990s to the broader connotations of environmental policies understood in terms of the sustainable development of resources and the complex linkages between environmental and economic policy areas, stretching from family activities to ozone depletion.[1]

This process of change and redefinition both helps and constrains the study of environmental policies and wider questions of resource use in developing countries, especially those like Indonesia, approaching NIC status. It serves to direct attention not only to policies designed to minimize the adverse environmental consequences of specific industrial or other projects, particularly air and water pollution, but also towards wider questions of political economy. In addition, it locates environmental problems in a triangular policy space along with both resources and population pressures. Such issues need to be examined in a number of different multidisciplinary contexts. Dwivedi has used the term *political ecology* to summarize the ways in which social, especially political, scientists can contribute to this process of promoting the expansion of scholarship and sound policy: Political ecology provides us with "a fresh framework for political scientists to analyze and examine the issues related to environmental politics in a more comprehensive manner."[2]

Indonesian approaches to environmental law and policy have to be viewed from the context of broader strategies of economic development. Article I of the 1982 act on the environment—the fundamental framework for Indonesian environmental regulation—aims for a balanced strategy emphasizing both economic development and environmental protection, that is, "a conscious and planned endeavor to utilize and manage resources wisely in continued development to improve the quality of life." This perspective is fundamental not only in terms of the priorities of government but also in the way key terms in environmental policy vocabularies are used in debates in Indonesia. Thus it was only during the 1980s that the term *environment* (*lingkungan*) came into wider usage in the Western environmentalist sense. Prior to that, the term tended to be used rather to refer to social environments, so that the qualifier "living" (*hidup*) has in practice often been used to make the distinction clear.[3]

Various meanings of important concepts are present in Indonesian legislation. The 1982 act defines environment in part in a geographical or territorial sense. In Article 2, the Indonesian living environment is defined as "based upon the Archipelagic concept" (*wawasan nusantara*). This concept has, since independence in the 1940s, been elevated into a general symbol of Indonesian nationhood, in part as a consequence of Javanese domination of the country's affairs. As applied to environmental law and policy, it has been interpreted officially to mean that

the living environment of Indonesia is none other than the area of the Archipelago, which lies at the juncture of two continents and two oceans, with a tropical climate, weather, and seasons providing natural conditions and a strategic position of great value, where the Indonesian nation and people live out their lives as a nation in all its aspects. Therefore, the concept encompassed in the management of the living environment of Indonesia is the Archipelagic Concept.[4]

This level of generality is useful as a philosophical orientation to Indonesian environmental policy, but it necessarily lacks specifics. Of the many complex elements in the population–resource–environment mix, Indonesia's population growth and distribution have historically posed serious constraints on the economy's resource base and on other aspects of its ecological carrying capacity.[5] Problems of overpopulation in Java were noted from the early nineteenth century under Dutch colonial rule. Today more than 60 percent of Indonesia's population lives on the main island of Java, which occupies only 7 percent of the land area of the country. The uneven distribution of population can be seen in the contrasting densities of Java (690 people per square kilometer) and Irian Jaya (3 people per square kilometer). Population growth rates, moreover, have steadily increased during recent decades: 1.5 percent in the period from 1930 to 1961, 2.1 percent between 1961 and 1971, and 2.3 percent from 1971 to 1980.[6] These demographic factors and Javanese interests have led to transmigration policies—primarily the movement of people from the Inner Islands of Java and Bali to the Outer Islands, such as Sumatra, which have been both highly controversial and also of doubtful effectiveness in terms of their ecological costs and of the problems they were designed to address.[7] This process has been cross-woven with a significant trend of migration from rural areas to cities.

A related demographic variable is diversity. Indonesia has been described as "probably the most ethnically and culturally heterogeneous of the world's largest nations."[8] The existence of more than 300 ethnic groups with over 250 distinct languages living on approximately 13,000 islands, combined with religious diversity in a largely but by no means exclusively Islamic state, is a traditional structural feature of the Indonesian polity with significant implications for the design and implementation of environmental and related policies. This has been one of the factors, for example, that

has led to a consistent emphasis by environmental officials on slow processes of consensus formation and public awareness and education as essential preliminaries to further progress in environmental regulation. Yet
the state, especially through the military, has remained dominant. Indeed,
academic observers have concluded that "the state's domination of political life is so far-reaching that the scope for extra-state groups to influence
policy in any direct way is minimal."[9]

Environmental problems—and the policy and political responses of
government in terms of legislation, regulations, institutions, and related
programs—have been a product of the interplay between demographic
factors and the modernization and economic development strategies of
the New Order period since 1966. Attention to these problems has resulted
from a number of more specific factors, including the impact of major international landmarks, particularly the 1972 United Nations Conference
on the Human Environment (UNCHE) in Stockholm and the 1992 U.N.
Conference on Environment and Development (UNCED) in Rio de Janeiro,
a steady growth of Indonesian and international environmental nongovernmental organizations (NGOs) and of environmental studies and research
at universities and specialized institutes (often encouraged by aid donors),
and the general conditions in Indonesia's political life that support an extensive bureaucracy grounded in technical expertise. These factors, and
the rise of Indonesia's environmental bureaucracy, are discussed later in
this chapter.

The kinds of environmental problems confronting Indonesia are many
and varied. The major environmental constraints have been categorized in
a 1988 report into problems of population growth, soils, deforestation, pollution of lower watersheds, hydrological constraints, and overexploitation
of coastal resources.[10] We look briefly at resource-use concerns, especially
in relation to forests, as well as air, inland water, and marine pollution.

Questions of land and resource use centered on Indonesia's forests account for a large part of environmental policy issues. In Indonesia (and
particularly Sumatra' and Borneo) and other countries of Southeast Asia
(especially Malaysia and the Philippines) are found approximately two-
thirds of the world's tropical rain forests. Indonesia, the Philippines, and
Malaysia were responsible for about 66 percent of worldwide exports of
hardwood and forest products during the 1970s, and into the 1980s, they
continued to provide the Indonesian economy with its second highest
source of export earnings.[11] Problems of overexploitation, compounded by
inadequate attention to reforestation and other sustainable-use management principles, have been evident since the nineteenth century. Forests
cleared for crops, for example, revealed unanticipated problems of low
and rapidly declining soil fertility evident in diminishing tobacco yields.[12]
The introduction under Dutch colonial rule of this and other export crops,
including sugar, indigo, coffee, tea, and rubber, started a historical process

of spreading deforestation and changing forest ecological cultures that is still continuing. This neglect of the ecological value of Indonesia's forests and of the danger of uncontrollable deforestation processes had broader consequences, too, in terms of the structures of village economies and gender relations. Much of the land taken over in this fashion had been a traditional source of food, firewood, and timber, and its loss created further pressures on forests from farmers excluded from these areas. One estimate by a Dutch scholar of the forest area lost between 1940 and 1973 for these reasons, as well as direct exploitation of the resource, puts it at two-thirds; the assessment of the Indonesian Forest Service is that "only half" was lost.[13]

More recently, the direct use of forest resources in an export economy has expanded, particularly following the so-called open-door foreign investment policies associated with the New Order economic programs from the late 1960s. This has focused both domestic and external criticism particularly on Japanese logging companies, partly for environmental reasons of too rapid resource depletion and partly for discouraging value-added processing inside Indonesia—an interesting combination of green and dependency arguments. Early Indonesian attempts to limit exports, for example, through the Council of Southeast Asian Lumber Producers Association (SEALPA), set up in 1974, had mixed results.[14] Later strategies have been just as controversial, especially with the rise of international NGO criticisms of the forest products utilization and exporting policies of Indonesia and other Southeast Asian countries. Indonesia participates in the workings of the International Tropical Timber Agreement (ITTA), in force since 1985. This has been subjected to numerous criticisms in Southeast Asia on ecological grounds, particularly in relation to problems of official data and documentation, the monitoring of approved projects, and the adequacy of environmental and social impact assessments. Hence it underwent a series of reforms in the early 1990s.[15] Indonesia in the 1990s is under increasing pressures in ITTA as a result of growing import restrictions imposed by Northern countries, a product of successful lobbying by environmental NGOs.[16]

When "environmental" issues were examined and prioritized in Indonesia in response to UNCHE, however, an important focus of government attention was not so much on questions of resource use as on the kinds of air and water pollution questions then increasingly dominant in Western environmental policy approaches. From this analytical and policy perspective, the threats were in general not seen by the Indonesian government to be serious. Indonesia's industrial and urban development in the late 1960s and early 1970s was not at a level that appeared to pose urgent dangers. Moreover, the modernization goals of the five-year plans, while containing general provisions for the protection of the environment and the abatement of pollution, tended to imply that pollution problems, when they arose, were a secondary priority in ranking environmental and economic development goals.

Official attention to environmental issues started mounting during the 1970s and paralleled the growing industrialization of the economy. Serious instances of pollution have arisen in relation to rivers, with consequences for pollution of offshore waters, especially shallow areas off Java and Sumatra. The Ministry of State for Population and Environment has reported acute pollution problems in twenty rivers, including problems arising from human waste and inadequate or nonexistent sewage treatment facilities. For example, many small- and medium-scale factories discharge effluents into the Ciliwung and Cipinang rivers in western Java, with a reported ten tons of chemical wastes dumped daily into the latter. Pollution from pulp and plywood factories has had serious impact on local fisheries, particularly in South Kalimantan. Many similar problems include damage to the shrimp fishery on the Bekasi River near Jakarta by a paper factory, and pollution of farmers' irrigation channels from a major government-owned chemical factory, also near Jakarta.[17] Jakarta and other cities experience substantial and chronic air pollution problems arising from traffic, emissions from factories, and burning of wastes.[18] These have led to a high and increasing incidence in some areas of respiratory ailments. Areas of Bali have experienced serious problems of pesticide pollution.[19]

Largely neglected until recently have been problems of marine pollution arising from land-based activities. This neglect has probably been a result of the common assumption, not unique to Indonesia, that coastal and other maritime environments have an infinite capacity to absorb wastes and other effluents without suffering irreversible damage. Expanded economic activities, particularly on Java, increasingly challenge this belief, especially in relation to more vulnerable areas, such as estuaries, bays, and semienclosed seas.[20] It is a perspective that has also been subjected to growing criticism in regional frameworks in Southeast Asia. Jakarta Bay itself, for example, has been described as "one of the world's most polluted coastal water areas [which] presents a major risk of serious environmental and economic damage associated with the destruction of fisheries and other marine and coastal resources."[21] The government set up an official marine pollution committee as early as 1972, one of the first steps in the elaboration of environmental policy frameworks, but the magnitude of the problem has outstretched the capabilities of Indonesia's minimal regulatory systems. While Indonesia's important oil sector has been affected by the decline in world prices since the late 1980s, related pollution threats are still linked with offshore oil exploration and exploitation activity, the passage of oil tankers in transit routes through vulnerable straits and across archipelagic seas, and pollution from refineries. Factors such as fishing by foreign fleets and the strategic significance for the Indonesian government of its vast seas suggest that the oceans generally will assume greater prominence in the 1990s. Tangsubkul has observed that "as an archipelagic nation which lies as a bridge of strategic importance between the Indian Ocean and the Pacific on the one hand, and between the Asian and Australian continents on the other, Indonesia, obviously, holds a tremendously important position with regard to ocean affairs."[22]

ENVIRONMENTAL POLICIES AND ECONOMIC DEVELOPMENT PLANNING

Indonesia's environmental legislation and policies have been formulated in the context of a series of five-year plans. Economic planning in Indonesia is thus juxtaposed with significant elements of market forces. From the mid-1970s, the planning process began to devote more space and a greater sense of urgency to the environmental problems associated with industrialization, urbanization, exploitation of forestry resources, agricultural development, and other economic sectors. A key role in the formulation of Indonesian environmental policy thinking has thus been played by the National Development Planning Agency (BAPPENAS).

The current phase of economic planning has followed the changes from the Guided Democracy of Soekarno—a classic case of a centralized-command political economy of the period—made by President Soeharto from the late 1960s under the general title of the New Order.[23] A central feature of this period, comparable to developments in other NICs, has been the opening up of the Indonesian economy to foreign investment and international trade, especially in the context of a larger series of measures designed to attack the high inflation rates of the late Soekarno period.[24] Asian NICs have more recently joined the line of foreign investors in Indonesia.[25] The plans (Repelita I-IV, 1969–1989) initially placed a strong emphasis on the agricultural sector, while the goal of a balanced budget, supported by the close association of the government planning apparatus with International Monetary Fund and World Bank officials, was sustained and successfully achieved. Through subsidies and other measures, Indonesian economic planning has also led to significant increases in food and other crop production figures.[26] As Indonesia applied "Green Revolution" lessons based on intensified use of fertilizers and other agricultural modernization technologies, the country was transformed from a rice importer to a rice exporter. Nonoil exports have expanded significantly since the late 1960s, particularly in the late 1980s, and primary commodity exports remain an important part of Indonesia's overall trade picture. In the 1990s, heavy government emphasis is placed on the requirement of expanding nonoil exports, including manufactured goods and sales in the growing regional agrichemical market in South and Southeast Asia, as a key stimulus for economic development.

Preparations in the mid-1970s for the Third Five-Year Plan (Repelita III) coincided with the growth of national and international interest in environmental issues. This plan, beginning in 1978, defined in broad terms a general commitment to protection of the environment. It was in the over-all framework of this plan that the main outlines of Indonesia's environmental legislation, in the form of an act passed in 1982, were developed. As noted already, a beginning was made earlier in the immediate aftermath of the 1972 U.N. conference; Indonesian environmental planning built on the experiences of this conference and on the Indonesian government's official report to the Stockholm meeting. In 1973 the general principles (GBHN) approved by the People's Consultative Assembly—a set of guidelines preceding the final drafting of the five-year plan—included the statement: "In the implementation of development, Indonesia's natural resources should be rationally utilized. The exploitation of these natural resources should not destroy the human environment and should be executed by a comprehensive policy which takes into account the needs of future generations."[27]

This early formulation of sustainable-development thinking represented an effective adaptation of contemporary Western and intergovernmental organization (IGO) thinking on environmental matters to Indonesian circumstances. The focus was on resources and their use, together with a strong implication that it was the role of the state to oversee this process. This guideline stems from the constitution of 1945, which includes (Article 33) a provision for natural resources to be "controlled by the State" and "utilized for the greatest welfare of the people." Approaches to environmental questions have thus tended to define these more broadly in terms of the use of resources, and within this general framework to locate specific sets of problems such as pollution of rivers. This general orientation has continued to shape subsequent five-year plans and the prior political statements of their philosophies and goals. The 1983 GBHN, for example, formulated shortly after the promulgation of Indonesia's Environment Act, noted among other things the need for the continuous conduct of "an accurate assessment of the impact of development on the living environment in the best possible way." This led during the mid-1980s to the development of Indonesia's first systematic attempt to incorporate EIA thinking into economic development planning.

The elaboration of legislation, regulations, and related programs that is outlined shortly indicates that in making such statements Indonesia's political elites were not merely paying lip service to an environmentalist philosophy that was becoming increasingly fashionable in Western and donor circles. Why did such approaches become embedded in economic development planning? Writing particularly about pollution control legislation in Indonesia, Cribb has suggested that external influences such as the increasingly proclaimed environmentalism of the World Bank have been important.[28] Both UNCHE and a key scientific and official conference held in Bandung the previous month[29] were significant in focusing Indonesian government attention on a variety of environmental questions. At Stockholm and at related preparatory meetings the Indonesian government had to submit reports on the state of progress in environmental protection. This requirement, reinforced by participation in the multilateral conferences of the early 1970s, was directly instrumental in leading to the guidelines of 1973 that placed environmental policy goals in the framework of the Second Five-Year Plan (Repelita II, 1974–1979). There was a comparable process of renewed attention, including presidential attention, to environmental issues in the preparatory work before UNCED in 1992.

Indeed, to the extent that New Order economic planning has been posited on a dependence on outside capital, technology, and markets, Indonesia has been almost inevitably drawn into policy ideas that reflect changing Western and IGO environmental policy priorities. The Western, largely U.S. (particularly Berkeley), graduate training of many of the Indonesian senior government officials in control of economic policy has served to reinforce this orientation. President Soeharto's cabinets from the outset included a significant number of such foreign-trained technocrats, while others assumed leading positions in the bureaucracy. This extended network of officials and ministers has thus included many who were inclined to be responsive to Western environmental and sustainable-development thinking and to be well connected with the relevant Western and multilateral policy settings. Some external influences from IGOs may, however, have different effects. Development project support for coconut production, for example (important in Indonesia for the processing of cooking oil) has involved the active discouragement of intercropping by farmers, despite ecological arguments that such practices tend to be more productive than reliance on monocropping.[30]

In addition, pollution has posed a set of problems that have in one way or another had far-reaching effects on middle-class constituencies, as well as on smaller farmers and fisheries; and this has created ready-made linkages with the main structures of political power. Important regional relationships in Southeast Asia have also been affected, for example, through the oil tanker threat to fisheries and vulnerable coastlines in the waters between Indonesia, Malaysia, and Singapore. These kinds of problems have set up an external regional dynamic for Indonesian environmental officials that has become increasingly important in fostering the continued development of policies and programs, as mechanisms have arisen or been implemented in response to specific incidents. In one such case, hazardous wastes, reported as "noodles," were exported from Singapore and dumped on Bintani Island in the Riau province; a government investigation led to a cleanup of the contaminated area and the imprisonment of the owner of the importing company.[31]

Since environmental policy thinking tends to be fundamentally regulatory and state centric in orientation, government intervention in these areas can also be argued to fit into a longer-term historical trend in Indonesian economic policy approaches. Under Dutch colonial rule, for example, a significant transition took place in the 1890s and early 1900s towards acceptance of the need for amanaged or directed economy and away from older laissez-faire principles.[32] The bureaucratic–military alliance through which Indonesia has been governed, particularly in the Soeharto period, and the historically special role of the military in Indonesian politics since the 1940s, have put a premium on technical expertise and legal training of just the kind that such an environmental policy orientation demands.[33] The bureaucratic momentum behind these environmental policies has survived, even thrived, for these reasons, despite the larger context of deregulation of the economy in the 1980s and 1990s, and has been strongly enough entrenched in government to overcome potential resistance from key resource sectors.[34] This strength may, however, be more apparent than real; the survival of a significant environmental policy dynamic has in part been a product of its limited efficacy. The environmental policy process was driven, too, by a particularly able and dynamic environment minister, Emil Salim, appointed to this new position in 1978, head of Indonesia's delegation to the 1972 Stockholm conference, and later a member of the U.N. World Commission on Environment and Development (the Brundtland Commission).

ENVIRONMENTAL LEGISLATION AND INSTITUTION BUILDING

Laws and regulations on what would now be termed "environmental" matters were an intrinsic part of colonial administration, in part because the low-lying character of Batavia had led to a need for water management measures. Regulations on the conservation of nature were introduced as early as 1841 by the Dutch.[35] A series of measures from 1924 was introduced to protect Indonesia's threatened forest areas from further exploitation. However these were inadequately enforced and were in practice often blocked in their implementation by either larger landowners or village leaders. Many of the foreigners then using the resource saw themselves in any case as temporary visitors (*niet-blijvers*) and thus lacked a long-term commitment to development on a sustainable basis.[36] Colonial officials also maintained an interest in preservation of Indonesian flora and fauna, some of the most spectacular in the world; and the colonial period saw the beginnings of the creation of a network of protected areas, especially as a result of laws passed in 1931 and 1941. This was closely associated with the international leadership role taken by Dutch scholars and colonial officials in the 1920s and 1930s on environmental conservation, especially with respect to threatened species of wildlife.[37] Various problems plagued enforcement of the antipollution regulations of the colonial era brought in from 1926 under "public nuisance" common law principles.[38]

Indonesia's current body of environmental laws and regulations dates from the mid-1970s when pollution control first began to be addressed as a serious legal and policy issue.[39] From this period also emerged a small core of government institutions at the national level dealing with environmental policy questions. In a top-down process, this framework of initial regulations and central agencies formed the background to the centerpiece of Indonesian legislation, the Environmental Management Act of 1982, and helped to usher in a steady flow of legal instruments and institutional development during the 1980s. It does not follow, however, that processes of practical implementation have been just as dynamic. We return to this larger question later, but first we treat each of these three phases of Indonesian environmental policy approaches in turn.

Early Approaches

Among the first indirect products of the 1973 guidelines and the environmental protection provisions of Repelita II (1974–1979) was a 1974 law on waterways. This covered a broad range of waters, including rivers and lakes, wetlands, and marine waters. It did not, however, focus on pollution problems as such; and this aspect was left largely for elaboration in later instruments. Pollution problems on the continental shelf, arising in the context of offshore oil and gas exploration and development, were similarly included in a more general 1973 law on the continental shelf. These provisions were further defined and amplified later, for example, in the 1983 law on the management of Indonesia's Exclusive Economic Zone (EEZ), a crucial, and also controversial, measure that also embraced the important archipelagic concept.[40] In a 1978 directive from the minister of industry, new industrial projects were for the first time required to carry out an environmental impact assessment (AMDAL [*analisa dampak lingkungan*]). This, however, was not backed up with an adequate legal or regulatory regime, and it lacked such elementary steps as effective definitions of procedures and monitoring capabilities. Indeed Cribb concludes that the measure "had a mainly educative role in that it signaled the government's future intentions and forced companies to confront the fact that the environmental impact of their operations was something they should consider."[41] In addition, during the 1970s, Indonesia was evaluating the implications for it of related developments in the Third U.N. Conference on the Law of the Sea (UNCLOS III), particularly through participation as a key archipelagic state; and in 1978 the government ratified the International Convention on Civil Liability for Oil Pollution Damage.

The key event of this important formative period, however, was the articulation, institutionalization, and centralization of environmental law and policy questions in the government of Jakarta. The planning agency, BAPPENAS, took a leading role in this process, with significant contributions from other government agencies.[42] A minister for the environment was appointed in 1978 (formally minister of state for development supervision and the environment, redesignated minister of state for population and environment [KLH] in 1983). Emil Salim became an influential figure in the development of Indonesia's environmental policy and the core legal framework of the 1980s. Significantly, the definition of environmental questions now shifted ground, partly through reinforcement by donor conditionalities and assistance. From the earlier focus on specific pollution questions, Salim increasingly used the new twofold—environment and development—definition of his ministry's mandate to broaden the appropriate scope of environmental policy in a resource economy. In particular, he put special emphasis in the early years of the ministry on general questions of population growth and its implications for Indonesia's resource base and on the problems associated with continued pressures on forests. This orientation led directly to the "sustainable development" approaches of the 1990s. This period also saw a substantial expansion of Indonesia's system of protected habitats. Historically it was an important period in the evolution of Indonesian environmental policy planning and coincided significantly with the early phases of industrialization and the wider impacts on the economy of the oil boom.

The Environmental Management Act (1982)

This institutional and legal background, as well as the renewed commitment to environmental policy goals enshrined in the Third Five-Year Plan (Repelita III, 1979–1984) and its earlier guidelines, set the scene for the creation of a more coherent and universal attack on the emerging body of laws and regulations. Part of Repelita III (Chapter 7) provided, among other things, for the drafting of an enabling act outlining basic principles and goals for the management of Indonesia's living environment.

Work on such an act had actually begun in 1976, but the appointment of Salim as the first environment minister in 1978 elevated this process to a much higher and more visible political level within the government. The drafting process was completed during 1981; the resulting document (for an Act on Basic Provisions for the Management of the Living Environment) was presented to parliament in January 1982, and Indonesia's planners embarked on a long-term process of industrialization stretching forward into the late 1980s and beyond—the NIC dream. It was already clear during the preparations for the Third Five-Year development plan that the successful achievement of industrialization goals required effective control of the costs in terms of pollution to avert the risk that the industrialization process might be significantly deflected or delayed by political opposition, external as well as internal.

The 1982 act was designed as a comprehensive environmental law. The intent was to define more general principles applicable to the more specific development later of detailed regulations in discrete environmental policy sectors. Hardjasoemantri has identified eleven main sets of principles underlying the approach taken by the drafters of the law. This summary follows his account: [43]

The Archipelagic Concept. According to Article 2 of the act, the Indonesian living environment is defined, as stated earlier, in archipelagic terms and "encompasses the space where the Republic of Indonesia holds sovereignty and exercises sovereign rights and jurisdiction."

Environmental Rights. Environmental rights ("to a good and healthy living environment") and obligations ("to maintain the living environment and to prevent and abate environmental damage and pollution") are defined in Article 5. The rights of victims of environmental abuses are also noted (Article 20).

Polluter Pays Principle. By the early 1980s, the polluter pays principle had become firmly established in Western and IGO thinking. This approach was set out in Article 20, paragraphs 1 and 3, and Article 21 of the act.

Environmental Impact Analysis. From its tentative beginnings in the 1978 industry ministry directive, EIA assumed much greater prominence in the 1982 act. Such an assessment is required for every development project likely to have a significant impact on the environment (Article 16). According to initial criteria developed in parallel with the act, among the specific categories of impacts to be considered were the number of people affected, the size of the area affected, the length of time involved, the intensity of the impact, other environmental factors, the cumulative character of the impact, and an evaluation of the reversibility of the impact.

Incentives and Disincentives. Under Article 8, the government can take steps, for example, through taxation policy, import and export regulations, or credit facilities, to support the promotion of environmental policy objectives. A basis for establishing pollution charges as an incentive for companies to control effluents is set up in Article 10.

Licensing. Similarly, regulation of business activities through the licensing system can be used (Article 7[2]) by the government as an instrument for insisting on compliance with environmental protection objectives.

Prevention and Abatement. Article 17 of the 1982 act calls for provisions in legislation on "the overall and sectoral prevention and abatement of damage and pollution of the living environment and its control."

Public Participation. The participation of the public in the formation of a consensus on environmental protection measures was strongly emphasized by Salim. According to Article 6(1), every person has "the right and obligation to participate in the management of the living environment."

Environmental Awareness. The government has the duty, according to Article 9 of the 1982 act, to promote public awareness of the living environment. This is to be achieved both through formal educational institutions and through other means.

Compensation and Restoration. Civil liability provisions are set out in Article 20, covering both the compensation of victims of pollution and measures to restore the health of the living environment.

Integration and Coordination. Finally, Article 18 attempts to define the basic principles governing the sound and uniform administration of environmental laws and regulations. The intent is to cover coordination both among different environmental policy sectors and between different levels of government (national and provincial). Appointment of a minister with environmental policy responsibilities in 1978 was the crucial first step in this complex process of multiple-layered coordination in the environmental policy field.[44]

It is important to emphasize that the act was designed as a framework for future laws and regulations. The drafters focused in 1980–1981 on important principles that should govern these, in conjunction with the general statements on environmental protection in successive five-year plans (and in the formal guidelines preceding each of these) and with official documents clarifying and expanding on specific clauses of the act. In addition, the act served to define a set of explicit policy objectives in a variety of environmental policy areas and, by emphasizing the requirement of coordination, underscored the government's commitment to the promotion and implementation of environmental rules governing both the utilization of Indonesia's natural resources and the process of industrialization. The task of constructing the regulatory framework had begun, as we have seen, before the act was promulgated. It continued during and after this work. The 1982 act itself did not establish enforcement mechanisms or wider implementing machinery. As legislation, it was binding on government departments and agencies; and they were thus placed under an obligation to design in succeeding years the required legal and regulatory frameworks in specific environmental policy areas. The upshot of this protracted process, which is still continuing, is that by the early 1990s Indonesia had in place one of the most detailed and extensive environmental regulatory regimes among developing countries. In many ways, however, this impressive edifice has not been buttressed since 1982 by effective sectoral enforcement regimes because of inadequate government resources at the national and provincial levels. This is a measure of official reluctance to tolerate the kind of public input required for fully functioning regimes, the ability of traditionally powerful, development-oriented agencies to check what are frequently perceived as environmental policy excesses contributed to the problem. Before evaluating this record, we must first look briefly at its scope.

Environmental Regulation in the Framework of the 1982 Act

Several measures have followed the pollution provisions of the framework of the 1982 act. These can for convenience be divided into two broad areas: first, sectoral pollution control strategies, for example, in relation to air or water pollution; and second, attempts to establish environmental impact assessment mechanisms for industry and other projects. Regulation of water was first dealt with in a systematic fashion in the 1974 law on irrigation and other aspects of the management of waters, including marine waters. In 1982, rules governing the disposal of wastes were drawn up, under which the appropriate minister (in this case the minister of public works) was given responsibility for monitoring water use and water quality, and also for preparing policies for water resources development. Following legislation passed in 1984, a decree of 1986 covered a variety of specific topics related to pollution by industrial enterprises, such as the handling of industrial wastes, providing information to companies, initiating relevant research, and so on, that were the responsibility of the minister of industry.[45] Further regulations on air pollution and water pollution followed in 1988.[46] Several related measures have treated other topics such as the specific problems related to toxic chemicals, including pesticides.

More ambitious in scope, and also more politically sensitive, have been the government's efforts in the field of environmental impact assessment.[47] The provisions on EIA (or AMDAL in Bahasa Indonesia) outlined in the 1982 act (Article 16) led to a major set of implementing regulations in 1986. Design of the regulations drew on the earlier experience gained by the Bureau for Natural Resources and Environment of BAPPENAS since the mid-1970s in investigating the environmental aspects and impacts of a variety of different kinds of development projects. This approach has in turn been further elaborated in decrees covering a number of policy sectors. For example, a 1988 decree of the minister of mining and energy specifies information to be submitted on the impact of mining activities, including activities in the areas of oil and natural gas and geothermal resources.[48] The 1986 AMDAL regulation is fairly broad in scope; but among other things, it identifies the main kinds of activities judged likely to have a significant impact on the environment (Article 2). This includes a provision for ministers and agency heads to list any of these activities that fall under their jurisdiction. Administratively, the AMDAL procedure was to be integrated into the existing extensive framework of government regulation and licensing (Article 5). Further, impact assessments are formally required to be made as early as possible in the process of planning a project. The impact assessment process is also designed as an open one (with some qualifications as far as confidential government data are concerned), so that a right of access to data relevant to determining whether there is a threat to the environment from a proposed project is clearly established.[49] In practice the achievement of this objective has been problematic. Finally, these and other environmental policy objectives were increasingly seen in the late 1980s in the emerging legal context of planning for major land use legislation and regulations in the 1990s, the ultimate effects of which in terms of Indonesia's sustainable development policies remain to be seen.

Paralleling this gradual growth of legal and regulatory capabilities has been a process of institutional development from the early 1970s. Giving the environmental portfolio minister of state rank in 1978—and confirming and strengthening of this position in the government reorganization of 1983—went a long way towards placing these issues at the center of government attention, even though officials have since had to contend, not always successfully, with counterpressures from more powerful ministries. This followed earlier developments, especially after the Indonesian government's report to the U.N. Environment Conference of 1972 officially anticipated the establishment of formal environmental policy machinery.[50] Thus, a national committee on the environment was set up in 1972, and a bureau for natural resources and environment was created in 1975 as part of the National Development Planning Agency.[51] However, the Ministry of State for Population and Environment, like its institutional predecessor, has not consistently had the political authority to press environmental causes successfully within government, either at the national or provincial level. During the 1980s, the ministry (KLH) gradually developed an institutional structure based on four main divisions: human resources, including questions of population development; natural resources; environmental disturbance, including environmental impact analysis; and coordination and support, including problems of community participation.[52]

A number of incremental changes have been made over the years, both inside the ministry and in the broader organization of government. Thus, a full account of the official institutional network at the national level in the early 1990s includes several important institutions centered on the environment ministry and the State Committee on the Environment.[53] An environmental impact management agency (BAPEDAL) was established in 1990 to coordinate government activities in the area of impact assessment and monitoring. Potential problems of overlap and duplication with KLH were largely averted by the appointment of Dr. Salim, the environment minister, as head of this agency too, and by the transfer to the new body of the environmental disturbance functions of the ministry.

More emphasis has been placed recently, too, on problems of environmental administration and coordination among Indonesia's central and provincial governments, of which there are 27. The early 1990s saw the tentative beginnings of more serious thought about decentralization—"deconcentration"—as a means of improving the efficacy of national and local implementation of environmental programs. The obstacles in the way of such a development, however, are considerable; the Indonesian political and administrative system is both highly centralized and also, paradoxically, one in which local and regional sensitivities can be a significant constraint on the emergence of genuinely national policy frameworks.

THE ECONOMIC AND POLITICAL CONTEXTS
OF ENVIRONMENTAL POLICY

The environmental policies of Jakarta have both helped to foster and been in part a response to an emerging environmental constituency. As in Malaysia, this has significant transnational aspects. The rise of environmental groups has to some extent reflected particular legislative provisions, such as the right-of-access principle in AMDAL, as well as the more general consensus-seeking approaches adopted from the outset by Environment Minister Salim. Thus the Indonesian Environmental Forum (Wahana Lingkungan Hidup Indonesia [WALHI]) comprises approximately 600 groups concerned with a variety of aspects of environmental policies. Its officers have been insistent that environmental policy should not be left for government alone: "The management of Indonesia's environment requires a new approach [that] must be based upon public awareness and community participation."[54] In addition, newspapers have been not only a forum of debate on environmental topics, particularly the pollution affecting farmers, fishermen, and inhabitants of the larger cities of Java but also an instrument for publicizing issues and government programs.

In general, Indonesia's hierarchical and controlled political system has nevertheless not been a nourishing foundation for this kind of development.[55] The capacity of groups to influence government policy is limited. Macintyre has suggested that there are "three basic types of linkage by which societal interests might be transmitted upwards to policy-makers: . . . patron–client relationships, corporatist channels and what we might term political input by 'osmosis' or absorption."[56] Thus the rise of environmental NGOs in Indonesia has to be seen in relation to significant constraints. First, it does not necessarily indicate a coherent and politically powerful body of opinion straddling most classes, regions, and economic activities. The characteristic focus on specific pollution problems—as in the various "clean rivers" or "clean cities" campaigns—or issues surrounding national parks and other protected areas, represents an important, but fairly narrowly defined (and also politically untroubling), attack on "environmental" questions. Larger issues of resource use, particularly of forests, have been less consistently a target for NGO or news media opinion-forming strategies. Donner, for example, has observed that the loss of Indonesia's forests and soil cover still "bothers relatively few people."[57] Second, the expression of public concerns has been to some extent directly or indirectly generated by government activity itself, and more particularly by the traditionally powerful New Order bureaucracy, and it has also to a significant extent been kept under careful control by the environmental bureaucracy. The need for public participation in the environmental impact assessment process, or as a means of bringing polluting enterprises to court, has been repeatedly emphasized by Dr. Salim. The success rate in practice, however, has been mixed. People or groups complaining about pollution, concludes Cribb, "have typically had to meet at best a wall of official indifference and disregard, and at worse potentially dangerous counteraccusations of nefarious political intent."[58]

Despite these substantial constraints, public, media, and NGO interest in the environment is an important and growing element of Indonesia's environmental regulatory capability. The scientific and legal expertise of the environmental bureaucracy is also supplemented by the rise since the early 1970s of research institutes dealing with environmental matters in leading universities, a process very much encouraged both by the environment ministry and by donors.[59] The mandates of these bodies include research, information dissemination, and environmental management. Some of their work is also reinforced by the environment-related research activities and conferences of the Indonesian Institute of Science.

Occasional evidence of the relative weakness of this ministry in relation to more powerful bureaucratic actors in Jakarta, however, has at times acted as a major brake on environmental programs. There persists in the cabinet a perception that environmentalism is inherently and irrevocably both expensive in financial terms and costly in the sense of being detrimental to the success of development projects in major resource and industrial sectors. At stake here are both political and administrative questions: first, the environment ministry is only one voice in the national government machinery, and it is not among the most powerful actors; second, even when there is broad governmental agreement on the desired form of environment policies, the implementation of decisions raises major problems of administrative coordination among government institutions, a process that is itself political.

Taking even a conventional definition of environmental policy, the field comprises activities of several government departments, including the ministries of Public Works,[60] Industry, Health, Mining and Energy, Agriculture, and Forestry. Each of these ministries has a significant role in relation to the central body for environmental impact assessment, the AMDAL Commission.[61] In relation to forestry, relevant government actors include, apart from the Department of Forestry itself, the departments of Public Works, Transmigration, and the Interior; and the ministries of Information, Institutional Reform, Trade, Industry, and Communications; and KLH.[62] The environment ministry is constitutionally not a policy-implementation agency of government. The task of implementation of programs is in the hands of other departments and ministries, which often have their own agendas and which may have fundamental reservations about the desirability of some environmental protection programs.[63] This historic fragmentation of responsibilities has compounded the difficulties of administrative coordination, which the continuing process of administrative reform—over which Salim significantly also had a vital role in his earlier position as minister of state for administrative reform—has in part been designed to address. Broader administrative coordination problems are paralleled in the diversity of external agencies involved with Indonesian environmental policies.[64]

One major obstacle to more effective national coordination of environmental programs has been at the provincial level. The environment ministry in Jakarta has traditionally been linked not with the environmental agencies of provincial governments but more indirectly via provincial governors. Environmental agencies of different kinds have been established in many provincial governments; formally, however, KLH has no direct link with these but must instead channel its relations with them through the central offices of provincial governors.[65] Problems of coordination and effective implementation have been compounded by a history of meager resources, both budgetary and personnel, at local and regional levels. There has nonetheless been growing recognition in the 1990s that environmental problems vary considerably between different provinces. Pollution issues associated with industrialization, for example, are concentrated in Java; oil and gas development in Sumatra and Kalimantan pose their own distinctive problems, as does tin in Sumatra; and regions in the east have been differentially affected by drought conditions. While a greater measure of decentralization in approaches to the implementation of national policies and in the design of appropriate local and regional environmental policy frameworks may seem a logical response, such an approach has to contend with major hurdles of both principle and practice in the Indonesian political system.

In relation to broader definitions of environmental policy hinging on sustainable-development criteria, the task far outweighs currently available government or community resources. There is considerable scope for improved methods of environmental and resource accounting, for example,[66] but the requirements in terms of data-gathering-and-analysis budgets and of administrative and monitoring capabilities would be considerable. In Indonesia, as in Southeast Asia generally, the effective management of coastal zones similarly requires a far more extensive investment in monitoring, laboratory, and other capabilities.[67] Many resource sectors remain essentially unregulated in practice, including fisheries, coral, and mangroves. The oceans have in the past received much less policy attention than rivers, cities, or forests, partly because of a traditional Javanese disregard for them and partly because of the value of their resources and the strategic significance placed on them by the Indonesian navy. Some projects designed with attention to environmental criteria, such as the World Bank–supported Kedung Ombo project, have met with unexpected and apparently uncontrollable ecological costs. Even present programs have been marked by an uneven or inadequate coverage of some areas, such as the control of marine and coastal waters pollution, the policing of reserves to combat wildlife smuggling, regulatory attempts to arrest or reverse deforestation, actions to stem overreliance on pesticides, improvement of water quality, or the management of toxic wastes. Without additional major funding, any additional legal and policy commitments may threaten the effectiveness or the viability of existing programs.

Environmentalism has thus made significant strides forward in Indonesia in the last two decades. Compared to its response to UNCHE in 1972, Indonesia approached UNCED in 1992 from a markedly different perspective. By the time of the Rio Conference, the government had put in place a still-evolving legal and institutional framework for handling a variety of environmental problems. Both in Indonesia and in multilateral settings in the U.N. system, definitions of environmental issues were by the early 1990s more centrally tied to the questions of natural resource use central to Indonesia's ecological predicament. The conference was significant. It provided a significant boost for both official and NGO environmental actors in Indonesia, not least by renewing President Soeharto's own interest in and appreciation of the principles of sustainable development. Agenda items on forestry and pollution were important focal points of Indonesian attention at UNCED. Officials were particularly active in the preparatory committee on the deforestation issue,[68] and in the work of the conference itself on conserving and sustaining forest resources.[69]

Overriding development objectives reinforce Indonesia's sustainable-development orientation to environmentalism but at the same time set powerful constraints on the vigor with which programs are pursued. Environmental policy in Indonesia is both in principle (in the 1982 law, for example, and in the thinking underlying the five-year plan process) and in government practice viewed as one element, albeit an increasingly substantial one, of overall economic development planning and growth.[70] Utilization of Indonesia's abundant natural resources is crucial to this wider task. Despite growing attention to concepts of sustainable development shaped by ecological wise-use criteria, this larger context will continue to shape the environmental regulatory framework. The Indonesian state is more unequivocally committed to economic growth than to environmental protection. This fact inevitably defines the limits beyond which environmental regulation cannot in practice be expected to affect the economic activities of a booming economy and beyond which allocation of scarce government and scientific resources becomes politically unacceptable. Tensions between green aspirations, on the one hand, and the drives and dreams of an ambitious NIC, on the other, will accordingly persist as increasingly important defining characteristics of Indonesia during the 1990s.

NOTES

1. J. MacNeill, "The Greening of International Relations," *International Journal* 45 (1990): 1–2.

2. O. P. Dwivedi, "Political Science and the Environment," *International Social Science Journal* (1989): 109.

3. Robert Cribb, "The Politics of Pollution Control in Indonesia," *Asian Survey* 30.12: 1116–1117.

4. Koesnadi Hardjasoemantri, *Environmental Legislation in Indonesia* (Yogyakarta, Indonesia: Gadjah Mada University Press, 1987).

5. *Population and Environment: An Exploration of Critical Linkages,* ed. Fay G. Cohen and Joan M. Campbell in cooperation with Dalhousie University (Halifax, Canada: Environmental Managememt Development in Indonesia, 1992).

6. Biro Pusat Statistik, *Penduduk Indonesia Dalam Gambar* (Jakarta: 1983), p. xxxii.

7. Graeme J. Hugo, Terence H. Hull, Valerie J. Hull, and Gavin W. Jones, *The Demographic Dimension in Indonesian Development* (Singapore: Oxford University Press, 1987), pp. 318–319; A. J. Whitten, "Indonesia's Transmigration Program and Its Role in the Loss of Tropical Rain Forests," *Conservation Biology* 1.3 (1987): 239–246.

8. Hugo et al., *Demographic Dimension*, p. 18.

9. Andrew Macintyre, *Business and Politics in Indonesia* (North Sydney: Allen and Unwin, 1991), p. 3.

10. Hans H. de Jongh et al., *Environmental Profile: West Java* (The Hague: Ministry of Foreign Affairs, 1988).

11. Eduardo Tadem, "Conflict over Land-Based Natural Resources in the ASEAN Countries," *Conflict over Natural Resources in South-east Asia and the Pacific*, ed. Lim Teck Ghee and Mark J. Valencia (Manila: Manila University Press, 1990), pp. 15–18.

12. Wolf Donner, *Land Use and Environment in Indonesia* (Honolulu: University of Hawaii Press, 1987), p. 94.

13. Ibid., pp. 109, 116.

14. Tadem, "Conflict," pp. 24–25.

15. Caroline Thomas, *The Environment in International Relations* (London: Royal Institute of International Affairs, 1992), pp. 270–271.

16. *The Economist*, 14 November 1992, p. 40.

17. Cribb, "Politics of Pollution," pp. 1124, 1129–1130.

18. Ibid., pp. 1124–1125.

19. Mohamad Soerjani, *Environmental Problems and Management in Indonesia* (Jakarta: University of Indonesia, Centre for Research of Human Resources and the Environment, 1992), p. 62.

20. Canadian International Development Agency (CIDA), *Marine and Coastal Sector Development in Indonesia*, Vol. 1, *A Strategy for Assistance* (Ottawa: The Agency, 1987), p. 21.

21. Ibid., p. 109.

22. Phiphat Tangsubkul, *ASEAN and the Law of the Sea* (Singapore: Institute of Southeast Asian Studies, 1982), p. 9.

23. *The Oil Boom and After: Indonesian Economic Policy and Performance in the Soeharto Era*, ed. Anne Booth (Singapore: Oxford University Press, 1992).

24. *The Economy of Indonesia*, ed. Bruce Glassburner (Ithaca: Cornell University Press, 1971); *The Indonesian Economy*, ed. Gustav F. Papanek (New York: Praeger, 1980).

25. Thee Kian Wie, "The Surge of Asian NIC Investment into Indonesia," *Bulletin of Indonesian Economic Studies*, 27.3 (1991): 55–88.

26. Sjahrir, *Basic Needs in Indonesia: Economics, Politics and Public Policy* (Singapore: Institute of Southeast Asian Studies, 1986), p. 21.

27. Hardjasoemantri, *Environmental Legislation*.

28. Cribb, "Politics of Pollution," p. 1128.

29. Otto Soemarwoto, *Ekologi, Lingkungan Hidup dan Pembangunan* (Djakarta: Djambatan, 1987), pp. 1–2.

30. Ricardo Godoy and C. P. A. Bennett, "The Economics of Monocropping and Intercropping by Smallholders: The Case of Coconuts in Indonesia," *Human Ecology* 19.1 (1991): 84–85.

31. *Environmental Profile of Indonesia 1990* (Jakarta: University of Indonesia, Centre for Research of Human Resources and the Environment, 1990), pp. 35–36.

32. Ge Prince, "Dutch Economic Policy in Indonesia, 1870–1942," *Economic Growth in Indonesia, 1820–1940,* ed. Angus Maddison and Ge Prince (Dordrecht: Foris, 1989), p. 220.

33. Salim Said, *Genesis of Power: General Sudirman and the Indonesian Military in Politics, 1945–49* (Singapore: Institute of Southeast Asian Studies, 1991).

34. Djisman S. Simandjuntak, "The Process of Deregulation and Privatization: The Indonesian Experience," *Asian Quarterly* 19.4 (1991): 363–370; Erik Thorbecke, "The Indonesian Adjustment Experience in an International Perspective," *Indonesian Economic Journal* April 1992: 76–116.

35. Herman Haeruman, "Conservation in Indonesia," *Ambio* 17.3 (1988): 220.

36. Donner, *Land Use*, p. 112.

37. Robert Boardman, *International Organization and the Conservation of Nature* (Bloomington: Indiana University Press, 1981), pp. 26–35.

38. Cribb, "Politics of Pollution," p. 1125.

39. Koesnadi Hardjasoemantri, "The Indonesian Approach," in *Environmental Law in Indonesia and Canada: Present Approaches and Future Trends,* ed. David VanderZwaag, Stephen Mills, and Barbara Patton (Halifax, Canada: Dalhousie University, School for Resource and Environmental Studies, 1987), pp. 9–16.

40. Moestadji, "Report on the Current State of Management of the Environment (Specifically the Legal Framework of Environmental Management)" (Jakarta: University of Indonesia, mimeo, 1989), pp. II/10, 21.

41. Cribb, "Politics of Pollution," p. 1126.

42. Shirley A. M. Conover and Arthur J. Hanson, "The Development of AMDAL (Environmental Impact Assessment) in Indonesia" (Halifax, Canada: Dalhousie University, School for Resource and Environmental Studies, 1988, draft).

43. Hardjasoemantri, *Environmental Law.*

44. Ibid., pp. 7–20.

45. Moestadji, "Current State," pp. II/12–16.

46. Ibid., pp. II/6, 12, 22.

47. Moestadji, "The Legal Framework for Environmental Assessment in Indonesia," in *Environmental Law in Indonesia and Canada,* ed. David VanderZwaag, Stephen Mills, and Barbara Patton (Halifax, Canada: Dalhousie University, School for Resource and Environmental Studies, 1987), pp. 130–144.

48. Moestadji, "Current State," p. VI/3.

49. Ibid., pp. VI/4–10.

50. Government of Indonesia, "Environmental Problems in Indonesia: A Country Report," Stockholm, June 1972.

51. Shirley A. M. Conover, "An Example of Institution Strengthening with EMDI Assistance" (Halifax, Canada: Dalhousie University, School for Resource and Environmental Studies, draft, 1992), pp. 7–11.

52. Ibid.

53. Soerjani, *Environmental Problems*, pp. 88–95.

54. Erma Witoelar, cited by Laurence Surendra, "Emerging Trends in Ecological and Environmental Movements in South and South-east Asia: Implications for Social Science and Social Theory," in *Protest Movements in South and South-east Asia: Traditional and Modern Idioms of Expression,* ed. Rajeshwari Ghose (Hong Kong: Centre of Asian Studies, University of Hong Kong, 1987), p. 213.

55. Richard Robison, "Authoritarian States, Capital-Owning Classes and the Poli-

tics of NICs: The Case of Indonesia," *World Politics* 41.1 (1988); Ian Chalmers, "Democratization and Social Forces in Indonesia," *Southeast Asian Affairs 1991* (Singapore: Institute of Southeast Asian Studies, 1991).

56. Macintyre, *Business and Politics*, p. 18.

57. Donner, *Land Use*, p. 232.

58. Cribb, "Politics of Pollution," p. 1132.

59. Mohamad Soerjani, "Promoting Environmental Study Centres in Indonesia in Support of Sustainable Development" (Jakarta: World Bank, 1989). The first was set up in 1972; see Soemarwoto, *Ekologi, Lingkungan Hidup*, pp. 2–3.

60. Liana Bratasida, "Environmental Management Development in the Ministry of Industry" (Jakarta: Ministry of Industry, mimeo, 1990).

61. Soerjani, "Environmental Study Centres," pp. 91–94.

62. *Review of Policies Affecting the Sustainable Development of Forest Lands in Indonesia* (Jakarta: Ministry of State for Population and Environment/Department of Forestry/Department of Interior, 1985).

63. Conover, "Institution Strengthening," p. 14.

64. *Toward Inter-Governmental and Inter-Agencies Cooperation on Indonesian Eco-Development*, ed. Herman Haeruman (Jakarta: Ministry of State for Population and Environment, 1979).

65. Conover, "Institution Strengthening," p. 10.

66. Henry Peskin, "Environmental and Non-Market Accounting in Developing Countries," *Environmental Accounting for Sustainable Income*, ed. Yusuf J. Ahmad, Salah El Serafy, and Ernst Lutz (Washington, D.C.: World Bank, 1989), pp. 59–64; Peter Bartelmus, E. Lutz, and S. Schweinfest, *Integrated Environmental and Economic Accounting: A Case Study for Papua New Guinea* (Washington, D.C.: World Bank, Environment Working Paper No. 54, 1992).

67. Manuwadi Hungspreugs, "Heavy Metals and Other Non-Oil Pollutants in Southeast Asia," *Ambio* 17.3 (1988): 182.

68. United Nations, *Report of the Preparatory Committee for the UNCED* (Doc. A/ 46/48, Pt. I, 25 May 1991), p. 57.

69. United Nations, "United Nations Conference on Environment and Development," Rio de Janeiro, 3–14 June 1992 (A/CONF.151/26, vol. II, 13 August 1992), p. 28.

70. Geoffrey B. Hainsworth, "Economic Growth, Basic Needs and Environment in Indonesia," *Southeast Asian Affairs 1985* (Singapore: Institute of Southeast Asian Studies, 1985), pp. 152–173.

Chapter 6

Environmental Problems, Policies, and Prospects in Africa: A Continental Overview

PETER J. STOETT

ENVIRONMENT IN AFRICA: THE PREDICAMENT

The environmental predicament in Africa is central to the future of that continent, and its extent is indeed difficult to exaggerate.

One of the chief problems in Africa today concerns its precarious water supply. Water is contaminated by two prime sources: human waste, typical along rivers which attract population settlements upstream and downstream; and industrial and agrochemical wastes, often dumped untreated into lakes and rivers. The latter is noticeable where there is advanced industrial development, as at the Nyamwamba River located near the Kilembe Mines in Uganda.[1] But the biggest water-related problem in Africa concerns the lack of access to clean drinking water, a condition that afflicts the majority of the underprivileged and is partly responsible for the high infant mortality rate and low life-expectancy throughout the region. As is discussed later in this chapter, dams and irrigation systems can, paradoxically, create further water-supply problems.

Africa's water supply is directly affected by periodic drought. Social conditions have often served to exacerbate, and not relieve, the suffering associated with drought cycles; in a highly stratified social structure, these calamities affect some more than others. Members of Africa's upper classes—whom some East Africans refer to in Swahilian as the *Wabenzi*, or "Mercedes-Benz tribe"—are less inclined to fear the diminution of the resources essential to their personal survival strategies. Water will be a source of conflict in the future, since most nations will lose considerable water per capita if present population trends continue. River systems, such as the Nile, whose basin touches ten countries, are potential hotspots that could well be the cause of future intraregional wars. A recent dispute between Mauritania and Senegal involved the Senegal River. However, water can also be the source of interstate cooperation: A tentative example is the Agreement on the Action Plan for the Environmentally Sound Management of the Common Zambezi River System, adopted in Harare on May 28, 1987, and signed by Mozambique, Zambia, Zimbabwe, Malawi, Tanzania, Botswana, and Namibia; and there are other more established agreements in effect (the Lake Chad Basin Commission dates back to 1964).[2]

Soil erosion remains the most visible African environmental threat, especially in eastern Africa. Though considerable international resources and scholarship have been committed to the problem, it continues to dominate discussions of African ecology. Desertification refers to the complete erosion of once-arable land, and a certain mythology surrounds perceptions of this process, often construed as natural, in the West. Though wind erosion and sand migration contribute, the Sahara's southern Sahel is advancing—and creating "environmental refugees" in the process—mainly because of negligent agricultural practices, such as overgrazing and haphazard irrigation schemes which induce salination. And purposive deforestation contributes, removing heat-deflecting shade. The results for agricultural output, herd maintenance, and wildlife dependent upon affected areas are disastrous. It is no surprise that the African delegates at the Earth Summit held in Brazil in June 1992, made desertification their priority, and a forthcoming international conference will address the issue directly.

Directly linked to soil erosion, deforestation is occurring throughout Africa as a result of population pressure (people using wood for fuel at unsustainable rates), timber exportation, land clearance for both cash-cropping and human settlement, overgrazing, and protracted warfare. Overall, the greatest pressure on Africa's trees is exerted by the exigencies of daily survival. It has become impossible in many areas to use wood for fuel without rapidly depleting local stocks of trees, though various types of agroforestry techniques are at present being utilized with noted success.[3] The forests most susceptible to logging (or, more precisely, the damage that follows the construction of roads for that purpose) include those in Côte d'Ivoire, Gambia, Burundi, Guinea-Bissau, Liberia, Malawi, and Nigeria, though many other countries are rapidly depleting forest reserves. In other words, it is not just the rain forests that are endangered; but they hold by far the greatest amount of biological diversity, which most concerns naturalists. Côte d'Ivoire has the highest tropical deforestation rate in the world; its forests could be completely destroyed within two generations.[4]

Though it appears that Africa's main environmental problems resulting from economic activity are principally related to agriculture, the continent is hardly free from the detrimental effects of industry. Mining produces significant water and air pollution, and diamond mining is perhaps the most wasteful of all (for example, only 0.89 carat of diamonds is found per ton of ground at the Orapa Mine in Botswana).[5] Africa is a virtual storebed of minerals, such as phosphates, iron ore, copper, and gold. As occurs in so much of the periphery of the world economy, industrial production often takes place with little regard for environmental protection. In this respect the chemical industry, which produces pesticides (often banned elsewhere) for local use has been infamous. Indeed, many analysts would argue that the much-heralded Green Revolution did little but sell the Third World a dangerous chemical illusion when Western methods were assumed superior to indigenous techniques. Pesticides and herbicides contribute to pollution at the stages of both industrial production and agricultural application.

Africa is growing increasingly familiar with advanced urban pollution, suffering the consequences of years of both intrastate and interstate migratory patterns of urbanization. Marginalized people have always sought opportunity in large cities, and in Africa this causes immediate problems because the influx of impoverished people is not usually accompanied with commensurate increases in city infrastructure. Inadequate urban sewage facilities present perhaps the greatest health problem. The sudden concentration of resource consumers puts unrealistic demands on the carrying capacity of local rural areas as well, and this is exacerbated by the political tendency, common in many postcolonial states, of urban bias in development policy.

Even such a brief survey as this would be incomplete without quick reference to Africa's wildlife and current conservation efforts aimed at its preservation. The controversial ban on trade in elephant products, promoted by Western nongovernment organizations and adopted at the Convention on International Trade of Endangered Species Meeting in 1989, has doubtlessly saved the African elephant from rapid decline; it may be too late to save the Black Rhino (whose numbers declined from almost 15,000 in 1980 to less than 4,000 by 1987).[6] The ban on ivory continues, despite the protestations of Tanzania and other nations which have recently sought its expiration. Related policy initiatives are discussed later, but ultimately African wildlife conservation depends upon the survival of African environments and citizens.

Global Linkages and Affects

One of Africa's biggest disadvantages may be that it does not threaten the global biosphere enough and, with a few conceivable exceptions in Northern Africa, African nations do not threaten neighbors with significant transboundary pollution. However, Africa is disproportionately affected by the contributions to global ecosystem deterioration (global warming, ozone depletion, and so on) made by others, most notably, of course, the affluent North Americans and Europeans. For example, it is believed that the people of the Sahel will suffer from changes in global weather:

Rainfall in the Sahel depends upon the reach of the Inter-Tropical Convergence Zone (ITCZ), the equatorial rendezvous for tropical air masses. In the summer months, warm maritime air condenses into monsoon clouds; how far north the clouds reach depends on the relative strength of atmospheric circulations over the oceans which in turn may be affected by small differences in sea temperatures between the North and South Atlantic. If the ITCZ contracts a fraction, the consequence for Sahelian farmers at the edge of the rainfall belt is certain crop failure.[7]

Of course, African ecology was and is affected by the global system in much more direct fashion. Indeed, the African experience includes the harshest of all resource extraction, that of indigenous peoples themselves, captured into slavery and transported north and overseas. Those darkest of days have passed. But the idea of an "ecological shadow" cast upon the less-developed world by advanced industrial nations has become commonplace in mainstream discourse. Such a process began in Africa as early as the Roman Empire, when Romans took wood for buildings and fuel (much of it to heat the famous Roman baths) from the Maghreb countries of Morocco, Algeria, and Tunisia. It is best to avoid the tired debate over the utility of dependency theory at this point, but we should stress the link between the enclave economy and the exploitation of local resources. This may not always explain local relative poverty, but it can often explain discernable patterns of environmental degradation.

Current trading practices in mineral resources reflect colonial ties: Belgium receives over 60 percent of its imported copper from Zaire, and Britain some 30 percent of it from Zambia.[8] Indeed, mining the Copper Belt dominates the Zambian economy in a typical enclave-dependency manner: Over 90 percent of foreign exchange is derived from copper (the price drop in copper in the 1970s was disastrous for the Zambian economy), and approximately 30,000 laborers working on some 700 large farms are required just to feed the miners and "associated urban population connected with the mineral economy." The belt attracts wage labor from Malawi, Tanzania, and Mozambique, draining villages of male workers and contributing to the increasing urbanization—and deforestation—of the area.[9]

It is not surprising, then, that in much of the world, and in Africa in particular, the colonial legacy dominates historical images. The arbitrary geopolitical division of Africa, an interior-to-coast trade pattern imposed by colonial powers, the development of export crops (as a commodity and, equally important, as a mode of production), the alienation of prime land (especially in South Africa, Zimbabwe, Kenya, Tanzania, and Zambia) from Africans: These conditions are continued today under present class formations.[10] British and French colonialism planted the "seeds of famine" by encouraging (with coercive taxation policies) the cash-cropping of peanuts and cotton in the Sahel, while the Belgians began the process of deforestation in Zaire by granting blanket exploitation rights to rubber and ivory companies.[11]

African ecologist Calestous Juma has summarized the ecological degradation that typically occurs in what he terms "raw material zones" used to feed both external nations and internal metropoles.[12] The advance of market capitalism, a process initiated by colonial powers and continued by development strategies and foreign aid, forces the activity of subsistence farming onto marginal lands, since the best land will be used for cash crops. Unequal exchange means that more produce must be exported to maintain current levels of imports; cash-cropped land will thus be overused, and there is a desire to employ fertilizers and pesticides that may pose serious occupational health problems and threaten local water supply. Deforestation is often a direct result of the effort to grow vegetation or raise livestock for eventual export; the chief cause of the rapid deforestation in Kenya, Mauritania, Botswana, Sudan, or Burkino Faso is not some "natural" process of desertification (as is often assumed in the West) but population pressure and the growth of export-oriented agriculture combined with the quite understandable need of people to use wood for fuel.

Despite its peripheral status within the world economy, Africa remains within its ideological orbit. African environmental problems may be illustrated with reference to the current influence of the International Monetary Fund. IMF requires trade liberalization, devaluation, antiinflationary measures such as the dismantling of price controls and control of wages, open-door policies on foreign investment, reduction of social services, and privatization. Debt-burdened nations are advised to concentrate upon exporting resources, which are viewed as economic variables only. Simply put, the IMF demands that the output of export commodities be raised in order to generate foreign exchange earnings. These resources often include timber; and, as noted earlier, intensified exploitation of forests at irreplaceable levels contributes much to deforestation. This is certainly the case in Ghana, according to P. A. Kwaku Kyem, who quotes that country's secretary for agriculture predicting that "if the drive to increase timber exports does not slacken, the carrying capacity of the country's soils which have already been stretched by poor methods of farming will be jeopardized."[13]

Africa has received substantial project aid from industrialized nations, a fact reflected by the heavy presence of World Bank initiatives and personnel. Rosenblum and Williamson write that "the trees slain in the service of printing advice to Africa, if restored to life, would likely stretch from Mauritania to Mozambique."[14] Many environmentalists have criticized

World Bank projects because they have often involved the installation of infrastructural designs that have not only proved troublesome in ecological terms but have disregarded the interests of indigenous populations. Examples abound. The construction of the Kariba project, between what is now Zambia and Zimbabwe, resulted in the forced resettlement of 56,000 inhabitants of both sides of the Zambezi River; and some 80,000 Ghanians were displaced as their residence was flooded by the lake created by the Akosomber Dam, built to supply cheap electricity to Kaiser Aluminum.[15]

One may note the deleterious effects of large-scale irrigation schemes, such as waterlogging and salination. It has been estimated that some three million Kenyans suffer from schistosomiasis because of the slow-moving water created by dams (which provides excellent breeding grounds for the snails that spread this debilitating disease).[16] The Kano River irrigation project in northern Nigeria eventually produced "major environmental effects. Wide-scale destruction of forests reduced the availability of fuel and sylvan produce to the poor. This inevitably increased the labor of poor women in fuel gathering. The destruction of economic trees reduced beer-brewing income, and deprived older women of income from the collection of firewood and water."[17]

On the positive side, there has been a definite shift in lending and aid institutions toward concern with the environment, as the latest World Bank report makes quite clear. Environmental problems have become an undeniable element of development planning, and it is changing perceptions of economic growth itself.[18] Still, the Global Environmental Facility, a fund for environmental technology designed to contribute to sustainable development under the auspices of the World Bank, has been criticized as an attempt to "tack environmental tails on very nasty dogs."[19]

Another connection with the world economy deserves noting. One of the groups most resilient to such conceptual change are African elites. A growing usage of the term "environmental imperialism" refers to the shipment of toxic waste from the West to less advantaged areas. This activity reached scandalous proportions in the 1980s; and though many nations have banned the export and import of such products and African nations have collectively signed the 1991 Bamako Convention (agreeing not to import hazardous waste), it is indeed difficult to gauge the level of covert activity that occurs in this area. Meanwhile, World Bank chief economist Lawrence Summers mused in a leaked internal memo that "the economic logic of dumping a load of toxic waste in the lowest-wage country is impeccable and we should face up to that."[20]

CONTINENTAL AND NATIONAL FACTORS

Obviously, the global linkages described in the previous section have regional and national counterparts. Exactly what these are is a matter of interpretation, but some broad comments may be made here. It has become an aphorism (in the West especially) that all of Africa's (indeed, all of the so-called Third World's) problems can be attributed to burgeoning over-population. Certainly, population pressure is real and growing, and this is exacerbated by poverty. But we cannot simply blame environmental problems on population augmentation itself.

One author who deals fairly with this issue is Paul Shaw who, before demonstrating the links between exponential population increase and ecological decay, makes several pertinent qualifications. First, most measurements are concerned only with growth rates, whereas population distribution and ratio to resources are as important. Second, global pollution problems, such as global warming and ozone depletion, are still the handiwork of the less-populated affluent North, not of the overpopulated South. This is also time for resource consumption; developed countries, with a quarter of the world population, consume some 75 percent of the world's energy, 79 percent of commercial fuels, 85 percent of wood products, and 72 percent of steel products.[21] It follows that we should be equally concerned with any substantial population rise in the North, since each additional child will become such a voracious consumer.

Shaw also mentions the need to take political factors into account before ascribing causal significance to population pressure within Africa, such as instability (over 200 coups or attempted coups in the last 20 years), class structures and preferential state treatment, and varieties across regions. The problem of refugees, who are usually the product of political or economic factors, is illustrative: "An influx of 100,000 refugees in rural sub-Saharan Africa initially desertifies about 875 acres and accounts for more than 100,000 tons of firewood annually . . . their negative impacts on the environment have little to do with population growth *per se*."[22] Neither Shaw nor the present author wishes to understate the problems associated with Africa's rising population: The need for extensive family planning programs to give African women reproductive choices is obvious. But other factors, inherently political, deserve equal emphasis.

Of all these factors, military conflict is perhaps the most visibly damaging of all. Beyond the obvious ecological destruction wrought by armed warfare, many environmental effects of conflict are indirect. The civil war in Mozambique, which has pitted the government there against South African–backed rebel guerrillas (the Mozambique National Resistance, or RENAMO), provides an unfortunate example. RENAMO has destroyed the infrastructure of most of the national conservation parks and has made work there unsafe. Greater environmental threats are longer term, resulting from "the pressure the displaced population exerts on the natural resources in safe areas, and from poaching of wildlife in rebel-held territories." Villagers have fled the war and settled in coastal zones and urban centers. Those suddenly settled in the coastal areas are putting major pressure on the vital mangrove ecosystem, a crucial habitat for the reproduction of shrimp and prawns, the largest contributor to foreign exchange. Many have settled in the relatively safe Biera Corridor near the Zimbabwe border, and the geographical differences between this area and village lowlands complicate matters further. The hilly Penhalonga region is well protected by government forces from both Mozambique and Zimbabwe since a telecommunications system is installed on the top of nearby Mount Xilunva, and the railroad linking the two nations runs through the area. This security zone has attracted villagers unfamiliar with cultivating high-slope land and, according to the Mozambique Ministry of Agriculture, they are "farming the slopes without terraces, greatly increasing soil erosion in a region that receives high rainfall."[23]

Civil strife and violent conflict are, unfortunately, too common a cause of extensive environmental damage in Africa, whether it be Angola, Chad, Sudan, Liberia, Somalia, Kenya, or elsewhere.

Under conditions of civil war, environmental policy is a luxury indeed. It is not so reasonable, however, that in the war against poverty—one that African nations have been waging collectively for many years—such policy should be considered luxurious, though it often is. In this context, the involvement of the developmentalist state is axiomatic in terms of both the causes of and solutions to ecological crises. The introduction and promotion of mechanized farming in eastern Africa, which coincides with the systemic marginalization in many countries of the nomadic peoples, was facilitated by the acceptance of inappropriate technology; but it was the outcome of political tensions within the state. As discussed earlier, exploitation of resources is often attributed to the legacy of colonialism and exogenous economic forces; there is some validity to this, but the collaboration of African governments, often corrupt and dictatorial themselves, is required. The forced "villigization" of the Oromos by the Mengista regime in Ethiopia is an extreme example of state complicity in the creation of refugees which, ultimately, puts unbearable pressure on scarce resources. It is also of obvious ethical concern that many African nations have been net exporters of food and yet have not sufficiently fed their own citizens (Sudan, Niger, Algeria). At the same time, however, African governments can stimulate proenvironmental organization and employment, and they are sources of political authority that may be able to mitigate potential damage caused by development projects.

This translates into the need for rigorous environmental impact assessment, which remains as subject to the political exigencies of the day as any other policy area. This is at best an imprecise yet vital science: Assessments not only must be concerned with the impact of development projects, agricultural and industrial, but also must consider superior alternatives and attempt to weigh environmental effects on some sort of common basis with economic and social costs and benefits. Governments, in regional coordination with the UNEP, have taken timid formal steps to universalize the assessment process: The Montevideo Program for the Development and

Periodic Review of Environmental Law was adopted in 1982, and the Goals and Principles of Environmental Impact Assessment, which in essence call for informational exchange and consultation in the event of potential transboundary effects, were adopted in 1987. Yet the hunger for foreign investment and drive toward trade liberalization, evident in many African nations, may render serious environmental impact assessments much more difficult. For example, in an attempt to speed up the rate of foreign investment in Morocco, a nation fast becoming heavily polluted because of extensive phosphate mining, a law was passed in 1990 that made it obligatory for authorities to respond to foreign industrial investment applications within two months. "If this is actually applied [as it needs to be to attract foreign investment], it will further constrain the authorities in pollution control measures."[24]

Impact assessments may also be construed as attempts to legitimize development plans by the state not only internally but for the sake of obtaining infrastructural aid packages.[25] When it emanates from centralized sources of public authority, environmental assessment gives rise to the further establishment of technocratic bureaucracy, by way of promoting what Andre Gorze terms "mandarin ideology: an ideology which claims that the holders of exceptional knowledge are responsible to their peers alone, and not to their neighbors, to the people."[26] This ideology extends to multinational corporations and development assistance programs. The World Bank is now emphasizing the necessity of local involvement at the planning stage. For example, the Burkina Faso national environmental management plan, developed over three years with bank (and other) assistance, "might have been quicker and cheaper to produce . . . using international consultants [but] the plan would not have been a Burkinabe product and would probably have joined other 'external' products on a backshelf instead of resulting in action."[27] It is clear that, as S. B. Akuffo asserts in the Ghanian case, ecological expertise should be fostered at the local community level.[28] But that there is a need for such regulation by state agencies (as well as autonomous nongovernment organizations) can hardly be debated: The modern state simply must play a major role in providing environmental security. This includes fiscal incentives, such as taxation policies that punish polluting and reward pollution abatement, educational activities, and legislation.

Indeed, this is a tall order for most African governments. Environmental policy is ultimately dependent upon the existence of a network of legislation that gives the assessment and management process its legitimacy. Even some of the most bureaucratized states have so far been unable to coordinate environmental protection with overall development plans. Two Kenyan authors lament the fact the there has been "no environmental protection law dealing with all aspects of environmental degradation and enhancement" though Kenya may have the most advanced environmental protection services in

Africa. Thus the Agricultural Act; Forests Act; Land Control Act; Crop Production and Livestock Act; Public Health Act; Factories Act; Water Act; Food, Drugs and Chemical Substances Act; and Pesticide Act serve as a fragmented environmental legislation, though there is a National Environment Secretariat to promote education and a Ministry of Environmental and Natural Resources which has jurisdiction over mineral and forestry resources.[29]

Two Nigerian analysts, writing about that country's growing water pollution problems, cite the "inability of Federal, State and Local agencies to co-ordinate their programs [and] the virtual non-existence of federal and state water laws."[30] One coordinating activity that has some support in the region is the adoption of national conservation strategies (NCS) prescribed in the World Conservation Strategy produced in 1980 by the International Union for the Conservation of Nature and Natural Resources (IUCNNR), UNEP, and World Wildlife Fund (WWF). Three constituent objectives of conservation are explicated: Nations should plan to develop and maintain essential ecological processes, ensure that the exploitation of natural resources is maintained at sustainable levels, and maintain biological diversity. Zambia has adopted an NCS following the policy decision to diversify the economy to include less copper mining and more agriculture; President Kaunda invited the IUCNNR to work with Zambians to prepare the strategy, which was approved by the Zambian cabinet in July 1985. According to one of its authors, the strategy has been successful: "NCSs were once viewed as a way of modifying development proposals. The Zambia NCS has been effective in actually creating" them.[31] But ultimately it is the people on the ground which must implement such initiatives.

LOCAL INITIATIVE AND SURVIVAL

While it appears obvious that the political revolutions that have taken place in Eastern Europe in recent times involved a great deal of substate sentiment and activity which eventually dispelled the legitimacy of many regimes, it should be noted that a similar transition, under very different circumstances, may be happening in Africa. Pierre Pradervand focuses not on state officials but on the voices of "the principal architects of the new Africa—its farmers" in his latest book.[32] And Nigel Cross writes of the growing recognition among developers and aid donors in the Sahel—people must be put first in development schemes—though he asserts the need to go beyond mere participation and begin thinking in terms of rights.[33] The twisted road toward official democracy continues, even in the apartheid state of South Africa. Political accountability is as essential, though often as elusive, as ever.

Although the overall situation in Africa seems desperate, we should stress that many grassroots development organizations, associated with a variety of other causes, are adopting environmentalist agendas. This includes organizations such as the Six-S in Burkino Faso and other Sahelian countries, the

Purros Project in Namibia, The Communal Areas Management Program for Indigenous Resources ("CAMPFIRE") in Zimbabwe, and the highly organized Utooni people of the Machakos district in Kenya. These groups manage to combine participation and conservation, throwing into question the Western assumption that only the state can be the proper center of authority that defines property regimes and allocates societal resources.[34]

Some of these groups make a further linkage between development and the heavy burden environmental degradation places on women. The "Green Belt" movement of Kenya, funded partly by the U.N. Development Fund for Women and private donations, employs some 50,000 rural women in tree-planting projects designed to stem the flow of the desert (it is estimated they have planted 10 million trees in ten years). The National Council of Women of Kenya has promoted a system of action which involves "women as equal participants and developers . . . communities become self-sufficient in fuelwood, and Kenyan women no longer spend hours each day in search of food."[35] There is also a firmly established Association of Women's Clubs in Zimbabwe which has begun planting drought-resistant indigenous trees. An International Fund for Agricultural Development (IFAD) project in Gambia "works to uphold traditional female cultivation rights under a new land-distribution scheme and establish day-care centers [necessary] with the introduction of double-cropping."[36] These movements are still subject to the vicissitudes of state control and often viewed as threats by those with a monopoly on defining national security. For example, the determined Wangari Maathai, famous founder of the Green Belt movement, and a popular speaker at the Global Forum (which paralleled the Earth Summit in Rio, 1992) is repeatedly harassed by Kenyan officials.[37] However, regional events such as the African Women's Assembly on Sustainable Development, held in Harare, Zimbabwe, February 1989, represent concrete beginnings.

But they are small ones. It is clear that the people of Africa have felt the effects of the shared assumption among policy and class elites that the key to widespread prosperity is the growth of industrialization. We see this in the infrastructural projects designed to attract foreign capital which will invest in the building of industry; and we see this in the hurried attempt to turn multiuse land into large-scale Botswanian beef factories or Sahelian peanut farms. The quest for economic growth is a fixation deeper than the ideological arguments that helped drive the Cold War, a central assumption few choose to question: Industrialize before the redistribution of wealth, before giving priority to ecology. This reflects the domination of a certain conception of human nature relations transplanted from industrial Europe to Africa and elsewhere.

Though it would be misleading to equate all precolonial African history with sustainable development, Africans have a long cultural history that has usually incorporated the environment as a central feature of life. The Swahilian term *mazingira*, the Arabic term *beea*, and the Ibo term *alaoma*, all refer to a conception of environment bereft of the axiomatic split between humans and nature made in the secular Eurocentric manner. Long-term hope lies in the ability of Africa's diverse and resilient peoples to recapture their respect for nature.

On a final note, we find that policy initiatives aimed at protecting Africa's wildlife are burgeoning. Wildlife management has become a political issue in many African countries; and various schemes—some of them involving community networks of management—have been implemented. It is also an area in which much regional cooperation is required: The East African Wildlife Society, for example, has been called "a model for building efficient organizations in areas in which wildlife needs protection on a sub-regional scale."[38] There is considerable access to Western funds in the name of "ecotourism" (which, if improperly managed, can prove disastrous for wildlife) and "big-game hunting." This can lead to unusual policy decisions: The Republic of South Africa, for example, recently announced that the Industrial Development Corporation would finance ecotourism, with a startup allocation of R600 million. Madagascar's environmental action plan, which seeks to protect the unique biological patrimony of that island nation from rapid desertification, has stimulated strong donor support.

Though the attraction of tourist dollars is obvious in places like Kenya, there is a bitter history of colonial powers displacing Africans for the sake of game reserves and wildlife preservation—for example, in British ruled Tanganyika—and modern efforts at preservation must involve complete ecosystems which, for better or worse, include humans.[39] "Debt-for-nature" swaps aimed at protecting biodiversity, though they are not free of problems themselves, will no doubt continue to gain popularity in the near future. However, their applicability in the African context is limited to the few African nations blessed with threatened rain forest, such as Gabon, Côte d'Ivoire, Zaire, and Madagascar. The IUCNNR's and UNESCO's "Man and Biosphere" projects, some of which are in Africa, are exciting developments in this regard. These internationally recognized conservation zones involve local human participation. A park to save the mountain gorilla involves three states: Rwanda, Zaire, and Uganda. It must be stressed, however, that human needs will invariably prevail over those of wildlife. Extensive droughts and the threat of famine will induce the purposeful, if tragic, slaughter even of elephants, as occurred in Zimbabwe in the summer of 1992.

CONCLUSION

Africa's ecopolitical future will depend on its people, organized at grass-roots levels, and their participation in forging a new approach to development on the continent. Granted, they need to be free from civil and international war to do this. They need some relief from the pressures of the world economic system, as well as limited technical assistance from the global community. Perhaps most of all, they need to live in societies where they are not systematically persecuted or robbed of their land. But just as important, they need be the focus of development projects that involve their considerable expertise and guidance. In a recent essay on state-run conservation efforts in Ethiopia, John Campbell stresses this point, salient to any discussion of the potential futures of African ecology. Afforestation programs were rigidly centralized under the Ministry of Agriculture and implemented in such a manner that the land upon which peasants were currently living was used without their permission or consultation with them.

At the same time, these peasants were expected to devote labor to the project. On at least one occasion, "Seedlings were deliberately planted upside down by tenants apparently to prevent the loss of land they would subsequently have had to face . . . without secure tenure tenants were unwilling to invest in soil conservation." Campbell concludes that "the centralized organization of afforestation programmes under the Ministry of Agriculture clearly gives the message to peasants that community forestry creates government forests. . . . The major decision affecting peasants appears to be whether they will have to plant the trees through paid or unpaid labor!"[40] Conservation policies must reflect an awareness of the survival strategies of people; and it may be argued that such strategies ultimately come from the community level. Unless people have a sense of personal commitment to their future, a further sense of local pride, and the promise of reasonable rewards, they will continue to plant seeds upside down.

Overall, it is most important that in Africa the very issue of environmental degradation not be marginalized. This is a distinct possibility as nation-states struggle with political change and conflict; and the situation is acute in Africa, whose continued environmental degradation, in the eyes of a self-interested humanity, threatens only itself.

NOTES

1. C. Okello-Oleng, "National Environmental Issues and Strategies in Uganda," *Integrated Management of Resources of Africa: A Reader* (Nairobi: United Nations Environmental Programs, 1989), pp. 120–123.

2. F. Visser, "Recent Developments in the Joint Management of International Non-Maritime Water Resources in Africa," *Comparative and International Law Journal of Southern Africa* 22.1 (1989): 59–92.

3. B. Munslow et al., *The Fuelwood Trap: A Study of the SADCC Region* (London: Earthscan, 1988).

4. W. Wood, "Tropical Deforestation: Balancing Regional Development Demands and Global Environmental Concerns," *Global Environmental Change* 1.1 (1990): 23–41, 26.

5. L. Lewis and L. Berry, *African Environments and Resources* (London: Unwin Hyman, 1988), p. 367.

6. J. Macgregor, "The Paradoxes of Wildlife Conservation in Africa," *Africa Insight* 19.4 (1989): 201–212.

7. N. Cross, *The Sahel: The People's Right to Development* (London: Minority Rights

Group, 1990), p. 16; also, T. Downing, "Vulnerability to Hunger in Africa: A Climate Change Perspective," *Global Environmental Change* 1.5 (1991): 365–380.

8. John Young, "Mining the Earth," *State of the World: 1992*, ed. L. Brown (New York: Norton, 1992), pp. 100–118.

9. Lewis and Berry, *African Environments*, pp. 369–373.

10. Paraphrased from ibid., p. 381.

11. R. W. Franke and B. Chasin, *Seeds of Famine: Ecological Destruction and the Development Dilemma in the West African Sahel* (Montclair, N.J.: Allanheld, 1980); also, J. Witte, "Deforestation in Zaire: Logging and Landlessness," *The Ecologist* 22.2 (1992): 58–64.

12. Juma's work is described by James O'Connor, "Uneven and Combined Development and Ecological Crisis: A Theoretical Introduction," *Race and Class: A Journal for Black and Third World Liberation* 30.3 (1989): 1–12.

13. P. A. Kwaku-Kyema, "Structural Adjustment and Sustainable Development in Sub-Saharan Africa: The Case of Ghana" (Ottawa: Carleton University, Department of Geography, 1991), p. 20.

14. M. Rosenblum and D. Williamson, *Squandering Eden: Africa at the Edge* (New York: Harcourt, 1987), p. 284.

15. Cheryl Payer, *The World Bank: A Critical Analysis* (New York: Monthly Review, 1982).

16. *The Social and Environmental Effects of Large Dams*, ed. E. Goldsmith and N. Hildyard (San Francisco: Sierra Club, 1984); also, for a condensed version by the same authors, "Large Scale Dams: A Special Report," *The Ecologist* 14.316 (1984). Kenyan statistic from M. Bell, *Contemporary Africa: Development, Culture and the State* (New York: Longman, 1986), p. 144.

17. G. Sen and C. Grown, *Development, Crises, and Alternative Visions: Third World Women's Perspectives* (New York: Monthly Review, 1987), pp. 42–43.

18. International Bank for Reconstruction and Development, *World Development Report 1992: Development and the Environment* (New York: Oxford, 1992).

19. Susan George, quoted in *The Ecologist* 22.3 (1992): 83.

20. *The Economist*, 8 Feb. 1992: 66.

21. *Population and the Environment: The Challenges Ahead* (New York: 1991), pp. 96–103.

22. R. P. Shaw, "The Impact of Population Growth on Environment: The Debate Heats Up," *Environmental Impact Assessment Review* 12.44 (1992): 11–36.

23. A. Dejene and J. Olivares, "Integrating Environmental Issues into a Strategy for Sustainable Agricultural Development," Washington, D.C., World Bank Technical Paper No. 146, 1991, p. 11.

24. *South* 14 Feb. 1991: 17.

25. R. Hirji and L. Ortolano, "Strategies for Managing Uncertainties Imposed by Environmental Impact Assessment: Analysis of the Kenyan River Development Authority," *Environmental Impact Assessment Review* 11.3 (1991): 203–230.

26. A. Gorze, *Ecology as Politics*, trans. P. Vigderman and J. Cloud (Montreal: Black Rose, 1980), pp. 190–191.

27. International Bank for Reconstruction and Development, *World Development Report 1992: Development and the Environment* (New York: Oxford, 1992), p. 89, Box 4.3.

28. S. Akuffo, *Pollution Control in a Developing Country: A Study of the Situation in Ghana* (Accra: Ghana Universities, 1989), pp. 102–103.

29. B. K'Omudha and C. Kamau, "The Needs and Methods of Including Environmental Concerns in Planning Development Programmes in Kenya," in United Nations Environmental Program, *Integrated Management of Resources of Africa: A Reader* (Nairobi: The Program, 1989), pp. 104–108.

30. M. Adeniyi and O. Odumade, "Some Examples of Pollution and Environmental Degradation in Nigeria and Strategies for Their Solution," United Nations Environmental Program, *Integrated Management of Resources of Africa: A Reader* (Nairobi: The Program, 1989), pp. 11–116; also, the perspective offered by Jaro Mayda, "Environmental Legislation in Developing Countries: Some Parameters and Constraints," *Ecological Law Quarterly* (1985): 977–1024.

31. S. Brass, "National Conservation Strategy: Zambia," in *The Greening of Aid: Sustainable Livelihoods in Practice,* ed. C. Conroy and M. Lituinoff (London: Earthscan, 1988), pp. 186–191.

32. Pierre Pradervand, *Listening to Africa: Developing Africa from the Grassroots* (New York: Praeger, 1989), p. 26.

33. Cross, *The Sahel*, p. 26.

34. Dharam Gai, "Conservation, Livelihood and Democracy: Social Dynamics of Environmental Changes in Africa," Geneva: United Nations Research Institute for Social Development, Discussion Paper 33, 1992.

35. I. Dankelman and J. Davidson, *Women and Environment in the Third World: Alliance for the Future* (London: 1988), p. 147.

36. S. Pastel, "Restoring Degraded Land," *The World-Watch Reader on Global Environmental Issues*, ed. L. Brown (New York: Norton, 1991), pp. 25–42.

37. "Activist Scorned in Kenya," *Toronto Globe and Mail* 9 June 1992: 12; Dr. Maathai "is certain that the Kenyan government will not honor its pledge to clean up the environment."

38. The World Bank, *Sub-Saharan Africa: From Crisis to Sustainable Growth* (Washington, D.C.: International Bank for Reconstruction and Development, 1989), p. 157.

39. J. S. Adams and T. McShane, *The Myth of Wild Africa: Conservation without Illusion* (New York: Norton, 1992) stresses the vital human dimension of conservation efforts.

40. J. Campbell, "Land or Peasants? The Dilemma Confronting Ethiopian Resource Conservation," *African Affairs* 90.358 (1991): 5–21.

Chapter 7

Nigeria's Environment: Crises, Consequences, and Responses

PITA OGABA AGBESE

It has been estimated that environmental degradation directly affects 50 million of Nigeria's 88.5 million people. E. O. Aina, the director of Nigeria's Federal Environmental Protection Agency (FEPA), puts the annual economic losses to Nigeria from environmental degradation at 25 billion Naira or 13 percent of the gross national product.[1] While environmental problems such as industrial pollution, uncontrolled discharge of industrial wastes, deforestation, oil spillage, soil erosion, desertification, and the dumping of toxic wastes have been major features of the Nigerian environment for a long time, it was only in December 1988 that the Nigerian government enacted a national policy to protect the nation's environment. The principal objective of this chapter is to critically analyze the Nigerian government's response to the country's ecological problems. Much of this response is embodied in the National Policy on the Environment, the Federal Environmental Protection Agency Decree (1988) and the Harmful Waste (Special Criminal Provisions) Decree of 1988. The author intends to assess the adequacy of these policy tools to the environmental disaster that confronts Nigeria. The analysis is divided into four sections. One section provides a general overview of the major environmental problems. The second section examines why they were ignored until 1988. The next discusses the details of the national policy on the environment, and the last develops a critique of the policy and argues that it is an inadequate response. This section also assesses the future of Nigeria's environment.

Fantu Cheru argues that much of Africa's environmental crisis had its origin in the European colonization of Africa.[2] From the European colonialists' perspective, African peoples and African resources existed to be exploited for the benefit of Europeans. Thus, the preindependence economic development model, as Cheru contends, was based on the economic logic which viewed "people and resources as capital to be exploited."[3] Accordingly, European imperialists felt no sense of social or moral responsibility towards Africans or their environment. Minerals were extracted without much thought to the ecological consequences of such extractions. Once the minerals had been depleted, the colonialists simply abandoned the mineral sites. Similarly, forests were cleared either for their lumber or for the growth of cash crops such as rubber, cocoa, coffee, and palm oil for export. Again, little or no attention was paid to the environmental impact of the resultant deforestation. What mattered to the Europeans was not the well-being of Africans but whether a particular economic activity was immediately profitable to European firms operating in Africa.

The postcolonial development model adopted by African leaders did not differ significantly from the European model. Much of its emphasis rested on attaining "quantitative goals at the expense of self-reliance, social justice, political autonomy and ecological harmony."[4] Like the colonial model, it was based on exporting African raw materials in return for the importation of manufactured goods to be consumed largely by a tiny elite class. Another characteristic of the postcolonial development model was that it relied very heavily on foreign capital, foreign technology, and foreign companies. As Cheru points out, postcolonial African rulers did not enact economic policies radically different from the colonial economic policies.[5]

Import-substitution industrialization, the main industrialization strategy pursued after colonialism, was embarked upon without environmental impact studies. Environmentally unsound mining practices put in place by the European colonialists were retained. For instance, ecological problems caused by the practice of open mining of tin and columbite in Nigeria were intensified after independence. Among other reasons, this resulted from the urgency of the Nigerian government to produce more tin and columbites for export to earn more revenue.

Not only did production of raw materials for exports cause environmental degradation in Africa; the proceeds from raw materials exports were not used to ameliorate some of the degradation. Moreover, the class interests of the emergent African bourgeoisie ensured that foreign exchange earnings were devoted to the consumption of manufactured goods from abroad. Since the main victims of ecological degradation were rural peasants who were marginalized from the political process, no attention was paid by African governments to the ecological dangers posed by the production of primary commodities.

All in all, the elite-oriented development strategies that African countries adopted after political independence intensified the ecological destruction begun in the colonial days. The development model ensured the continuation of the environmentally unsound policies of the colonial period.

Even as the postcolonial economic development model was intensifying ecological degradation in rural areas, it was causing greater damages in the urban areas. The concentration of industries, social services, and state power in the cities resulted in rapid rates of urbanization, largely through rural–urban migration. P. K. Makinwa and A. O. Ozo have estimated that Nigerian towns grow at about twice the rate of population growth rate.[6] One of the immediate consequences of the rapid growth of cities is massive unemployment among migrants with low education and low skills. Thus, urbanization in Nigeria, as in other Third World countries, accentuates mass poverty. Urban poverty in turn produces several environmental problems. A. N. Nzeako argues that there is degradation of all sorts

in the Nigerian ghettos of the urban poor, leading to despair and a degraded environment. Thus in the crowded urban communities that have mushroomed in recent years, mounds of refuse (including human wastes) that litter everywhere— gutters, schools, roads, market places and town squares—have been accepted as part of the way of life. Normally these refuse heaps are composed of inflammable cellulose and synthetic matter which are very easily ignited into frightening conflagrations.[7]

Urban congestion places severe strains on existing meager social services. For instance, John Nwaobi's analysis of urban water supply in Nigeria indicates that much of the water "contains carcinogenic nitrosoamine . . . benzene from leaking underground storage tanks, trihalomethanes from chlorine and lead and copper which are often washed down into underground water by torrential rains."[8] Nwaobi argues that as a result of "a sharp drop in the quality of chemicals used for chlorination, germs and toxins are pumped" daily into city dwellers' water supply.[9]

While Nigeria's ecological crises are traceable to colonial economic policies, much of the current environmental degradation resulted from the industrialization strategy adopted in the 1970s. In the 1960s, agriculture was the mainstay of the economy. Over 70 percent of the population was engaged in agricultural production. Crops such as cocoa, cotton, peanuts, and palm oil were produced for export. The bulk of the country's foreign exchange receipts was derived from the export of these and other agricultural commodities. While minerals such as tin, columbite, oil, and coal were also mined, they did not constitute major sources of foreign exchange earnings. Although these activities also posed ecological hazards, their effects were generally localized. Moreover, much of the agricultural system was peasant-based production which posed no permanent damage to the ecology.

The increasing reliance on crude oil production significantly changed the environmental picture in Nigeria. Oil exploration, production, and refining cause serious ecological damage. In addition, the huge foreign exchange that began to accrue after the quadrupling of oil prices in the 1970s financed the import-substitution industrialization strategy adopted by the federal government. Many of the industries attracted in the 1970s are heavy environmental polluters. Oil revenues also financed gigantic agricultural development projects that have produced ecological nightmares.

NIGERIA'S ENVIRONMENTAL CRISES

As mentioned previously, Nigeria faces several ecological problems. This section discusses the most important of these problems. The importance of this discussion is to provide a backdrop against which to examine the government's response to the crisis of the Nigerian environment.

Indiscriminate Discharge of Industrial Wastes

In 1980, the federal Ministry of Housing and Environment drew attention to the dangers to the Nigerian environment of the indiscriminate discharge of industrial wastes on land and rivers. The report pointed out the high rate of wanton dumping of industrial wastes in Lagos, then the capital. It noted: "The improper management of industrial wastes in Lagos has reached a stage where it has constituted potential and real danger to human health, natural resources and marine life."[10] President Ibrahim Babangida has affirmed that one of the most pressing ecological problems in Nigeria is the "uncontrolled discharge of harmful industrial wastes, untreated human sewage, industrial and household refuse into drains, streams, lagoons and shorelines."[11] He stated that Nigeria is faced with high risks from the "indiscriminate discharge of hazardous fumes and particulate matter into the atmosphere by industries."[12]

Among the major industrial polluters are the petroleum refineries, the automobile assembly plants, textile companies, tanneries, fertilizer manufacturers, and detergent makers. For instance, the petroleum refineries at Kaduna, Warri, and Port Harcourt discharge crude oil effluents directly into nearby bodies of water. The Kaduna refinery discharges oil and other effluents directly into River Roni. As Louisa Aguiyi-Ironsi has pointed out, the effluents discharged by the refinery contain "lead and other dangerous metals."[13] She also pointed out that the level of toxicity of the resultant discharge was so high that aquatic life in River Roni and River Kaduna (of which the Roni is a tributary) has been destroyed.

Kaduna is a major industrial city in northern Nigeria. It is home to several textile companies, including Arewa Textiles, United Nigeria Textiles, Arewa Textiles, and Kaduna Textiles. The Peugeot Assembly Plant and the

Federal Superphosphate Fertilizer Company, among other industries, are also located in Kaduna. What most of these industries have in common other than their location in Kaduna is the fact that they discharge their untreated industrial wastes directly into River Kaduna. The textile mills dump concentrated dyes, acidic and caustic wastes, into the river. The Peugeot plant discharges oil and plant effluents. As for the fertilizer plant, it is responsible for uncontrolled sulphur dioxide emissions. It is estimated that these and other industries in Kaduna dump as much as 50 to 60 metric tons of hazardous industrial wastes annually.[14]

Kano, another major industrial city, suffers from similar indiscriminate dumping of industrial wastes. Kano is home to major textile, brewing, vegetable oil, tanning, and plastic-manufacturing companies. Yet it does not have a single industrial waste treatment plant. Some of the industries, like the tannery, Intertan, simply dig large open pits within their industrial premises into which they dump their wastes. Effluents from Intertan's waste pit spill over into the nearby River Chalawa. Although Chalawa is the main water source for the city, it has been heavily contaminated by effluents from Intertan and other industries. The scale of industrial pollution in Kano is so high that the city has been described as a "pollution time bomb."[15]

Agbara Industrial Estate in Ogun State exhibits one of the worst cases of industrial pollution in Nigeria. Industries in the estate discharge their untreated wastes into River Ologe. Effluents from the many industries at the estate have almost wiped out aquatic life in the river. Yomi Lawal, an environmentalist who has conducted studies on the impact of industrial wastes on marine life in River Ologe, has concluded that fish in the river have been bleached by the industrial effluents.[16] He also calculates that industrial effluents have raised the water temperature to a level that cannot be tolerated by most fish. In addition, the effluents have diminished the level of dissolved oxygen to between 0.8 and 0.9 milligram per liter—making it difficult for fish to survive in the river.

Several cement companies at Nkalagu, Ewekoro, Sokoto, Gboko, and elsewhere freely emit cement dust into the atmosphere. Villages and farms within the vicinity of the cement plants are literally coated with fine cement particles. Cement dust, freely discharged into the atmosphere, has seriously reduced soil fertility in these villages. The complaints of villagers about the consequences of cement dust on their major economic activities are simply ignored by the cement companies.

Petroleum companies in Nigeria burn off natural gas in the process of extracting crude oil. It is estimated that over 16.8 billion cubic meters of natural gas are burned off each year. In turn, the burnoff produces annual emissions of 2,700 metric tons of particulate matter, 160 metric tons of sulphur oxides, 5,400 metric tons of carbon monoxide, and 27,000 metric tons of nitrogen oxides.[17] Ken Saro-Wiwa charges that Shell, one of the major oil companies in Nigeria, "flares all its gas and has destroyed the Ogoni environment in the process."[18] Saro-Wiwa also notes that the farmlands of Ogoni and other communities from where crude oil is extracted "have been completely devastated."[19] Similarly, Etim Anim contends that oil exploration and the attendant neglect of communities in which oil is extracted have inflicted untold misery on the people. As he puts it: "What they used to call upon for their livelihood and well-being have been wrecked for eternity by the coming of oil—they cannot fish because marine lives have been flushed out; they cannot hunt because the game fled a long time ago, thanks to the oil hunters; and their land no longer yields good harvests. In short, neglect, poverty and deprivation."[20]

In March 1988, the NAFCON, a fertilizer company based at Onne, discharged huge quantities of water containing a high ammonia level into River Okrika. This action created a substantial loss of fish and other aquatic life. It is common knowledge that Nigeria's waters around industrial zones "contain concentrations of ammonia high enough to be toxic."[21]

Crude Oil Spills

Nigeria is a major crude oil producer. One of the negative consequences of petroleum production is oil spillage. From 1971 to 1975 alone, there were 347 oil spills. Between 1976 and 1980, there were a total of 784 spills.[22] The Nigerian Environmental Society has estimated that between 1970 and 1983, over 1.7 million barrels of crude oil were spilled over Nigerian land and waters.[23] In January 1980, Funiwa-5, an oil well jointly owned by the Nigerian National Petroleum Corporation (NNPC), Chevron, and Texaco, blew up spilling over 146,000 barrels of crude oil. According to Eboe Hutchful, oil industry activities such as exploration, production, refining, and transportation produce "widespread social and ecological disturbance" in Nigeria.[24] Hutchful observes that the ecological disturbance results from such things as "explosions from seismic surveys, pollution from pipeline leaks, blowouts, drilling fluids and refinery effluents as well as land alienation and widespread disruption of the natural terrain from construction of industry infrastructure and installations."[25] In his analysis of the impact of oil exploration on the Nigerian environment, Paul Nwabuikwu concludes that even though petroleum is the mainstay of the Nigerian economy, the petroleum industry exacts a high price on many Nigerians, "especially those who inhabit the areas where petroleum is drilled."[26] According to Nwabuikwu, Nigerian communities in Rivers, Cross River, and Imo States (the main areas of oil exploration) "fight a daily battle with oil spillage which destroys their rivers and farms."[27]

Oil prospecting in general and its associated spillage in particular, have had disastrous consequence on the environment. Etim Anim argues that "the pipelines, the wells, the gas flaring, the human and mechanical activities involved in the business of oil prospecting and production leave a tell-ing effect on the land and its people."[28] Nigerians who live near oil wells have suffered untold hardships from oil spillage and other pernicious effects of oil production. Francis Okpozo observes that "we have continued to suffer huge losses in our farmlands and fish ponds because of the activities of oil prospecting companies. Oil spillages have rendered almost completely useless our economic live-wire."[29]

Dumping Toxic Wastes on Nigeria

In June 1988, Nigerian students in Italy alerted the Nigerian public to the fact that an Italian businessman, Gianfrance Raffaelli, had dumped over 4,000 tons of Italian, Dutch, American, Norwegian, and British toxic wastes at the fishing port of Koko in Nigeria. Over 8,000 barrels containing the most deadly substances, including radioactive materials and polychlorinate biphenyl (PCBs) were dumped at Koko. The toxic wastes were dumped for over a year before reports of the dumping surfaced in Italy. Raffaelli paid very little money for dumping such a huge quantity of toxic wastes. He paid an elderly peasant, Sunday Nana, about $100 per month rental fee to dump the wastes on his land. In addition, he paid a number of young men about ten cents per hour to off-load them from ships. It is also believed that he paid a few hundred dollars in bribe money to some customs and port officials. Raffaelli reportedly made a profit of about 800 million Italian Lira from the first two shipments alone.[30] This means that while Raffaelli received millions of dollars for dumping the wastes on Nigeria, he paid his Nigerian accomplices only a pittance. FEPA says that the environmental implications of the Koko toxic waste dumping "are yet to be fully realized."[31] Nevertheless, it should be noted that Sunday Nana, who harbored the wastes, has since died.

Several attempts to sell highly contaminated European beef and milk to Nigeria and other African countries have also been uncovered in recent years. Among other things, dumping hazardous and other wastes on Africa led the Organization of African Unity (OAU) to adopt a resolution in May 1988 prohibiting the importation and dumping of wastes in Africa. However, as the Koko episode clearly illustrates, poverty and corruption make it relatively easy to secretly dump hazardous and other substances on Nigeria.[32]

Desertification, Deforestation, and Soil Erosion

The Nigerian government admits that deforestation, desertification, and soil erosion constitute significant threats to the country's environment. As President Babangida has noted, "the rapid southern advance of the desert, aggravated by the uncontrolled felling of trees to provide fuel wood and overgrazing of pasture lands" represents one of the prevalent forms of ecological damage in Nigeria.[33] Mamman Kontagora, the federal minister of works and housing, has argued that desert encroachment has reached an alarming stage. He points out that parts of Katsina, Kano, Kaduna, Sokoto, and other states in the north which have become integral parts of the Sahara Desert had trees and other forms of vegetation just 50 years ago.[34] It is estimated that in Bauchi, Borno, Jigawa, Kano, Kebbi, Sokoto, Katsina, and Yobe states, the Sahara Desert spreads southward at 3 to 5 km per year.

David Okali, coordinator of the Nigerian Environmental Study/Action Team, in an unpublished study, has asserted that soil erosion "either by water or wind, is clearly the most serious form of environmental deterioration across the country associated with deforestation." He estimates that Nigeria loses about 23,000 hectares of officially gazetted forests per annum. Okali estimates that between 1979 and 1986 alone, Bauchi State lost 22,301 hectares and Bendel State lost 14,650 hectares. In addition, the construction of the Army School of Artillery and the Nigerian Defense Academy at Kaduna caused the loss of over 12,000 hectares.[35]

Onome Osifo-Whiskey, commenting on soil erosion and other forms of ecological degradation in Nigeria, contends that many parts of the country, particularly in Anambra, Imo, Benue, Akwa-Ibom, and Bendel states have serious problems with erosion, which, he contends, has ruined "farmlands, residential quarters and highways, imposing adverse economic calamities running into billions of Naira."[36]

In recent years, soil degradation has been accentuated by large-scale agricultural development projects all over the country. In a study on the ecological impacts of the Hadejia-Jama'are Project, K. Kimmage and W. M. Adams have concluded that the "economy and ecology of the Hadejia-Jama'are floodplains are threatened by development projects both upstream and downstream."[37] Other massive dam and irrigation projects such as the Kainji and the Bakalori projects have had similar devastating impact on the ecology of surrounding areas.

Overall, the social costs of ecological neglect have been quite heavy in Nigeria. These are easily discernible in reduced soil fertility, which in turn has increased reliance on pesticides and fertilizers, massive destruction of forest lands, poisoning of land and waters. One of the consequences of declining sustainable agriculture is the massive influx of immigrants from the rural to urban areas. This influx creates its own environmental problems in the form of urban squalor and congestion. For instance, congestion has led to poor drainage and encouraged human settlement in marginal lands in Ibadan and other major cities. When "poor urban planning and indiscriminate encroachment on the land" in Ibadan led to the flooding of River Ogunpa in 1978, over 30 people drowned, and properties worth millions of naira were destroyed.[38] In a repeat performance two years later, Ogunpa claimed over 300 lives, rendered over 50,000 people homeless, and caused over 300 million naira in property damage. Similarly, poor planning contributed to the collapse of the Bagauda Dam in 1988. The resultant flood killed over 146 people, destroyed 18,000 houses, caused other property damage of about 650 million Naira, and rendered over 200,000 people homeless.[39]

STATE AND ENVIRONMENT: THE FAILURE TO RESPOND

Despite the enormity of Nigeria's ecological problems, no serious attention was paid to the hazards of environmental destruction until 1988. It took the national embarrassment caused by the Koko dumping episode to wake up the Nigerian government to its environmental responsibilities. As President Babangida has himself admitted:

The Koko toxic waste episode, sad as it was, became the crucial test of the will of the government and the people of this nation to protect the national environment in a more comprehensive and enduring manner than had been done hitherto. Since no responsible government would stand by and allow a repeat of the Koko episode or permit its territory to become a dumping ground for all types of hazardous substances and wastes, this administration rose decisively to the challenge by creating the appropriate and enduring machinery that can effectively manage and protect the Nigerian environment.[40]

Several factors behind the failure to respond to Nigeria's ecological crises can be identified. First, there was an implicit assumption that ecological damage is a price that must be paid for Nigeria's rapid economic development. This assumption was itself anchored on the belief that a country has to make a choice between development and the preservation of the environment. Consequently, since Nigeria was in a hurry to develop, it had no choice but to reject environmental preservation in favor of rapid economic development.

The assumption that ecological damage is a price for economic development is explicit in the various national development plans. Despite the comprehensive and elaborate economic planning in the four national development plan documents, there was no mention about the consequences of the envisaged development projects on the environment. Similarly, no proper environmental impact assessment was ever conducted before massive dam projects were built at Kainji, Bakalori, Bagauda, and other places.

There was also an implicit assumption that whatever ecological damage resulted from economic development projects would be more than offset by the enormous benefits accruing from these projects. In addition, it was naively assumed that such damages could either be corrected in the future or that the payment of appropriate compensation to those adversely affected would rectify the damage. This later assumption was particularly strong with respect to ecological disasters from oil compensation. Both the oil companies and the Nigerian government saw their responsibility with respect to oil spills as limited to paying compensation for farms and homes destroyed by the spills.

A second factor for the government's indifference to the country's environmental crises lies in the weaknesses of the Nigerian state vis-à-vis the multinational corporations. The developmental option favored by the state was dependent on foreign investments. The state would do almost anything to attract and keep foreign investments. Within this mind-set, it was unthinkable to expect multinational corporations, which were largely responsible for much of the ecological damage, to be held accountable for their actions.

Therefore, no effective sanctions could be contemplated against industrial polluters for fear that they would pull up their stakes and go to other places that did not have environmental regulations. In addition, the tight control the multinationals exercised over their production processes, coupled with Nigeria's lack of requisite technical skills to monitor these activities, gave multinationals a free rein to pollute the environment.

Yet another factor in the failure of the Nigerian government to properly manage the environment was lax enforcement of existing regulations against pollution. The Oil Navigable Waters Act of 1968 requires that no more than 100 parts of oil be discharged within 30 nautical miles off the Nigerian coast. Yet, as Louisa Aguiyi-Ironsi has observed, "Oil tankers routinely wash processed petroleum out of their tanks into Nigerian harbors."[41] No one has ever been charged with contravening this act, even though oil tankers contravene the act in full view of harbor police and other law enforcement officers.

Autocratic military rule also facilitates ecological damage. Several Nigerian communities in the oil-producing areas have, over the years, attempted to force oil companies to live up to their environmental responsibilities; but the government has frustrated their efforts each time. For instance, when the people of Iko protested against the wreckage of their environment by Shell Oil Company by disrupting its prospecting activities, the government sent in police to break up the protest. The police burned down 38 houses, assaulted Iko women, and brutalized many of the protesting young people.[42] The lack of democracy epitomized by military rule means that there is no public input in economic policies. Consequently, the interests of the poor, who are usually the main victims of ecological destruction, are not taken into consideration in planning economic development projects.

Given these factors, the only thing that passed for a national policy on the environment prior to December 1988 was the public sanitation program introduced by the Buhari military government in 1984 as part of the general effort to inculcate "discipline" in Nigerians. The program requires every Nigerian to devote one Saturday every month to cleaning and beautifying his or her surroundings. An effective curfew from 7:00 A.M. until 1:00 P.M. is imposed on each National Sanitation Day. In reality, this program has made no contribution to sanitation. In the first place, it is based on the assumption that the greatest threat to the environment does not emanate from Nigeria's particular mode of production but from the unsanitary habits of Nigerians. Second, the autocratic implementation of the program has alienated millions of Nigerians and prevented them from taking the program seriously. Third, the program was anchored on the untenable stand that it was the undisciplined nature of Nigerians that was responsible for the country's ecological crises. Hence the need for the government to operate the program on the military "discipline" to make Nigeria a more sanitary country.

Prior to 1988, a second state response to ecological damage, particularly damage resulting from desertification, was the national campaign for tree planting. Usually, the president or military governors would take well-publicized trips to areas experiencing the most rapid forms of desert encroachment to plant trees. In reality, tree-planting campaigns by the president or military governors is largely symbolic. While one cannot discount the importance of symbolism in politics, as Joseph Amali Shekwo has aptly observed, tree-planting campaigns are very wasteful and ultimately counterproductive.[43] The president and his entire entourage would, for instance, fly hundreds of miles from Lagos to Maiduguri so the president could plant a single tree. The amount of fossil fuel consumed by the flight and the fact that virtually all economic activities would be paralyzed that day on account of the president's visit make tree-planting campaigns very expensive propositions. Moreover, there is no indication that any Nigerian has ever been inspired to plant trees because Shehu Shagari, Ibrahim Babangida, or any other president symbolically planted trees under the glare of television lights. One can even make a case that felling trees to make newsprint for publicizing political leaders' tree-planting campaigns has destroyed more trees than all the trees that Nigeria's presidents and other government officials have cumulatively planted since the tree-planting campaign was started over a decade ago.

ECOLOGICAL CRISES AND NEW RESPONSES

The Koko hazardous-waste dumping incident forced the Nigerian government seriously to address the dangers posed by their numerous ecological crises. The dumping was revealed at a particularly awkward time. Nigeria was excoriating African countries that had accepted toxic wastes from the United States and Western Europe. The revelation of the Koko incident proved very embarrassing, at best. In fact, it occurred as Ike Nwachukwu, the minister of external affairs, was addressing the United Nations in New York on the iniquities of dumping toxic wastes on Africa. Before the revelation was made, Nigeria had largely succeeded in convincing the OAU and the Economic Community of

West African States (ECOWAS) to pass resolutions prohibiting the dumping of toxic wastes on Africa.

The fact that the Koko wastes contained radioactive substances and PCBs created national alarm and anxiety. Moreover, the inability of the government to detect the presence of these wastes for over one year suggested huge lapses in the country's security system. Many Nigerians were left wondering if there were other undetected cases all over the country.

The Koko incident and the actions various communities, particularly in the oil-prospecting areas, were taking to safeguard their environment compelled the government to adopt a more comprehensive approach to safeguarding Nigeria's environment. In 1980, Mkpanak community barricaded the offices of Mobil Oil, demanding compensation for damage inflicted on their land. The community halted oil production for three weeks. Mobil lost millions of naira in oil revenues and was forced to provide amenities such as roads, water, and electricity to Mkpanak. The people of Iko used similar tactics in 1987 in their struggle against Shell Oil Company. In 1982, the people of Egbema barricaded the roads leading to the premises of the Nigerian Agip Oil Company (NOAC) to protest nonpayment for damage to their environment. Other communities were taking similar actions, demanding compensation from oil companies and other polluters.

The government was alarmed by the assertive actions of these communities. Its initial response to such actions was to send in the police to put down any revolts against polluters. However, this did little to discourage protests against polluters. The government was forced to make nominal provisions to tackle ecological disasters by setting aside 1.5 percent of the federal revenues each year as an ecological fund. The amount was grossly inadequate, and its distribution was flawed. On few occasions when proceeds from this fund were used to pay compensation to victims of oil spills, the victims received only a tiny fraction of the losses they suffered.

Apart from the precipitate actions various communities were taking in defense of their environments, another factor that induced a change in the government's attitude to the environment was the emergence of several environmentalist groups (e.g., the Nigerian Environmental Study/Action Team was created to exert pressures on the government to implement concrete actions to safeguard the environment).

Under pressure, the government promulgated the Harmful Wastes (Special Criminal Provisions, etc.) Decree on November 25, 1988.[44] It was issued largely in response to the Koko dumping episode. The decree makes it a criminal offense, punishable by life imprisonment, for anyone to carry, deposit, dump, transport, import, sell, buy, or negotiate trade in harmful wastes within Nigerian territory and the Exclusive Economic Zone of Nigeria. The decree gives police officers the power to search, without warrant, "any land, building or carrier, including aircraft, vehicle, container or any other thing whatsoever which he has reason to believe is related to the commission" of the crime of dumping toxic wastes on Nigeria.[45]

In December 1988, FEPA was established through Decree No. 58.[46] The agency has responsibilities to control and oversee the state of the nation's environment. Among its major functions are (1) initiate and undertake environmental research and development studies; (2) prescribe national environmental standards; (3) supervise and enforce compliance with environmental regulations; (4) establish such environmental criteria, guidelines, specifications, or standards for the protection of Nigeria's air and interstate waters as may be necessary to protect the health and welfare of the population from environmental degradation. Other duties assigned to FEPA include (1) advising the federal government on national environmental policies and priorities and on scientific and technological activities affecting the environment; (2) preparing periodic master plans for the development of environmental science and technology and advising the government on the financial requirements for the implementation of such plans; (3) promoting cooperation in environmental science and technology with similar bodies in other countries and with international bodies connected with the protection of the environment; and (4) cooperating with federal and state ministries, local government councils, statutory bodies, and research agencies on matters and facilities relating to environmental protection.[47]

FEPA is the sole agency authorized to establish guidelines, criteria, and standards for such things as water quality, effluent limitations, air quality and atmospheric protection, protection of the ozone layer, noise control, control of hazardous substances, and prescription of removal methods. The decree under which FEPA was established also authorizes the agency to "collect and make available, through publications and other appropriate means and in co-operation with public or private organizations, basic scientific data and other information pertaining to pollution and environmental protection matters."[48]

Membership of FEPA consists of a chairman "a person with wide knowledge in environmental matters," four "distinguished scientists," one representative each from the federal ministries of Health; Science and Technology; Works and Housing; Agriculture, Water Resources and Rural Development; Industries; Mines, Power and Steel; Employment, Labor and Productivity; Petroleum Resources; Transport; Aviation, as well as a director who is chief executive. The chairman, the director, and four scientists are appointed directly by the president of Nigeria.

While direct grants from the federal government constitute the main source of finance for FEPA, the agency is authorized to raise additional funds by way of gifts, sale of publications, and fees and charges for its services. The federal government has given over 60 million Naira to the agency since its inception in 1988. Much of the money was spent on the construction of seven national laboratories and other capital investments.

In order to get state governments and local government councils to enforce environmental laws, FEPA requested each of the 30 state governments to establish state environmental protection boards. Many of the state governments have duly created such boards, but they have not proved effective in enforcing FEPA's environmental regulations. For instance, a recent communiqué issued by the National Council on the Environment noted that many states in the federation "lack appropriate institutional framework to effectively tackle environmental issues."[49] The council is an institution created to harmonize environmental policies between FEPA and the states. It is composed of state commissioner-directors in charge of environmental matters, representatives of the federal Ministry of Works and Housing, and officials of FEPA. The council meets regularly to adopt a common approach to national environmental issues.

In December 1988, the government enacted a national policy on the environment. With the enactment, the federal government proclaims Nigeria's "commit[ment] to a policy that ensures sustainable development based on proper management of the environment in order to meet the needs of the present and future generations."[50] The government admits that the national policy on the environment represented a "fundamental re-thinking and a clearer appreciation of the interdependent linkages among development processes, environmental factors as well as human and natural resources."[51] It further admitted that in the past, environmental issues were either completely neglected or given short shrift in the belief that economic development was more important than the environmental devastation it engenders. The federal government further claims that the new thinking rejects the old dogma of development at any cost. Instead, the new national creed is based on sustainable development. It views sustainable development as a developmental strategy that integrates environmental considerations in the planning and implementation of development projects and meets the needs of the present generation without compromising the ecological needs of the future.[52]

President Babangida stated that the new policy was aimed at rectifying the "damage already done to our sensitive environment through decades of uncontrolled exploitation of our endowed natural resources and to initiate and enforce conservation measures, deemed necessary and expedient for the protection and preservation of this vital heritage."[53] The specific goals of the new national policy on the environment are to

1. secure for all Nigerians a quality of environment adequate for their health and well-being;
2. conserve and use the environment and natural resources for the benefit of present and future generations;
3. restore, maintain, and enhance the ecosystems and ecological processes essential

for the functioning of the biosphere to preserve biological diversity and the principle of optimum sustainable use of living natural resources and ecosystems;

4. raise public awareness, promote understanding of essential linkages between environment and development, and encourage individual and community participation in environmental improvement efforts; and

5. cooperate in good faith with other countries, international organizations, and agencies to achieve optimal use of transboundary natural resources and effective prevention or abatement of transboundary environmental pollution.

The policy details specific actions and strategies to be adopted with respect to major environmental issues. Thus, strategies and courses of action on land use and soil conservation, water resource management, forestry, and wildlife and marine and coastal area resources are provided. In addition, guidelines on sanitation and waste management, toxic and hazardous substances, and air and noise pollution were spelled out. Here are some of the major strategies for various ecological problems.

Land Use and Soil Conservation

Strategies designed to enhance the proper use and management of land include

1. encouraging soil conservation principles in highway and other construction activities;

2. developing programs to ensure the rational application of fertilizers and other soil conditioners appropriate to the improvement and sustained use of the soils;

3. enlarging and improving available arable land through irrigation, reforestation, and reclamation of saline, flooded, and otherwise unproductive land;

4. regulating agricultural mechanization and other agroforestry techniques to reduce soil erosion;

5. providing guidelines for traditional grazing systems to reduce environmental degradation through overgrazing; and

6. supporting research to develop farming systems that combine optimum production with land-resource protection and are compatible with the socioeconomic conditions of all people.

Water Resources Management

Strategies to be employed in the rational management of water resources include

1. ensuring the provision of water in adequate quantity and acceptable quality to meet domestic, industrial, agricultural, and recreational needs;

2. conducting environmental impact assessments on water resources development projects;

3. encouraging efficient water usage;

4. specifying water-quality criteria for different water uses;

5. conducting studies on public health implications of water resource development projects, such as dams and irrigation schemes;

6. establishing adequate controls and enforcement procedures to prevent contamination and depletion of water resources; and

7. providing water-damage prevention measures through flood control, drainage water collection, and treatment.

Forestry, Wildlife, and Protected Areas

The goals of the national policy with respect to forestry and wildlife are to sustain the productivity of natural vegetation, protect wildlife, maintain genetic diversity, and avoid forest and soil degradation. Strategies that would help attain these objectives are clearly spelled out. These include

1. promoting the "rational exploitation of forest resources to meet domestic consumption needs and to achieve a significant export activity on a long-term basis";

2. regulating forestry activities to enhance conservation and environmentally sound management practices;

3. protecting flora and fauna in danger of extinction, as well as forest reserves, for scientific, recreational, and other cultural purposes;

4. promoting the development of alternative sources of energy while supporting programs for the development of more efficient methods of wood energy use;

5. protecting forests from bush and forest fires and taking measures to discourage wanton destruction of forest resources; and

6. strengthening forest protection programs to ensure adequate vegetation cover in critical areas and to discourage developments likely to cause harmful changes.

Sanitation and Waste Management

Under the national policy on the environment, the discharge of industrial effluents, raw sewage, and domestic wastes will henceforth be strictly regulated. Specific strategies to provide safe environments against wastes include setting up and enforcing standards for adequate sanitary facilities for the disposal of human and other solid wastes in dwellings, housing estates, and public facilities in both urban and rural areas; regulating, registering, and licensing all major land-based waste disposal sites and systems; and establishing a mechanism for the identification and cleanup of abandoned land-based hazardous waste dumps.

The new policy also permits the setting up of state environmental protection boards. It mandates that environmental impact assessment be conducted for all new development projects in housing estates, dam construction, industrial development, large-scale farming, and highway construction.

The minister of works and housing, whose ministry is responsible for environmental matters, is authorized by the Environmental Protection Agency Decree to make regulations on environmental matters. In this connection, in August 1991, General Mamman Kontagora issued two regulations on pollution abatement and effluent limitations.[54]

All industries, according to the new regulations, shall henceforth install approved waste-minimization and pollution-prevention systems to ensure the proper treatment of all industrial and municipal wastes before they are discharged into the ecosystem. The regulation on effluent limitation has set up standards for effluent discharge for all categories of industries in Nigeria. Any individual who contravenes the regulation is to be punished by a fine not exceeding 20,000 Naira or a term of imprisonment not exceeding two years or both. A corporate body found guilty of contravening the regulations is liable to a fine of 500,000 Naira and must pay compensation for any resulting damage to the environment.[55]

ENVIRONMENTAL POLICY: CONSTRAINTS AND CONTRADICTIONS

Despite the prompt promulgation of the Harmful Wastes (Special Criminal Provisions) Decree in the wake of the Koko toxic waste dumping and the setting up of the Federal Environmental Protection Agency and its ancillary regulations against environmental destruction, the Nigerian government's responses to the country's ecological crises are grossly inadequate. In the first place, the measures were panicky and designed to reassure a nation that had become jittery about the dangers to its environment. Being essentially ad hoc crisis-management techniques, these measures eschew a comprehensive, systematic, and long-term approach to ecological problems.

The new environmental policy looks good on paper, but there is no indication that it will be vigorously implemented. Only very little money has so far been budgeted for FEPA. Moreover, the Babangida government, through its economic structural adjustment program, is committed to lessening the regulatory role of the state in the economy. Thus, ironically, the dangers of environmental degradation are becoming more widely known precisely when there is an intense assault on the role of the state in the economy. Within the context in which the regulatory role of the state is increasingly denigrated, the commitment of the state to industrial regulation is highly suspect.

The Babangida's commitment to provide a safe haven for foreign investors is more important than its commitment to safeguarding the environment. Moreover, various economic policies that have encouraged land speculation will do more damage to the environment.[56] In addition, the intense pressures to export agricultural and other raw materials will aggravate Nigeria's ecological crises.

Several actions of the Babangida regime betray its lack of commitment to safeguarding Nigeria's environment. For instance, it has increased the price of natural gas and kerosene. Unable to pay the new exorbitant prices for these commodities, poor people have resorted to felling more trees for firewood. This defeats the goal of discouraging the indiscriminate felling of trees. While the government reiterates that it was committed to reducing air pollution, it has enacted the contradictory policy of allowing individuals and corporate bodies to import used automobiles that contribute immensely to air pollution.

The new policy does not assign responsibility for past ecological devastation, even though the culprits are well known. The new policy is excessively forward looking rather than attempting to rectify the serious ecological problems created by thousands of industries in Nigeria. There was little public input in the new environmental policies. Without active public involvement, environmental standards cannot be enforced. Focus on environmental issues has, ironically, legitimized environmental protectionist groups: The responses of the Babangida regime to Nigeria's environmental crises has succeeded in elevating environmental degradation to a national concern.

The imperative for rapid growth meant that resources were exploited regardless of their ecological impact. Natural resources were therefore overexploited and misused. Ecological hazard and degradation were viewed as necessary tradeoffs to development. The national policy on the environment now proclaims that this assumption is no longer part of Nigeria's development strategy. Nevertheless, for many decades, Nigeria's political leaders based their economic policy decisions on the ground that there was a tradeoff between environmental degradation and economic development. Nigeria's stand on Agenda 21 and on the Biodiversity Treaty at the recent UNCED Conference in Rio also affirms the change in Nigeria's perspective on the relationship between economic development and the environment. Nevertheless, Nigeria's environmental degradation is not only a reflection of the country's underdevelopment but a big contributor to its continuing underdevelopment.

Despite the establishment of FEPA and the enactment of a national policy on the environment, the prospects for Nigeria's environment are still cloudy. For one thing, FEPA does not have the technical capacity for monitoring Nigeria's environment or for enforcing its environmental regulations. Second, given the abject poverty to which the economic Structural Adjustment Program (SAP) has subjected many Nigerians, the sheer imperative to survive will discourage any concern for environmental protection.

The responsibility for safeguarding Nigeria's environment should not lie with the government. Accordingly, to make environmental regulations more effective, the public must be intensely involved in making and implementing environmental policies. While this may have to wait until the full democratization of the political process takes place, a temporary solution is to give communities as collectives the power to sue companies and individuals for ecological degradation. FEPA does not have the resources or the personnel to sufficiently monitor the Nigerian environment by itself. Moreover, like other public institutions in Nigeria, its regulatory role may be obviated by bribery and corruption. Therefore, it is imperative that the actual victims of ecological destruction be given the right to monitor their own environment and to have the power to sue violators for huge compensation.

NOTES

1. Federal Environmental Protection Agency, "National Counsel on the Environment Declares Program-Oriented Concern about Environmental Degradation and Pollution," *Nigerian Environment* 3.1 (1991): 2.

2. Fantu Cheru, "Structural Adjustment, Primary Resource Trade and Sustainable Development in Sub-Saharan Africa," *World Development* 20.4 (1992): 497–512.

3. Ibid., p. 499.

4. Ibid., p. 498.

5. Ibid.

6. P. K. Makinwa and A. O. Ozo, Introduction to *The Urban Poor in Nigeria*, ed. P. K. Makinwa and O. A. Ozo (Ibadan: Evans Brothers Publishers, 1987), p. x.

7. A. N. Nzeako, "Fire Outbreaks as Socio-Economic Consequences of Urban Poverty in Nigeria: An Empirical Case Study," in *The Urban Poor in Nigeria*, ed. P. K. Makinwa and O. A. Ozo (Ibadan: Evans Brothers Publishers, 1987), p. 10.

8. John Nwaobi, "No More Water of Life," *The African Guardian* 7 Aug. 1989: 15.

9. Ibid.

10. Quoted in Louisa Aguiyi-Ironsi, "The Looming Shadow," *Newswatch* 18 July 1988: 15.

11. Ibrahim Babangida, *Our National Environmental Goals* (Lagos: Federal Environmental Protection Agency, 1989), p. 16.

12. Ibid.

13. Aguiyi-Ironsi, "Looming Shadow," p. 13.

14. Niyi Beecroft et al., *Report of the Kaduna River Pollution Study* (Zaria: Department of Chemical Engineering, Ahmadu Bello University, 1986).

15. Aguiyi-Ironsi, "Looming Shadow," p. 18.

16. Paul Nwabuikwu, "A Threatened Future," *The African Guardian* 20 June 1988: 19.

17. Onome Osifo-Whiskey, "Finding the Mean," *Newswatch* 11 June 1990: 18.

18. Ken Saro-Wiwa, *On a Darkling Plain: An Account of the Nigerian Civil War* (London: Saros International Publishers, 1989), p. 12.

19. Quoted in *Newswatch* 2 July 1990: 18.

20. Etim Anim, "Sticky, Oily Problem," *Newswatch* 2 July 1990: 16.

21. Nwabuikwu, "Threatened Future," p. 18.

22. S. A. Awobajo, "An Analysis of Oil Spill Incidents in Nigeria: 1976–1980," paper presented at the Seminar on the Petroleum Industry and the Nigerian Environment, Warri, Petroleum Training Institute, 9–12 November 1981.

23. *Newswatch* 18 July 1988: 13.

24. Eboe Hutchful, "Oil Companies and Environmental Pollution in Nigeria," in *Political Economy of Nigeria*, ed. Claude Ake (London: Longman, 1985), p. 115.

25. Ibid.

26. Ibid., p. 19.

27. Ibid.

28. Anim, "Sticky, Oily Problem," p. 16.

29. Quoted in *Newswatch*, 2 July 1990: 15.

30. *The African Guardian*, 20 June 1988: 15.

31. Nigeria, Federal Environmental Protection Agency, *Guidelines and Standards for Environmental Pollution Control in Nigeria* (Lagos: The Agency, 1991), p. 72.

32. On the relationship between poverty, corruption, and dumping toxic wastes on Africa, see Diana Johnstone, "Western Developmental Overdose Makes Africa Chemically Dependent," *In These Times* 8 November 1989, p. 17.

33. Babangida, *National Environmental Goals*, p. 16.

34. Nwabuikwu, "Threatened Future," p. 20.

35. Nigerian Environmental Study/Action Team, "Nigerian Environmental Profile" (unpublished study).

36. Osifo-Whiskey, "Finding the Mean," p. 21.

37. K. Kimmage and W. M. Adams, "Wetland Agricultural Production and River Basin Development in the Hadejia-Jama'are Vallet, Nigeria," *The Geography Journal* 158.1 (1992): 4.

38. *Newswatch* 11 June 1990: 21.

39. Ibid.

40. Babangida, *National Environmental Goals*, p. 18.

41. Aguiyi-Ironsi, "Looming Shadow," p. 13.

42. For details on this protest, see *Newswatch* 2 July 1990: 18.

43. Private communication, Abuja, August 1991.

44. Federal Republic of Nigeria, *Official Gazette* 75.79 (1988): A779–A783.

45. Ibid., p. A781.

46. For full details on the decree, see *Federal Republic of Nigeria, Federal Environmental Protection Agency Decree, 1988* (Lagos: Ministry of Information and Culture, 1988).

47. Ibid., pp. A912–A913.

48. Ibid., p. A913.

49. Federal Environmental Protection Agency, *Nigerian Environment* 3.1 (1991): 4.

50. Federal Republic of Nigeria, *National Policy on the Environment* (Lagos: Federal Environmental Protection Agency, 1989), p. 5.

51. Ibid.

52. D. Pearce, "An Economic Perspective on Sustainable Development," *Journal of the Society for International Development* 2.3 (1989): 17–19.

53. Babangida, *National Environmental Goals*, p. 16.

54. Federal Republic of Nigeria, *Official Gazette* 78.42 (1991): B15–B38.

55. Environmental Protection Agency, *Nigerian Environment*, p. A920.

56. J. A. Ariyo and D. O. Ogbonna, "The Effects of Land Speculation on Agricultural Production among Peasants in Kachia Local Government Area of Kaduna State, Nigeria," *Applied Geography* 12 (1992): 31–46.

Chapter 8

Environmental Policy and Politics in Chile: A Latin-American Case Study

JORGE NEF

The study of environmental policy and administration in Latin America offers a convenient window to view the intricate relationships between politics, social forces, and the pursuit of sustainable development. The purpose of this chapter is to provide an overview of environmental policy and administration in one country—Chile—which has become a "model" of Third World development. The perspective taken is broadly systemic,[1] as well as interpretative.[2] It uses a political economy framework,[3] attempting to link environmental policies with the broader development model, the constellation of socioeconomic forces affecting these policies, the institutional constraints and mechanisms to policy formulation and implementation, and the overall outcomes of the policy process.[4] We explore a number of operational questions:[5]

1. Which are the basic environmental problems that have characterized Chilean development strategies, and how have these problems been articulated by diverse social actors?

I wish to thank Dr. Patricia Adams from Probe International for giving me access to correspondence, memos, and studies regarding Chile. Likewise, I would like to express my gratitude to Ms. Kim Gharabaghi for collecting the documentary information for my research.

2. Which are the main alliances and coalitions supporting and opposing various environmental perspectives, and how are they organized in the Chilean political arena?

3. Which are the main ideological and programmatic underpinnings of such policy options?

4. Which are the principal channels of influence and mechanisms through which these environmental perspectives and policy options became both public policy objectives and official policy instruments?

5. Which is the current environmental policy menu (the articulated alternatives, problem definitions, and courses of action offered as options within a given power interplay among political brokers, constituting either part of one or many broader political agendas), and how is it connected with the larger developmental model and in particular with the issue of sustainable development?

6. What are the consequences of these policies over the economic development strategies, the different sociopolitical actors, and ultimately upon the existing environmental problems and development process?

7. Finally, as a conclusion, what are the nomothetic "lessons" one could generalize from an idiographic case study of Chile for the Latin American region?

To analyze Chilean public policy and administration, one needs to come to grips with a number of distinctive traits that permeate the country's administrative culture and institutions.[6] The first is the high degree of bureaucratic salience and continuity conditioned by a highly legalistic and formalistic administrative culture. Despite a pervasive neoliberal orientation grafted on the state apparatus since the counterrevolution of 1973, the Chilean public sector is still by far more decisive in national life than that of any other country in Latin America, with the sole exception of socialist Cuba.[7] The second trait is that in one generation Chile has undergone a dramatic reshaping of public policies and priorities. These various phases have included Keynesian import-substitution industrialization (1938–1970), a short-lived experiment with democratic to socialism (1970–1973), the forceful establishment of unbridled neoliberalism under military rule (1973–1989), and finally redemocratization with economic orthodoxy. The third trait is the obvious fact that Chile is an underdeveloped (albeit outwardly modernized) and dependent country, subject to the "boom-and-bust" oscillations of commodity export cycles.

HISTORICAL OVERVIEW

These observations are particularly relevant to understanding the place of a relatively "new" policy area in the Chilean agenda. This is not to say that Chile's environmental problem is new. What is new is the codification of a number of otherwise symptomatic dysfunctions (land degradation, air pollution, sewage and chemical contamination of streams and water resources, fauna and flora depletion, and the consequent health hazards and decline of quality of life associated with these) under the terms *environmental problems and policies*. In Chile, as in many other places, the very existence of the environmental problem in the political agenda is contingent upon the administrative, political, and legal semantics that label and structure the problem as a goal to be tackled by government intervention. Brokerage and agency are essential here, for labeling and constructive (as well as deconstructive) problematization also shapes public views and attitudes. Until recently, there was no significant unifying concept to deal with environmental issues. These issues were traditionally handled in diverse levels and jurisdictions. They were attended by diverse territorial (national or municipal) and functional legislation—health and sanitation, agriculture, forestry, public works, industry, transportation, fisheries, and the like.

Nature and the love of landscape played an important part in the romanticized ideas of independence. Creole elites had been influenced by the accounts of the dramatic Chilean geography and nature contained in the writings of Jesuit Abbot Juan Ignacio Molina (1740–1829) and later by the reports on the exploration of the Chilean coast by the renowned Prussian scientist Alexander von Humboldt. This construction of the Chilean natural environment as a rich preserve was further enhanced by Charles Darwin's field-trip to Southern Chile. The lyrics of the Chilean National Anthem, a product of postindependence territorial patriotism, read from their beginning as an environmentalist's hymn, with reference to "pure, clean skies," vast flowered fields, the majesty of white mountains, and the bounty of the oceans.

But this contemplative view of nature, one that permeated a good deal of the nationalist and folklorist literature, coexisted with a highly pragmatic predisposition. This ambivalence expressed itself in a growing separation between rhetoric and practice that would characterize both elite and popular attitudes towards nature. From the 1830s onwards, the agricultural, commercial, and mining elites that built the early republic were organized into powerful interest groups focused upon the exploitation and export of natural resources. The National Society of Agriculture, the National Society of Mining, and later the Industrial Development Society espoused a "progressive" liberal ideology, heavily influenced by positivism, which looked upon nature as resources for exploitation and embraced an ethos of manifest destiny.[8]

With the creation of the University of Chile in 1842—molded in part on the Napoleonic concept of the polytechnic—the formation of engineering cadres (especially in the mining and civil fields) became a national priority. It was also decisive in shaping the intellectual "culture" pertaining to the relationships between society, economy, and polity on the one hand, with environment ("nature") on the other. This early development in scientific and technological training was decisively influenced by numerous scientific missions of European scientists. The latter were invited by the Chilean government and played important roles in the modernization of the country's educational system.[9] The new scientists and engineers trained at the University of Chile and at the School of Mining in Copiapó were imbued with a modernist ethos amalgamating—but not synthesizing— these tendencies. A metaphysical and almost poetic belief in "civilization" and "progress" coexisted with a reliance on engineering technique to transform and harness nature for commercial purposes. This conceptual software, or mind-set, in university curriculums soon transcended the realm of things mechanical or electrical. It became the intellectual matrix of professionalism and university education well into the twentieth century. It manifested itself in agronomy, medicine, law, education, and other careers.

Since the past century, Chilean elites have shared a positivist view of progress: The environment-as-resources paradigm has been hegemonic. It has been shared by right-wingers, centrists, center-leftists (radicals, Christian democrats, moderate socialists), and Marxist-Leninists, irrespective of their specific utopias and, of course, the political methods to reach those utopias. As a Chilean analyst observed: "To a certain extent all these models share the basic fallacies of modern industrialism and the limitations of short-term, non-ecological thinking. Moreover, each model is supported by, and supports in turn, political and economic interests the aims of which are rarely in accordance with the interests of the natural environment."[10]

This sort of Spencerian liberalism was decisive in the highly elitist and racist policies of "pacification," "resettlement," and immigration that opened and "tamed" the Southern Frontier, after the War of the Pacific (1879–1883). From this view, "nature," including of course "nature people" (Amerindians) had to succumb to "civilization." The theme of "civilization versus barbarism" also played a major part in the aforementioned war, in which Chile took over the rich Bolivian and Peruvian nitrate fields. These perceptions, which had been shaped in no small manner by Comtism, were not confined to Chile. Brazilian, Mexican, and Argentine liberal oligarchs shared a common world-view and, to a large extent, pursued similar development strategies.

The world Depression of 1929 put an end to the "old" export economy, whose cornerstone had been the export of minerals, especially nitrates and copper ores. The response by the ruling elites to the challenge posed by economic catastrophe was a mixture of Keynesian import-substitution industrialization (ISI) with populism. This recovery strategy was based upon an expansion of the administrative state into the realm of parastatals. State corporations were entrusted with both planning and financing substitutive industrial activities and with implementing development projects. The centerpiece of the strategy was the creation of a TVA-like development corporation (Corporación de Fomento de la Producción [CORFO]). It was established in 1939 by the Popular Front government of Pedro Aguirre

Cerda (1938–1941) and based upon a study prepared by the College of Engineers. CORFO's approach favored megaprojects and heavy industry to boost development. Over the next three decades, under the aegis of Keynesian strategies, a number of other sectorial corporations emerged from the CORFO hub. These included ENAP, the National Petroleum Enterprise, charged with the exploration, exploitation, and refining of oil; ENDESA, the National Electrical Corporation, building large generating plants and harnessing the country's considerable hydroelectric potential; CAP, the Pacific Steel Company; ENAMI, the National Mining Company, with smelters for medium-sized copper mines. There were also numerous mixed economic ventures in manufacturing, processing, and the like partly financed with CORFO monies.

These policies, borne out to the necessity to arrest economic recession, often failed to take a look—let alone a comprehensive look—at environmental impacts. In the 1960s, it became apparent that industries were having severe effects on air quality in large industrial centers. This was especially the case in Santiago, the capital, but it was also a problem in the area near the Southern city of Concepción, the port of Talcahuano, and the Bay of San Vicente where CAP's Huachipato steel mills were located. But the damming of rivers for ENDESA's use, the wholesale exploitation of forests, strip-mining, and other practices hardly raised an eyebrow. Chile's present environmental crisis was shaped during these years—a crisis that combined, as in most underdeveloped nations, the worst of both worlds—"modern" contamination of high chemical toxicity with "traditional" bacterial pollution; underutilized resources side by side with indiscriminate resource depletion.

With increasing industrialization, urbanization, and the expansion of government and business activities into industry, environmental damage also increased. This lack of environmental concern cut across political barriers. It was shared by such dissimilar political coalitions as those of the populist administration of Carlos Ibáñez (1952–1958), the rightist government of Jorge Alessandri (1958–1964), the reformism of Eduardo Frei's Christian Democrats (1964–1970), the brief Socialist experiment of Salvador Allende (1970–1973), and the protofascist military dictatorship of General Augusto Pinochet (1973–1990). Until then, outside the pioneering work undertaken at the U.N. Economic Commission for Latin America (ECLA) by Osvaldo Sunkel, Pablo Bifani, and Nicolo Gligo, environment had not evolved into a distinctively political issue, nor had environmental problems been put in a larger developmental context.[11] The need to present a clear alternative to the policies of the dictatorship politicized environmental concerns. Paradoxically, however, it was the military regime that elevated the rhetoric of environmentalism to unprecedented heights. It included in Articles 19 (No. 24) and especially Article 20 of its own "tailor-made" authoritarian constitution of 1980, a provision guaranteeing citizens the "right to live in an environment free of contamination."[12] Obviously, this statement had little to do with the real public policies pursued. That section of the constitution meant first and foremost an entrenchment of the absolute right to private property. It constituted, however, good public relations and asserted that Chile was "in tune with the times."

By the mid-1980s, what had been pyrotechnics and political opportunism had taken the form of an important component of the political agenda. The timing was right, since the country had already plunged into a real environmental crisis that defied rhetoric. The discourse had finally caught up with reality. Moreover, the growing opposition to the regime had become both more unified and more internationalized. On the one hand, environmental organizations were receiving significant external supports in financing, technical cooperation, and ideas. On the other, the very phenomenon of exile had meant that numerous Chilean intellectuals had been exposed to global issues to an extent hard to imagine scarcely a decade before and had become "cosmopolitanized."

When the prohibition for dissidents to come back was gradually lifted, many foreign-educated Chilean academics and professionals returned home. Among them there were ambientalistas—physicians, engineers, economists, geographers, anthropologists, sociologists, and physical scientists—with a new professional agenda and a more holistic outlook. They had been influenced by "environmental studies" in Europe and North America, by the U.N. efforts,[13] especially by the aforementioned studies by ECLA,[14] and by the Brundtland Report.[15] Departing from the established Chilean tradition, democratic politics came to converge with a "clean" environmental posture. In fact, it could be argued that "environment"—and in particular the relationship between environment and development—had become a paradigm or surrogate for ECLA-style structuralism[16] vis-à-vis the onslaught of the neoliberal monetarism pursued by the authoritarian regime.[17]

THE PRESENT CRISIS

By the late 1980s, it was increasingly obvious that most of Chile was affected by a host of interrelated environmental dysfunctions. Even a sketchy list is impressive:

1. There is a dangerous air pollution problem (particle and carbon monoxide as well as dust resulting from soil erosion) in metropolitan areas. In Santiago, it approaches the levels of Mexico City.[18] In other cities, such as Rancagua or Concepción, both south of Santiago, the source of the problem varied, being industrial smokestacks rather than connected with transportation.

2. There is also a water pollution problem: Untreated sewage combined with industrial waste is dumped into rivers, whose waters are used to irrigate vegetables. Both the Mapocho River, which divides Santiago, and the Zanjón de la Aguada, have become, for all intents and purposes, open sewers where fecal

and industrial refuse end up irrigating Santiago's green belt. In the northern city of Antofagasta and in numerous mining centers in the north, mining by-products (such as arsenic) have been finding their way into the limited water resources, as with some CODELCO (Copper Corporation) and ENAMI operations, while in Concepción, Arauco, Bio-Bio, and Valdivia, wood-processing and paper mills had contaminated lakes and streams in varying degrees.[19]

3. The aforementioned poisonous mixture finally makes its way to the coast, creating an ocean pollution problem affecting flora, fauna, resort areas, and the food chain. The most contaminated area has been the central zone (the San Antonio-Algarrobo resort area and the long coastal strip from Valparaíso to Quintero). But in the Eighth Region, some 500 kilometers to the South (Concepción; Talcahuano; and Lota, with its steel mills, refineries, wood-processing plants, and canneries), the level of contamination has reached disastrous proportions.[20] In addition, oil extraction, transportation, and refining have compounded the problem both in the southernmost Magellanic region and in the south-central and central ports, where petroleum is transported and refined.

4. Industrial and vehicle-originated air pollution had brought about an acid rain problem, concentrated especially in Santiago, but not exclusively limited to it. The main effects have been on trees, but overall water acidity levels have also increased.

5. The rapid expansion of the forestry industry in recent years has created a severe, and growing deforestation problem. This currently affects mostly the central-south regions, and in particular the araucaria, alerce, and other native-tree forests further south. It should be remembered, however, that the near-northern semiarid regions of Atacama, Coquimbo, and Aconcagua are suffering today drought and desertification resulting mainly from deforestation started in colonial times.

6. The increasing demand for electricity for both industrial and domestic use has brought about the development of hydroelectric megaprojects such as the Rapel, Laja, and Pangue dams. The damming of rivers has affected flora, fauna, and the lives of peasant cultivators, many of whom are native peoples, whose livelihoods have been severely and arbitrarily disrupted.[21]

7. In recent years, with the export-led policy concentrating upon nontraditional agricultural exports—mostly fruits—an increase of toxic substances has taken place. The use of pesticides, fertilizers, and other substances to preserve or improve the appearance, texture, and longevity of the products has been on the rise. Many of these substances—such as Alar or DDT or its local equivalent, TANAX—are widely employed in the industry. Recently there have been reports of fertilizers reaching the water table in the fruit-growing regions. A related problem is posed here by the expansion of cold-storage facilities and the wide use of fluorocarbon-based refrigeration.

8. The most recent and threatening environmental problem only became known in 1989: the thinning, or "hole" in the protective ozone layer. Its effects, so far concentrated in the far southern regions of Aysén and Magallanes and the Argentinean and Chilean Patagonia, have been visible in sheep and cattle (causing blindness) and in wild animals. Direct effects on humans have not been so far evaluated, but they are potentially alarming. Unlike the other seven categories, the ozone problem is one whose causes are mostly "external": the massive use of fluorocarbons by industrial countries.

There are even more potential environmental dysfunctions looming in the horizon. Two of these future environmental threats are worth mentioning. One is the eventual processing of rare metals, such as uranium, molybdenum, and especially lithium, of which Chile has a large supply. The processing of these rare metals releases highly toxic substances. The other threat is perhaps more pressing. Since the coup, the military has had a free hand in controlling what is today a significant "military–industrial complex." Firms such as the Army's Factory of Materiel and Equipment (FAMAE), the National Explosives Enterprise (ENAEX), and the privately owned Cardoen Enterprises are reportedly engaged in the development of lethal substances. In 1991, there were reports of an industrial accident with loss of life in the town of Melipilla, in which allegedly nerve gas was released from an army factory. The military is also involved in the development of an intermediate-range missile, the *"Rayo,"* the nature of its warhead still unspecified.

More ominous is the fact that since 1970, three years before the military coup, the army took a constant and almost obsessive interest in the development of nuclear power. This despite the technical reports indicating that nuclear generators were both economically marginal and geologically unsafe for Chilean conditions. Late in 1972, the army's Nuclear Energy Council (CENE) was created. After the coup, the army took direct control of all nuclear research; it appointed officers—some of whom had been trained in nuclear engineering—to the top posts in the Chilean Atomic Energy Commission, and in 1974 it started an immediate action plan to reach criticality at its nuclear reactor at La Reina. This occurred on October 13, 1974.[22]

In the following years, numerous steps were taken to hasten the pace of nuclear development. In 1980, a new and more modern accelerator in Lo Aguirre entered in operation. The plant was geared to uranium enrichment and concentration by means of ionic exchanges and the use of solvents.[23] The same year, the Centre for Research in Nuclear Energy (CIEN) established a network to collect rain water, ostensibly to obtain "heavy water." Installations and research facilities were effectively transformed into military zones, the condition in which they still remain. On January 23, 1985, a "second criticality with enriched uranium at 45% in a 235 isotope" was accomplished.[24] The nuclear genie was seemingly out of the bottle. The alarming question is what use are the Chilean military making of intensive nuclear research. Given the totalitarian and secretive nature of the institution, with its callous contempt for civilian control and human life, the answer is at best disturbing.[25]

The manner in which these multiple dysfunctions reciprocate and interact is quite complex. The mere physical chain of events (e.g., the complex interconnection between soil erosion, dust, transportation, air pollution, and acid rain and the last's impact upon flora and water acidity) is, however, far less complicated than the economic, social, and political linkages underpinning Chile's environmental crisis. For these are issues of culture and perception, of "economic rationality" and interests, and above all, power or, more to the point, lack of power. While Chile's environmental problems have a long historical lineage, the present crisis is distinctively connected with the acceleration and multiplications of contradictions of the present modality of development. As Sunkel observed more than a decade ago, there is a definite relationship between present development styles and environmental problems.[26]

THE POLITICS OF ENVIRONMENT

Most orthodox economists and their associates in the international business community describe Chile as an "economic miracle"[27] to be imitated by other countries.[28] Yet this view is not always shared. As a recent report by the U.S.-based Natural Resources Defense Council stated:

Two decades of rapid economic growth have had significant impacts on the quality of Chile's environment and natural resources. Santiago, for example, suffers from the second worst air quality in the Western hemisphere, following Mexico City. Copper smelting operations in northern Chile have produced dangerous blood levels of arsenic among local populations. Commercial logging of southern Chile's native forests is rapidly eliminating some of the world's oldest temperate rain forest ecosystems. Over-fishing has left all of Chile's important commercial fisheries in critical condition. . . . Chile's environmental problems are largely a legacy of the Pinochet's government, which aggressively encouraged private sector economic development, drastically reduced government control over the use of natural resources and failed to establish a regulatory structure for environmental protection.[29]

What clearly emerges from the preceding analysis is that the country's current environmental crisis has been related to the country's development policy—one characterized by a policy of nondecision on environmental matters. In my opinion, the Pinochet regime did not create the necessary conditions for environmental catastrophe. It accelerated environmental dysfunctions present in the development style by imposing an extreme view of "cowboy" capitalism and by eradicating the possibilities for a meaningful democratic debate on issues of human concern. The democratically elected government of the *Concertación*,[30] under President Patricio Aylwin "declared a commitment to improve the environmental situation [but] his government's overriding concern for continued economic growth has delayed progress in developing an effective environmental regulatory program."[31]

Actors, Alliances, and Agendas

The constellation of actors that partake in the environmental policy process is relatively large and complex. It is also characterized by a significant level of transnationalization, that is, the boundary between the "domestic" and the "international–regional" dimensions of environmental issues and alliances is unclear. For the sake of simplicity, we could identify three major blocs of agents in the process, all possessing transnational linkages. The first is what, for lack of a better term could be called the "antiregulation" or "prodevelopment" bloc, formed by public, parastatal, and large business concerns and their associates at home and abroad. Second, there is the equally transnationalized "proregulatory" or "environmentalist" alliance, of numerous research centers, NGOs, and grassroots groups and constituencies. Third, there is what can be vaguely referred to as "the government." It is constituted by a number of policymaking institutions and public bodies where conflicting interests eventually become regulatory norms and where rule making, rule-implementing, rule-adjudication (arbitration), and rule-enforcement take place. The military establishment, even under the present democratic administration, has to be considered quite outside "the government." They are extremely powerful and autonomous, maintaining close personal, institutional, and ideological ties with Chile's aristocracy and business classes. The Pinochet regime forged an enduring "reactionary coalition" between the officer corps, capitalists, and U.S. military and business constituencies. Pinochet still remains as the commander-in-chief of the army. His large, loyal, and disciplined organization, in alliance with the other branches of the armed forces, is the warrantor of last resort to maintain the order created by the military regime.

The "Environmentalists." Glenn Prickett has identified a vast web of environment-related organizations as participants in the policy process. Although his "mapping" was originally intended to describe the main official and NGO participants with regards to hydroelectric projects, this "environmental network" offers an insight into the structure and modus operandi of environmental groups in Chile. Although from afar environmentalist groups and their allies may appear to be a highly cohesive coalition, they in fact suffer many of the same problems present in NGOs worldwide—magnified in the Chilean setting. They experience the chronic underfinancing of underdevelopment—their supports coming mostly from outside sources. In addition, while there is a good degree of cooperation and solidarity among the groups, there are also profound cleavages stemming from ideology, as well as professional or personal distrust, compounded by fierce competition for scarce resources.

The largest, oldest, best organized, and most influential environmental interest group in Chile is the National Committee for the Defense of Fauna and Flora (CODEFF). It was formed in 1968 during the Christian Democratic administration of Eduardo Frei. Because of its "technical" conservationist (and seemingly "apolitical") orientation, the organization has been able to function under dramatically different development projects.[32] Today it constitutes a sort of "nodal" organization, able to network with more functionally or geographically specific environmental groups. Among its successes, CODEFF coordinated an effective research and advocacy campaign to win legal protection for the araucaria and alerce trees. They also took an interest in the legal challenges to mining companies using desert waters. More recently, the committee participated in the early stages of the study of the impact of hydro projects on the Bio-Bio river in southern Chile. Subsequently it devoted less attention to the issue, choosing instead to endorse the action of a regional group, the Bio-Bio Action Group (GABB) to which it provides assistance upon request.

Another environmental group is the Centre for Environmental Research and Planning (CIPMA), established in 1979 as a think-tank studying the relationships between economic development and environment. It is a policy-oriented group, seeking economically efficient and socially equitable solutions to environmental problems. It acts as host to annual symposiums on environmental policy and publishes a journal, *Ambiente y Desarrollo* (Environment and Development). There is also a National Network for Ecological Action (RENACE) affiliated to the Institute of Political Ecology (IEP), an advocacy group that publishes a bulletin, *Ecoprensa*, and also holds seminars and workshops. RENACE serves as a liaison and information exchange among ecologically oriented NGOs, independent research centers, and the public. Other environmental organizations include the Centre for Ecological Extension (GAIA), geared to public education, and the Ecological Centre Canelo de Nos, an experimental program implementing alternative pilot projects for popular sector organizations (especially Popular Economic Organizations [OEPs]),[33] both urban and rural.

These organizations interact with "external linkage groups"[34] such as the Natural Resources Defense Council in the United States, Probe International in Canada, and Greenpeace. The last has a Chilean chapter, while representatives of the council and of Probe have visited Chile on several occasions. International NGOs have been instrumental in developing an "environmental partnership."[35] They coordinate and assist in lobbying foreign governments, international organizations (such as the World Bank or the Inter-American Development Bank), foreign business, and transnational corporations.

The environmental coalition in Chile involves much more than environmental interest groups. It comprises a myriad of other organizations that either have environmental components in their agendas or share some of the environmentalists' interests and concerns. These concerns range from specific technical or social issues to broader considerations such as "sustainable development." Those whose mandates encompass "sustainable development" include the Corporation for Economic Research in Latin America (CIEPLAN), and the Center for Alternative Research (CEPAUR). The largest and most influential of these is CIEPLAN, associated with the Christian Democratic Party.[36] It was created in 1976 as a public research institute, with significant external support, including a large and sustained contribution from the International Development Research Center (IDRC). The corporation's mandate is to identify and promote equitable, democratic, and sustainable economic development policies. Smaller but equally important, CEPAUR is a policy research group whose efforts are also concentrated upon the formulation of sustainable development strategies. Manfred Max-Neef, the winner of the "alternative Nobel Prize" is active within the organization. CEPAUR enjoys high international visibility and has many contacts at home and abroad, especially with European research centers and organizations (such as the Dag Hammarskjold Foundation).

Several independent technology-research centers are also part of the environmental coalition. These include the Center for the Study of Alternative Technologies for Latin America (CETAL), the Energy Research Program (PRIEN) and a U.S. group with offices in Santiago—the International Institute for Energy Conservation (IIEC). The CETAL was established in the main port city of Valparaíso as a technology research group promoting the development of alternative energy technologies, including energy-efficient and nonconventional renewable energy. It provides support to other groups on the issue of energy and environment. PRIEN is a group constituted by engineers from the University of Chile conducting research on energy production, use, and conservation. It has carried on studies at the local (municipal) level in Santiago and in other cities. It also provides technical advice to authorities and electric utilities in energy-saving measures, especially in integrating end-use energy-efficient programs into investment planning.

An effective functional linkage has evolved between environmental interest groups and the Chilean Human Rights Commission (CCHDH) created in 1976. The commission, which has a Program for Indian Peoples, has acted as a catalyst for environmental rights, especially with regard to natives' claims. In this respect, CCHDH has been a bridge-builder between legal, social, and technical concerns on environment. Likewise, through the active membership of José Aylwin, a young human rights attorney—who is also a member of the Bio-Bio Action Group and a son of President Aylwin—international linkages have been established between native Pehuenche representatives and Cree Indian leaders in Canada struggling against the James Bay II hydroelectric development.

This list is not exhaustive, since there are numerous regional and more issue-specific groups. Most significant among these is the aforementioned GABB, which has carried the environmental banner in the proposed ENDESA hydroelectric Pangue project in the Bio-Bio River. Other groups such as *Vida Magallánica* (Magellanic Life) in the southernmost region and the Institute for Andean Development in the Andean ranges of the far north are associations dealing with sustainable local development.

The environmental network, despite the "elite," upper-middle-class nature of most environmental interest groups, has been able to connect successfully with civic action (e.g., Citizen's Action Assembly), NGOs, and grassroots movements. In the specific cases of forests, land, and rivers, an important collaboration has developed between environmentalists, human rights activists, and native peoples' associations. These associations represent aboriginal ethnic minorities within Chile: *Aymara* in the North Andean region, *Rapa-Nui* in Easter Island, *Mapuche* (*Pehuenche* and *Huilliche*) in the south, and *Kawashkar* in the far south. This new role for groups that had been historically relegated, discriminated against, and often brutalized, entails a drastic change for a society marred by deep-seated racism. Native and pronative organizations include the Aymara Studies Workshop (TEA), *Pacha Aru*, the Regional Institute for Aymara Development and Promotion (IRPA), the Coordinating Body of *Mapuche* Institutions (CIM), the *Pehuen Mapu* Guild Association, the *Mapuche* Council for All the Lands, the umbrella organization National Native Commission (1989), and the government-appointed National Commission for Native Peoples (CEPI, established in 1990) to mention just a few.[37]

The "Developers." The category under the "developer" label is perhaps even more complex than the environmental network. On the surface it comprises a multiplicity of firms of all sizes, both public and private, associational interest groups to which these firms are linked, foreign corporations and financial organizations with participation in the firms' operations, international organizations, and foreign governments' development agencies. It is by and large a loose and seemingly disjointed alliance constructed specifically to overcome opposition to projects and support deregulation.

But this appearance is deceiving. Despite the looseness, the "developers' bloc" still possesses a hard-core power center and is capable of mustering an enormous amount of power and resources. The developers' bloc is extremely influential. Leaving aside the outer rims of the alliance constituted by associated small firms and support groups, the developers' main constituencies are linked among themselves by interrelated activities, common interests, interlocking directorships, associational bonds, access to official channels, control of the media, common ideology, and often party affiliation.[38] In other words, this is the Chilean "establishment."[39] Its interests are articulated in the private-sector-wide National Confederation of Production and Commerce (CNPC or COPROCO, established in 1932). COPROCO, in turn, encompasses seven interest groups covering all of Chile's major productive and financial activities, all of them with strong transnational links and representation in numerous boards and commissions in the parastatal sector. These are the National Agricultural Society (SNA, 1838), the National Mining Society (SONAMI, 1883), the Society for Industrial Development (SOFOFA, 1883), the Chilean Chamber of Construction (CCHC, 1951), the National Chamber of Commerce (CNC, 1857), the Association of Banks and Financial Institutions (ABIF, 1980), and the Santiago Stock Exchange (BCS).[40]

The mining sector comprises all major extractive corporations. The largest is the autonomous parastatal CODELCO, established in 1965. CODELCO is one of Chile's "sacred cows," dealing with the country's single most important export commodity. With over 30,000 employees, upwards of $1.5 billion in sales, net assets of over $500 million, and high profitability, CODELCO is charged with the exploration, exploitation, and international marketing of the largest share of Chile's copper market. In a way CODELCO is an anomaly. Despite drives to privatize and denationalize the corporation following the 1973 coup, it maintained control over the country's largest mines, expropriated from the U.S. consortia by the Allende administration. The retention of the public corporation status was essentially a consequence of pressure from "hard-line," corporatist sectors within the military, resisting the influence of the regime's "economic team." For them, copper was a strategic resource whose control was in the "national interest." CODELCO became both a means to provide the military with extrabudgetary resources and a protected source of employment upon retirement from the ranks.[41]

CODELCO and another parastatal, ENAMI—charged with processing and smelting—are currently contributing in large scale to air and water contamination in the northern First and Second Regions as well as in the Ventana and Rancagua areas west and south of Santiago. Other mining parastatals include the National Coal Company (ENACAR), the Aysén Mining Enterprise. Though they are functionally dependent on either the Ministry of Mining or that of Economics, there is very little public control and real accountability of these entities. In practice, each agency is directly responsible to a board of directors, many of whose members were appointed to tenured positions by the previous regime. The dictatorship also drafted these parastatals' organic legislation, one the Aylwin government agreed not to touch. Other companies are quickly being privatized. Privately owned medium- and small-sized mines throughout the territory equally share a rather spotty environmental record. Most privately owned mining companies are represented by SONAMI, one of the seven major business interest groups mentioned earlier.

In the industry and manufacturing sector, a constellation of semiprivate and private corporations dominates the scene. Many of the largest are privatized detachments from the CORFO hub. Others are privately owned, varying in size from large-scale to small operations. The largest industrial concern is the Pacific Steel conglomerate, today an investment company centered in the production of steel at its Huachipato mills. CAP "owns 19 firms—enterprises ranging from mines to real estate to forestry—with annual sales of $600 million. Exports account for half of these revenues. CAP's steel division claims to be among the most efficient producers in the world"[42] yet it is a main contributor to the contamination of air, sea, and water in the Concepción region. In a similar vein, there is ENAP. With extraction operations in the southernmost island of Tierra del Fuego and off the Strait of Magellan and with several refineries along the Chilean coast, ENAP's activities are far from "clean." The same could be said about the expanding canneries, fishmeal processors, paper mills, and petrochemical plants. Vertically integrated corporations such as the Paper and Cardboard Manufacturing Company (CMPC) and highly diversified conglomerates such as the Luskic Group function by and large on the logic of production and profits, with little or no concern for environmental or social impact. But the rather cavalier use of toxic substances does not stop here.

The widespread deregulation that characterizes the post-1973 economic model has allowed both a lack of strict controls for formal industries and a total absence of controls for the mushrooming "informal sector." This sector—often a form of disguised unemployment—exists at the margins of labor, sanitary, taxation, and environmental regulations, however weak. It contributes in no small manner to air pollution and to the dumping of toxic waste into sewers and rivers. The deregulatory ideology enshrined in the legislation enhances the antienvironmental effects of industrial and manufacturing operations. The principal association representing the manufacturing sector is SOFOFA, though there are more industry-specific lobbies.

Forestry and forestry-related industries have been one of the fastest growing sectors in the Chilean export economy. Three megaprojects—Celpac, Arauco II, and Santa Fe—are being started to increase the volume of exports. "The production of pulp and paper . . . is controlled by two economic groups, the *Angelini* (or *Compañía de Petroleos de Chile*, COPEC) group and the *Matte* (or *Compañía Manufacturera de Papeles y Cartones*, CMPC . . .) group."[43] Foreign investment in the wood-producing area of Bio-Bio far exceeds $450 million, most of it coming from the Ibn Mafuz, Fletcher Challenge, and Shell consortia.[44]

The public sector, through CORFO holding operations, has retained a small presence in the field, such as the *Panguipulli* Forestry and Wood Complex. This and other interests have been increasingly sold to private foreign investors by means of "debt-for-equity" swap mechanisms. In fact, a high degree of integration between domestic and foreign capital has taken place. The interests of forestry and related industries are represented by a powerful lobby and research entity, the Wood Corporation (CORMA), an affiliate of SOFOFA. It reportedly had direct access to government agencies such as the National Forestry and Renewable Resources Corporation (COMAF), the executive and members of the legislature.

The expansion of electrification is a fundamental component of Chile's energy-intensive development strategy. For the 1979–1989 period, the rate of increase in energy consumption (at 5.2 percent per year) outpaced the average rate of economic growth (4.2 percent annually). "The main users are transportation, industry and mining (copper, petro-chemicals, paper and cellulose, steel, sugar, iron, cement and nitrates). Growth in electricity demand has been even greater, averaging more than 6 percent per year."[45] ENDESA, established in 1943 as a CORFO-affiliated parastatal, is a gigantic power monopoly. Its annual output is 7,550 GWh (equivalent to 45 percent of the country's total needs), which it sells to the equally monopolistic retailing utility, CHILECTRA.

In 1990, ENDESA was completely privatized. At present, its stock—divided among some 50,000 stockholders—is heavily concentrated in a handful of private financial conglomerates related to insurance, medical services, and the like, known as financiers. The company owns several subsidiaries such as INGENDESA (engineering services), the *Pehuenche* Corporation of Maule and Curanilahue, and the *Pangue* Corporation in Bio-Bio. "ENDESA is the holding company for about 1600 MW of hydro capacity and 320 MW of thermal plant and remains the leading power producer in the country."[46] The company's megaprojects involve a comprehensive scheme for the expansion and interconnection of hydropower, by damming Chile's major river systems in the south. This development is expected to double the country's electrical capacity before the end of the century. Needless to say, the ecological and social impact of these projects is potentially devastating. Opposition to these plans has been growing. However, ENDESA's power is more than electricity. It is a financial conglomerate connected with dominant economic and political groups and with an enormous capacity to lobby, both inside and outside the government and through its linkages with other sectors of the business community. It enjoys a reputation of being "invulnerable" and "free from public oversight."[47]

As with the environmentalist bloc, the structure of the "prodevelopment," antiregulation lobby includes a myriad of other groups. One of the important sectors partaking in both the problem and the controversy surrounding environmental effects is the transport sector. The processes of economic and urban expansion, including sectoral changes privileging exports and technological transformations from trains to diesel-powered trucks, has had a serious effect on air pollution. Also, as cities and private automobiles have expanded, particle contamination has dramatically increased. Santiago possesses a gigantic, unregulated complex and an inefficient, privately owned public transportation system. Private automobiles have compounded the problem. The city has probably twice as many buses and cars as are warranted for a city of its size—most of them obsolete, poorly maintained, and sources of high levels of emissions. Since the "military, following radical neo-liberal policies, regarded such measures as control of the buses and industry as anathema," it has been extremely difficult to bring bus and truck owners into line.[48]

Transportistas are a relatively powerful group, with a demonstrated ability to paralyze the country. For instance the thoroughly corporatist National Confederation of Truck-Owners (CNDC), with CIA support was able, first in 1972 and finally in 1973, to organize a nationwide strike that shut down the country, paving the way for the military coup. Bus strikes—some with support of the owners' associations—contributed to some extent to the "civic protests" against the Pinochet regime in 1988. At any rate, the owners' power to blackmail depends to a considerable extent on their ability to elicit support from their employees. At any rate, the bus owners have been far less cohesive and clear in their corporate positions than the truck owners. They have also been more politically and factionally divided.

Other groups that can be included in the "developer" and antiregulation side are large export-promotion associations, such as the *Fundación Chile* (Chile Foundation) and fruit producers and packers. Rural entrepreneurs use large amounts of fertilizer and pesticides and rely heavily upon fluorocarbon-based refrigeration. The land is being gradually poisoned, and birds are disappearing. Farmers have become part of a highly "competitive world market in fresh produce; they thus are pressured to use ever-increasing amounts of pesticides as well as fertilizers."[49] Likewise, large-scale producers at the edge of technological innovation have largely depended upon hybridization, which threatens the genetic variability of many local crops. For as long as there is a profitable market for exports, these environmental dangers are often dismissed by large and small agricultural producers alike. Commercial agriculture is represented by the established National Society of Agriculture (SNA), while some smaller and medium-sized producers articulate their interests in the Confederation of Guild Associations and Federation of Chilean Farmers, both of right-wing persuasion.

Last, but not least, three sectors are of crucial importance in the developer side. The first consists of the large Chilean financial institutions (banks and financiers) that provide the internal capital for large-scale ventures and their corporate mouthpiece, ABIF. Second, and in close collaboration with the local finance capital, there are the international private businesses— including foreign banks, joint-venture capitalists, and transnational corporations—with operations in Chile—names such as Citicorp, Aetna, Dole, The Bond Group, or the aforementioned Shell, Fletcher Challenge, and Ibn Mafuz. These groups are particularly influential with, and have direct access to, the third sector: foreign government and international organizations that participate in the financing of development projects. These include entities such as the World Bank, the IDB, and the International Finance Corporation (IFC). The previously mentioned international sector acts as an external linkage group for the "developer" alliance, giving its constituencies a distinctive transnational dimension.

The Government Framework. Government involvement in the environmental field is generally weak and fragmented. There is not a single agency dealing with environmental issues, let alone one with the capacity to act and regulate. In the intricate body of administrative law and municipal law that regulates the functioning of Chile's bureaucracy, there are very few and indirect references to environment other than the vague constitutional provisions of articles 19 and 20 of the charter: "A newly established Comisión Nacional del Medio Ambiente

(CONAMA) is only now preparing to submit comprehensive environmental legislation to Chile's Congress. Meanwhile, the government faces a formidable backlog in other critical areas. The Administration and Congress have signalled their intent to rewrite the country's forestry law and water code, establish a national energy policy, and enact a new law to protect the rights of indigenous peoples."[50]

Other pieces of legislation, such as the Fisheries Law—now passed through Congress with drastic concessions to the antiregulation forces of the right—contain some important environmental dispositions, such as the notion of common property management. Most of these initiatives, however, have encountered the relentless opposition by the forces of the ancien régime and have been stalemated. This has been made possible through a number of legalistic "tricks" in the Pinochet constitution, such as the appointment of senators, the quorums required to change basic legislation, the appointment of tenured pro-regime individuals to the constitutional tribunal, the supreme court, the comptroller's office, the boards of most parastatals, the civil service, the military, and the police. Thus, despite public opinion, the present government is tied to the old policies.

The alternatives for the constitutional government are few. It could "violate" either the transition accords or the fraudulent constitution itself, which would give the military a "legal" reason to intervene. Conversely, it could pursue a painfully slow process of negotiating and watering down more "radical" proposals, as it is currently doing. This gives the forces of deregulation and the status quo an overwhelming advantage from the start. Even should a negotiation begin, the sheer power of the "developers," not to mention their "legal" ability to stalemate and veto initiatives or to sabotage the process, gives them once again the upper hand.

In this context, the regulatory structure remains extremely weak and fragmented. There is no such thing as an "environmental management system." Rather, there are series of discrete bodies dealing with very partial aspects of environmental regulation. The most important of these is the aforementioned National Commission on the Environment (CONAMA), created in June 1990. The commission is attached to the minuscule Ministry of the National Patrimony, the least powerful of all the cabinet portfolios. It lacks personnel and finances, being staffed with six qualified experts in its Santiago headquarters. In addition, CONAMA has small "field offices" spread among the country's thirteen territorial administrative zones. It is presided over by the minister of national patrimony and managed by a commission secretary. Its mission is basically to draft the environmental legislation, or framework, for environmental regulation and management.

So far, the most "executive" of Chile's environmental offices is the Santiago Special Commission on Decontamination (CDS). The office has a territorial jurisdiction limited to the metropolitan region, the largest urban concentration in Chile. Its prime directive is to deal with the dramatic and persistent smog problem. CDS functions as both an interministerial and an intergovernmental (municipal and central) entity and has a special working relationship with the Ministry of Transport. It is vested with emergency powers to pursue an active plan to curtail carbon monoxide and particle emissions by establishing restrictions in burning, vehicle circulation, pollution control, and dust-prevention measures. Private vehicular traffic and emissions are regularly checked with some success, though it has been more difficult to deal with smokestacks and diesel contamination.

Early in 1992, the commission claimed a significant victory when one of Santiago's major bus associations started to fit new converters to its bus fleet, and trolley buses went into operation.[51] Contamination levels had been the lowest in many years.[52] However, this early optimism proved to be premature; by mid-year, pollution levels surpassed the 300 preemergency mark and approached the 500 emergency level. Acute respiratory infections nowadays constitute the highest cause of death among children under five in poor urban areas.[53]

In addition to these new agencies, there is a handful of established semiregulatory bodies with a potential influence in implementing environmental programs. One of the most important is the National Energy Commission (CNE). The agency is preparing "a national energy strategy, with assistance from the U.S. Department of Energy (DOE). As part of this strategy, CNE hopes to propose administrative and policy reforms, that would transform CNE into a true regulatory agency."[54] Another is the Directorate-General of Waters (DGA) of the Ministry of Public Works. DGA is given the authority to grant water rights to any prospective engineering work. The agency must verify that the use of the water will not affect the security of third parties or produce contamination. Yet in practice, its power is very limited. The Superintendency of Electrical and Fuel Services, the Economic Regulatory Agency, and the National Irrigation Commission, all from the Ministry of Economics, have a limited power in granting "concessions" to enterprises. Other agencies include more than 300 autonomous municipalities and the National Sewers and Sanitation Services of the Ministry of Public Works.

Two other mechanisms of an institutional nature deserve to be mentioned. One is, of course, the legislature. In theory all general normative matters fall within the jurisdiction of parliament, and it is there that the aforementioned environmental legislation is being debated. However, in a presidential system, most of the initiative in legislation rests with the executive; and the political agenda is established by the president and the cabinet, with the approval of the ruling party coalition. As party configuration changes, so do the nature of the cabinet and of the government agenda. Most pressure-group activity is directed to executive agencies, with parliamentarians playing second fiddle.

The other is the judiciary. This is a relatively novel aspect in Chile, which is unlike the countries under British common law in that courts have played a minor role, except for that of strictly dealing with conflicts between contending parties or in the field of criminal law. A most interesting case occurred in 1985. A farmer in the northern Valley of Azapa sued the Ministry of Public Works for having authorized the utilization of a natural water reservoir by the large parastatal SONAMI.[55] The challenge was supported by CODEFF, and a clever legal strategy was adopted based upon the precepts of the 1981 constitution. The Court of Appeals of Arica decided for the plaintiff. What is important in this case is that the challenge took place during the dictatorship years, under a supreme court that usually rubber-stamped all decisions from the executive, and involved a major parastatal enterprise. "The Supreme Court by verdict of 19 December 1985, confirmed the previous verdict with some declarations that complement it."[56] The confirmation was based upon constitutional grounds. As the "comment" indicates: "It is, as well, of great interest the use by Chilean law of precepts contained in international treaties which, eventually, contributed in a very important way to the judicial decision. . . . This is, without doubt, one of the most interesting verdicts dictated regarding resources of protection in the last [few] years."[57]

While this case is quite remarkable in legal terms, its overall impact on Chilean practices regarding environmental protection can be overestimated. So far, there is no such thing as "environmental judicial review": The operation of the Chilean judicial system is not like that of its Anglo-American counterpart. The courts have limited jurisdiction, applicable only to the specific case before them. Moreover, jurisprudence in Chile is only a minor source of court decisions, relevant only after an exhaustive literal interpretation of the codified legislation is undertaken. Supreme court decisions on constitutionality like the one on Chungará, are not of general and automatic application to analogous cases. Each instance requires a specific judgment.

Policy Process and Effects

In the context of Chilean bureaucratic politics, public-sector agencies often find themselves, by design or default, advocating one or the other side of the debate (and the two main alliances). In some cases, there are strong clientelistic and parentalistic ties between agencies and interest groups.[58] The policy process, though relatively fluid and not devoid of a degree of "pragmatism," does not occur on a "level playing field." The possibilities for consensus-building, cooperation, and compromise between the sides exist, providing two conditions are met. One is that the specific issue at hand does not radically challenge the neoliberal economic model. The other is that the issue discussed be either narrowly "technical" or of such dramatic magnitude (e.g., smog in Santiago, the cholera epidemic of 1991, or—more to the point—the ozone "hole" over the Antarctic region) that some declaratory agreement could occur.

Limited Bargaining and Intersectoral Cooperation. Given the heterogeneous nature of the blocs, it is also possible that some weaker actors (e.g., bus owners' associations) may agree to move away from a relentless opposition to regulation. The same could be said with regards to farmers. The opposite is also the case: "environmentalists" and their likely allies in the government becoming increasingly willing to accept the "pragmatic" and "realistic" fact that they cannot implement their agendas. The model that seems to characterize best the Chilean policy process regarding environmental issues is that of small changes in the correlations of forces, resulting from shifts in the outer rims of both the environmentalist and the developer alliances, ultimately affecting government action (or inaction). The different configurations of alliances and menus result from a combination and recombination preeminently among elites and around usually narrow issues. Popular groups, though formally represented in the alliance (e.g., natives in the case of hydro projects), have little to say as far as final decisions go. In this context, the process is exceedingly slow and frustrating. The most common policy outcome is either a nondecision or a decision resembling the status quo.

An example of intersectoral cooperation was the Fourth Scientific Conference on the Environment held in Valdivia in April 1992: a minisummit in preparation for the Rio Earth Summit. Organized by the Center for Environmental Planning and Research (CIPMA), and cosponsored by the Chilean Academy of Sciences, the Austral University of Chile, and SOFOFA, it was attended by scientists, businesspeople, nonprofit organizations, and government representatives. Five key topics were considered: renewable natural resources, ecological impact in business, environmental information, environmental preservation efforts, and national policy for sustainable development. The consensus emerged that it was necessary to move from study and denunciation to action—hardly a ground-breaking exercise.[59]

Intersectoral Conflicts. More common, however, are situations of profound disagreement. An example is the discussion of the Development and Recovery of Native Forests Law, also known as the Forestry Law. Although CODEFF played an important role in developing the proposals for the conservation of native forests, early in 1992 the environmental group asked the government to review substantial parts of the executive's draft sent to parliament for discussion in April of that year. CODEFF strongly criticized those parts of the legislation making possible the substitution of native forests for forestry plantations.[60] The committee charged that the draft appeared "to be directly dictated by the wood chip industry."[61] It proposed instead a comprehensive and sustainable management system for native forests, recommending grants in aid for their "protection and development, an immediate end to the use of native woods in the wood chip industry, greater control by the state of exploitation permits and more resources to the organizations designed to enforce these measures."[62] The committee's view was that industry should be able to develop the country without destroying its heritage.

This motivated a response by the socialist (PPD) president of the Chamber of Deputies, who had been among those most critical of the deregulatory policies of the former military regime: "The bill is of such importance that it is incumbent upon members of Parliament to find the means to reconcile the opposing positions of the Wood Corporation (CORMA) which thinks the bill goes too far, and ecologists, who feel it falls short."[63]

He called upon the parties "to find a happy medium to allow rational forest exploitation without destroying native species."[64] Heavy pressures on parliament may have been coming from the executive, via the "development" ministries of finance and economics, as well as from those in the government coalition negotiating a series of delicate balances with the right-wing opposition. This conciliatory stand was apparently timed as well with the opening of the first International Conference on the Commercialization of Forestry Products in the Pacific Basin, organized by the Forestry Department of the *Fundación Chile*. More than 100 businessmen from all over the world were meeting to create new opportunities and improve communication among their industries.[65] Environmental protection had apparently been traded off for political stability and growth. The overall attempt seems to have been geared to prevent "rocking the boat," especially at a critical time in the process of democratic consolidation, requiring business support.

Another example of the dynamics of the environmental policy process is the case of one of ENDESA's affiliates, the Pangue Dam project. It is part of the enterprise's long-term energy development strategy, which contemplates a series of dams in the Bio-Bio River—Pangue, Ralco, and Huenquecura. The initial stage of the project (Pangue) will entail flooding some 1,250 acres of land along the river banks, with a peak generating capacity of 450 MW. According to environmental studies, the effects will be devastating for an extremely fragile ecosystem, with destruction of forests and of land and river species, as well as soil erosion and the traumatic uprooting of three communities of Pehuenche Indians who see the dams as "the end of Pehuenche life."[66]

The cost of the operation is upwards of $470 million, and it is to be financed with foreign loans. One loan for $125 million is to come from the World Bank, and its feasibility is being studied by the IFC. Another loan of $50 million is to come from the IDB. There is another tied loan negotiated with the Spanish government. The approval of the World Bank loan is strategic, since it would clear the way for an international finance package.[67]

Prior to that, ENDESA obtains all the required authorizations from the pertinent agencies—the Ministry of Public Works' Directorate-General of Waters, the Ministry of Economics, and the National Energy Commission.[68]

GABB was formed in 1991, specifically to coordinate a campaign to protect the river and the populations living within its confines. The group has been extremely successful in providing public education, articulating the public interest, and establishing a wide national and international network, along the lines discussed earlier. Despite ENDESA's powerful public relations machine, which dismissed criticisms as the actions of "wealthy whitewater rafters," GABB has been able to maintain the interest on the issue and to generate a good deal of external support.

The Bio-Bio has become perhaps symbolic of a struggle to "save the planet." The tactics have also changed from the domestic—as in the case of Chungará and the Forestry Law—to the international arena. Since the ostensible weak link in the process is external finance, in particular the environmental assessment required from IFC prior to its recommendation to the World Bank, pressure by organized environmental groups in North America has been brought to bear upon both IBRD and IFC. It should be remembered that such environmental assessments of international agencies were the consequence of heavy pressure by public interest groups in Europe and North America upon the "development establishment." Thus, while formal environmental reviews and assessments are, so far, inoperative in Chile, external assessments of project financing are not. It was, however, a case of too little too late, or worse, a case of too powerful a developmental coalition against a well-organized yet outgunned environmental campaign. Despite contradictory and optimistic indications for the environmentalists, the development side was to prevail in the long run.[69]

CONCLUSION

Whatever their outcome, campaigns of this nature have a number of secondary and unintended effects. One of these is the institutionalization in Chile's governmental process of an environmental policy agenda, as well as mechanisms around which future political debates are likely to emerge. Here there have been some encouraging signs. For instance, in a speech at the International Seminar on Mining and the Environment organized by the Chilean Copper Commission, the Institute for International Studies of the University of Chile, and the International Law Institute, Mining Minister Juan Hamilton was quite blunt. He expressed the view that companies "that fail to respect environmental protection regulations" or those with poor environmental records in their own countries will not be tolerated.[70]

He indicated that his ministry was ready to implement "environmental protection measures in new mining enterprises and that in the near future CODELCO and ENAMI must present their decontamination plans for their

Chuquicamata and Ventana plants, in accordance with the Mining Ministry's Decree 185."[71] He added that a number of foreign companies have already made significant investments for controlling their impact upon the environment. The minister also expressed optimism about the possibilities of getting through parliament a legislative package "to regulate substances harmful to the ozone layer, such as the use of combustibles with high sulphur content, related to mining and industrial production."[72]

Another latent effect of environmental campaigns is the establishment of an organizational network of brokers, especially on the public interest side, which allows for learning new strategies and for advancing environmental goals. This is particularly the case with both the incorporation of "base" organizations, such as those advancing the natives' cause, and the external constituencies made up of environmental groups in industrialized countries. Until not too long ago, transnationalization had benefited large business conglomerates or the military but not popular organizations and public interest associations.

A less discussed, but equally important, consequence of bringing the environmental debate to the public is the increased salience of environmental issues among the population at large. Public attention generates an "environmental awareness" (or consciousness) in the public mind. My own assessment of the Chilean situation is that the culture is still dominated by a "predatory" attitude towards the natural environment. Conservation and environmentally friendly behavior are not highly developed. As indicated at the beginning of this chapter, modernism and the engineering mode have been hegemonic in Chilean culture. Concern for environment at the mass level—perhaps with the exception of a minuscule and vanishing Amerindian subculture—was often confused with elite snobbism: a "keep-it-green, keep-it-clean" kind of discourse. Since 1989, this has begun to change. Environment has been incorporated, as in Europe and North America, into the political menu and has become part of the normal, everyday discourse and practice. There is still a long way to go, but the qualitative nature of the change is significant. Prickett's optimistic assessment may not be too far off: "Public concern about the environment is widespread and rapidly growing. A large number of environmental organizations have formed to channel this public sentiment into action by the government and the private sector. These groups have had a number of notable victories."[73]

There is, however, another less optimistic perspective. Chile's present predicament is clearly one where environment could be easily pushed aside for economic considerations, which is currently happening. As I indicated earlier, for as long as the social construction of environment does not appear threatening and for as long as it does not involve the mobilization of popular actors who could upset the pact of elites, it will be permissible. Should it fail to remain within what the socioeconomic and military establishment define as "acceptable bounds," it could be disposed of by extreme means. After all, this menu-restructuring happened to the "old" discourse of democracy, social justice, import substitution, and the welfare state.

In addition, there are powerful regional forces that have a crucial impact upon environmental policies and more broadly speaking on human security.[74] In this sense, one needs to keep in mind the fact that Chile, like the rest of Latin America, is highly vulnerable to external pressures as far as policy formulation and implementation go. The lure of a free trade agreement between Chile and the United States,[75] modeled upon the United States–Canada and the United States–Mexico agreements (NAFTA), could either water down or enhance the current environmental agenda, depending on who is in control in Washington. The Bush administration represented a clear antienvironmentalist position at the ill-fated Rio Summit. Because of "pressure from the United States"[76] even the proposed "Agenda 21," which committed "nations to carrying out environmental protection measures, [lacked] reference to any concrete programs in terms of energy conservation and ozone layer protection."[77] In fact, the outcome of the conference surpassed some of the worst predictions, signaling the corporate world that the status quo is acceptable. To add it up, 1992 U.S. Supreme Court decisions limiting class action suits and virtually erasing the possibilities of U.S. environmental groups launching legal challenges on behalf of foreign groups has been a clear victory for environmental conservatism. Thus, the chances for effective interlinking and environmental partnership have been dealt a severe setback. Yet the election of President Clinton in 1992, as well as his administration's efforts to give priority to environmental goals, are signaling a significant departure from the previous antiregulatory record. Current environmental initiatives in Chile reflect this new international climate.

In a way, the Chilean experience is relevant to other countries in the region to the extent that its "development model" is being hailed by the international business community as the "best case" for Third World development. As suggested already, its environmental record and policy are a reflection of this development style. The latter, in turn, is conditioned by the country's modality of insertion into a global and regional political economy of development. The preceding exploration may have already shed some light into the relationships between environment and development that such "best case" really implies. As John Sheahan observed of the Chilean economic experiment before the end of the dictatorship:

Perhaps the main economic problem in Chile has not been the recourse to free markets so much as the particular monetarist model imposed on the country. This approach is **not** a helpful guide to economic policy in any country, whether Chile, England, or the United States. In democratic countries, monetarist policies are either modified in practice or drag down the economy concerned until the voters get rid of the government unwise enough to rely on them. The monetarist approach applied in Chile is inconsistent with democracy because an informed majority would reject it. . . . The main reasons it cannot win popular support are that it neither assures employment opportunities nor provides any other way to ensure that lower income groups can participate in economic growth.[78]

The problem now seems that after the dictatorship under the present restricted democracy, the economic model and its environmental corollaries have become entrenched.[79] However, the consolidation of an environmentally dysfunctional economic model is not limited to Chile, Latin America, or the two-thirds of humanity once referred to as the Third World. Developed and fully democratic countries without the traumatic political adjustments experienced by Chile appear to be caught in a similar "no-choice" predicament.

NOTES

1. Harold Lasswell, *Politics: Who Gets What When and How* (New York: McGraw Hill, 1950), passim; also David Easton, "An Approach to the Analysis of Political Systems," *World Politics* 9.3 (1957): 389–395.

2. For an elaboration of Max Weber's notion of "interpretative" analysis, see his *Theory of Social and Economic Organizations*, trans. A. M. Henderson and Talcott Parsons (Glencoe, Ill.: The Free Press, 1974), pp. 90–92.

3. Martin Staniland, *What Is Political Economy? A Study of Social Theory and Underdevelopment* (New Haven: Yale University Press, 1985), pp. 1–9.

4. Barbara Stallings, *Class Conflicts and Economic Development in Chile, 1958–1973* (Stanford: Stanford University Press, 1978), pp. 5–10, 21–23, 51–52; also J. Nef, "Development Crisis and State Crisis: Lessons from the Latin American Experience," in *Development Administration in Papua New Guinea*, ed. O. P. Dwivedi and P. Pitil (Boroko: Administrative College of New Guinea, 1991), p. 11.

5. J. Nef, "Política, administración y políticas públicas: un análisis sistémico," *Política* 28 (1991): 155–184.

6. Peter Cleaves, *Bureaucratic Politics and Administration in Chile* (Berkeley: University of California Press, 1974), passim; also Ferrell Heady, *Public Administration: A Comparative Perspective*, 3rd ed. rev. (New York: Marcel Dekker, 1984), pp. 355–356.

7. J. Nef, "Latin America: The Southern Cone," *Public Administration in the Third World*, ed. V. Subramaniam (Westport, Conn.: Greenwood Press, 1989), pp. 352–384, especially 371–373.

8. E. Bradford Burns, *Latin America: A Concise Interpretative History*, 4th ed. (Englewood Cliffs, N.J.: Prentice-Hall, 1986), pp. 161–162.

9. Among these were the French-born naturalist Claude Gay (1800–1872), author of *Physical and Political History of Chile*; the Polish chemist and geologist Ignatious Domeyko (1802–1889), who wrote the first definitive treatise on Chilean mineralogy; and his associate, the German naturalist Rudolf Armand Philippi (1809–1904), who became the founder of the National Museum.

10. Godofredo Stutzin, "A Note on Conservation and Politics," *Environmental Policy and Law* 1 (1975): 38.

11. Osvaldo Sunkel, "The Interaction between Styles of Development and the Environment in Latin America," *CEPAL Review* 12 (1980): 15–50; also Nicolo Gligo, "The Environmental Dimension in Agricultural Development in Latin America," *CEPAL Review* 12 (1980): 129–144; a more comprehensive treatment can be found in *Estilos de vida y medio ambiente en América Latina*, ed. Osvaldo Sunkel and Nicolo Gligo, vols. 1 and 2 (Mexico City: Fondo de Cultura Económica, 1980), passim; also Nicolo Gligo, "Estilos de modernización y medio ambiente en la agricultura Latinoamericana," *Estudios e informes CEPAL* 4 (Santiago: EPAL, 1981); Pablo Bifani's main work is contained in his *Desarrollo y medio ambiente*, vols. 1, 2, and 3, nos. 24, 25, and 26 of *Cuadernos del centro internacional en ciencias ambientales (CIFCA)* (Madrid: Linoexpres S.A., 1982), passim.

12. J. Nef, "Economic Liberalism and Political Repression in Chile," in *Latin American Prospects for the 1980s: Equity, Democratization, and Development*, ed. Archibald Ritter and David Pollock (New York: Praeger, 1983), pp. 314–316.

13. UNEP was established in 1973 after the Stockholm meeting of 1972. It served as a center for a series of official and NGO initiatives in Europe and the Americas. Several organizations in Europe, especially in Sweden (under the umbrella of the Dag Hammarksjold Foundation) and Spain (CIFCA, Centro Internacional de Ciencias Ambientales, established in 1975), as well as in the Netherlands, France, and the United Kingdom, among others, served as pivotal points for a network of Chilean scholars dealing with environmental issues and constituting the vast intellectual diaspora under the military regime.

14. *CEPAL Review* December 1980, where a good sample of the U.N. Economic Commission for Latin America regarding environment is displayed. The entire issue is devoted to the relationship between environment and development.

15. World Commission on Environment and Development (WCED), *Our Common Future* (New York: Oxford University Press, 1987), passim.

16. John Sheahan, *Patterns of Development in Latin America: Poverty, Repression, and Economic Strategy* (Princeton: Princeton University Press, 1987), pp. 103–110.

17. In a conversation with Osvaldo Sunkel at ECLA in 1991, he explained to me that after the military coup of 1973 many left-of-center academics, mostly economists like himself, shifted the focus to environment as a safer and more fruitful realm of permissible critical analysis, still not taken over forcefully by right-wing monetarists. In this sense, "environment" became the main venue for an alternative discourse to neoliberalism.

18. Glenn Prickett, "Partnership Opportunities to Protect Chile's Bio-Bio River," Memo from Natural Resources Defense Council to Probe International, 26 February 1992, p. 2.

19. For an assessment of environmental damage in the Eight Regions, see Patricia Tomic and Ricardo Trumper, "The Contradictions of Neo-Liberalism in Chile, 1973–1989: The Case of the Concepción Region," *Canadian Journal of Latin American and Caribbean Studies* 15.30 (1990): 233–235.

20. Ibid.

21. "Fight for Bio-Bio Wages On," *International Rivers Network* Special Briefing, December 1991: 2; also September 1991: 10; December 1990: 6; March 1992: 11.

22. An official document prepared by Chilean Brigadier General J. Mir Dupouy,

Executive Director of the Chilean Nuclear Energy Commission, *La evolución de la energía nuclear en Chile* (Santiago: Comisión Chilena de Energía Nuclear, 1985), p. 7. The text contains a most interesting chronology, especially of the crucial years of military rule.

23. Ibid., p. 9.

24. Ibid., p. 12.

25. J. Nef, "The Politics of Repression: The Social Pathology of the Chilean Military," *Latin American Perspectives* 1.2 (1974): 55–77.

26. Sunkel, "Interaction," pp. 15–49.

27. Jonathan Kandell, "Prosperity Born of Pain," *The New York Times Magazine* 7 July 1991, pp. 15–18, 33, 35.

28. Carol Graham, "A Development Strategy for Latin America?" *Brookings Review* Fall 1991, reprinted in Paul Goodwin, *Global Studies: Latin America*, 5th ed. (Guilford, Conn.: Sluice Dock, Dushkin Publishing Co., 1992), pp. 173–174.

29. Prickett, "Partnership Opportunities," p. 2.

30. An alliance that includes the centrist Christian democrats, the left-of-center socialists of various brands, the traditionally centrist and minuscule Radical party, and other miniparties, such as the Humanists and the Ecologist (Green) party won the presidency by a wide margin, with over 56 percent of the popular vote and obtained a commanding majority in the Chamber of Deputies and a simple majority in the Senate. As a result of the constitutional manipulation of the previous regime, it lacks the capacity to implement legislation past the Senate. Likewise, in other instances of decision making, such as the Constitutional Tribunal, the Comptroller's Office, the Central Bank, the National Security Council, the Telecommunications Commission, the vast senior levels of the bureaucracy, the military and police establishment (stacked with hand-picked appointees of the Pinochet regime), the elected government does not have the necessary power to rule.

31. Prickett, "Partnership Opportunities," p. 2.

32. Stutzin, "Note on Conservation," p. 38.

33. Nef, "Development Crisis," pp. 22–25.

34. For a conceptualization of "linkage groups" see Douglas Chalmers, "Developing in the Periphery: External Factors in Latin American Politics," *Contemporary Inter American Relations: A Reader in Theory and Issues*, ed. Yale Ferguson (Englewood Cliffs, N.J.: Prentice-Hall, 1972), pp. 11–16.

35. Prickett, "Partnership Opportunities," pp. 10–11.

36. CIEPLAN provided institutional support for important Christian democratic researchers and intellectuals who became President Aylwin's close associates, cabinet ministers, or advisors (such as Finance Minister Alejandro Foxley). The corporation's openly critical stands against the neoliberalism of the Pinochet regime have been quickly toned down as a neoliberal "pragmatism" has increasingly permeated the government's "economic growth policies," with which CIEPLAN has become identified.

37. Presentation by GABB and other organizations to the International Finance Corporation, 27 February 1992, p. 10. For an overview of native politics with special emphasis on the Aymaras, see María-Inés Arratia, "Khistispxtansa? Who Are We? Rethinking Aymaraness and Chileanness in the Nineties," in *Forging Identities and Patterns of Development in Latin America and the Caribbean*, ed. Harry P. Díaz et al. (Toronto: Canadian Scholars' Press, 1991), pp. 253–262.

38. In the past, the connection between the CNPC (COPROCO) and the right (conservatives, liberals, since 1965 fused into the National party) was axiomatic. Today, close contacts exist between the National Renovation party (RN), which recycled and modernized the old Liberal-Conservative and National "old guard" and the various components of the National Confederation of Production and Commerce. The same is the case between CNPC and the more ideological and corporatist Democratic Independent Union (UDI). Most empresario sectors have been supportive of the military regime, while distancing themselves from its "excesses." Pinochetismo is still very strong in these quarters.

39. For an analysis of the Chilean ruling class, see Maurice Zeitlin and Richard Earl Ratcliff, *Landlords and Capitalists: The Dominant Class of Chile* (Princeton: Princeton University Press, 1988), passim.

40. *Canadian Journal of Latin American and Caribbean Studies* 15.30 (1990): 310–311.

41. Ibid., p. 320. By law, 9 percent of all proceeds from copper exports go directly to financing the armed forces. The estimate for 1988 was U.S. $200 million. See Ruth Leger Sivard, *World Military and Social Expenditures 1987–88* (Washington, D.C.: World Priorities, 1987), p. 46.

42. Kandell, "Prosperity," p. 18.

43. Tomic and Trumper, "Contradictions," p. 230. Emphasis added.

44. Ibid.

45. Prickett, "Partnership Opportunities," p. 3.

46. H. Zavaleta, "Recent hydro development in Chile," *Water, Power & Dam Construction* December 1991, p. 22.

47. Prickett, "Partnership Opportunities," p. 1.

48. "No End in Sight to Santiago's Pollution," *La Nación* 18 June 1992.

49. Goodwin, *Latin America*, p. 67.

50. Prickett, "Partnership Opportunities," pp. 2–3. Emphasis added.

51. "Chile Buys 50 Trolleys from Russia," *La Nación* April 1992.

52. "Buses Fitted with New Filters in Santiago," and "Changes in Make up of Santiago Pollution," *El Mercurio* 25 April 1992.

53. *La Nación* 18 June 1992.

54. Prickett, "Partnership Opportunities," p. 8.

55. Humberto Palza Carvacho subsequently ran as a Christian Democrat and was elected to Congress as a Deputy in 1989.

56. Supreme Court, trans. copy of verdict, 19 December 1985: 252–257.

57. "Comments" to the verdict, pp. 252–257.

58. Joseph La Palombara, *Interest Groups in Italian Politics* (Princeton: Princeton University Press, 1964), passim.

59. "CODEFF Criticizes Government Proposals," "Native Forest Parties Must Come to Terms," "Natural Environment Mini-Summit Opens," *La Nación* 25 April 1992.

60. Ibid.

61. Ibid.

62. Ibid.

63. Ibid.

64. Ibid.

65. Ibid.

66. "World Bank Loan to Private Sector Spells Doom for Famed Chilean River, Pehuenche People," *Probe International* April 1992, p. 1.

67. "Six Dams Threaten Chilean River," *International Rivers Network* Special Report: The Bio-Bio: A River in Peril, December 1990, p. 3.

68. Susana Kunkar, "Represas en Alto Bio-Bio. 'Si el rio suena . . . '," *Análisis* 1–7 July 1991, p. 16.

69. "World Bank to Take Decision on Pangue in Next 60 Days," *El Diario* 25 April 1992.

70. "Chile Will Not Harbour Companies That Harm Environment," *La Época* 25 April 1992.

71. Ibid.

72. Ibid.

73. Prickett, "Partnership Opportunities," p. 3.

74. "Governability, Governance and Human Security: A Framework for Comparison," paper presented to the First Workshop on the Impact of International Adjustment on the Caribbean Basin Countries, AVANCSO/CELA, Tlaxcala, Mexico, 14–17 May 1992, passim.

75. "Possibility of Free Trade Agreement with the United States," *El Mercurio* 25 April 1992.

76. "Greenpeace Criticizes U.N. Earth Letter," *La Época* 13 April 1992.

77. Ibid.

78. Sheahan, *Patterns of Development*, p. 234. Emphasis added in third line.

79. J. Nef and H. Bensabat, "'Governability' and the Receiver State in Latin America: Analysis and Prospects," in *Latin America to the Year 2000: Reactivating Growth, Improving Equity, Sustaining Democracy*, ed. Archibald Ritter, Maxwell Cameron, and David Pollock (New York: Praeger, 1992), pp. 161-176; also J. Nef and N. Galleguillos, "Chile: Redemocratization or the Entrenchment of Counter-revolution," in idem, pp. 177–193.

National Environmental Policy and Programs in Mexico

MARÍA EMILIA JANETTI-DÍAZ,
JOSÉ MARIO HERNÁNDEZ-QUEZADA, AND
CHADWICK BENJAMIN DeWAARD

Ecological balance and environmental protection are among the most critical issues on the agenda of the world community. These issues have a tremendous impact at the regional and local levels and demand urgent policy responses from national governments. Mexico is no exception to this general trend.

By 1989, after almost 50 years of rapid industrialization, Mexico ranked in the top one-third of the economies in the world.[1] This "economic miracle" came at a high environmental cost. Indeed, Mexico now faces an environmental crisis of significant proportions, including a virtual environmental wasteland along the United States–Mexico border, severe air pollution in Mexico City, and the extermination of various plant and animal species. To counter this crisis, over the last few years, Mexico has designed an aggressive environmental policy that aims at achieving sustainable development and economic and social modernization by protecting its natural resources. Such an approach was advocated and strongly supported by Mexico at the 1992 Earth Summit held in Rio de Janeiro.[2] Like many other countries, Mexico faces difficulties in implementing these policies.

In this chapter, the authors analyze some of the most important elements of the National Policy on Ecology and the Environment pursued by the government of President Carlos Salinas de Gortari, discuss progress made in specific areas of that policy, identify relevant issues yet to be dealt with, and review Mexico's recent environmental record.

Environmental degradation in Mexico had several causes. Among the most important was the import-substitution model of development pursued from the mid-1930s until the foreign debt crisis of 1982. This model was based on a protectionist foreign trade policy and government support for the national private sector through the expansion of infrastructure, cheap energy supply, mass consumption stimuli, low tax rates, and an agricultural policy primarily intended to support industrialization. This development strategy was mainly directed at the achievement of quantitative growth; and until 1981 Mexico's economy grew at a spectacular rate, recording a 6 percent annual increase in the nation's GNP.[3] It facilitated the concentration of industry in a few metropolitan areas, especially Mexico City, and failed to take into account the ecological externalities and costs associated with the import-substitution industrialization model.

Second, as a consequence of this development strategy, inadequate attention was given to the agricultural sector; this contributed to the explosive growth of urban areas through massive migration and to the overexploitation of limited natural resources in rural areas by people facing extreme poverty. The third element was the state-subsidized consumption of natural resources (water, electricity, gas, and petroleum). The state subsidization of natural resources was expanded in the 1970s to give a strong stimulus to the consumption of these resources by the urban upper and middle classes.

Finally, there was an absence in the past of a coherent and systematic public policy regarding environmental protection and ecological balance. For most of the 1950s and 1960s, environmental concerns were largely ignored by public policy. However, environmental issues became a growing concern in government spheres in the late 1960s. They acquired more relevance in the 1970s, and showed a dramatic increase in the 1980s.

In 1981–1982, the Mexican economy, protected from serious competition and lacking substantial internal and external investment, collapsed. Faced with a deep economic crisis and very serious environmental problems, President Miguel de la Madrid-Hurtado (1982–1988) initiated structural changes in the Mexican economy, government, and society. He would be the first Mexican president to give greater national priority to environmental issues.[4] Environmental legislation, however, preceded de la Madrid's presidency.

The first Mexican environmental law, the Federal Law to Prevent and Control Environmental Pollution, was issued in 1971 by President Luis Echeverría-Alvarez (1970–1976). It had several provisions regarding air, water, and land pollution. The Secretariat of Health and Assistance (now the Secretariat of

Health) was made responsible for its implementation. Because of the lack of clearly defined functions and responsibilities among government units, as well as the lack of sufficient financial resources, the ecological policy at that time concentrated on the propagation of regulations and norms. Environmental policy tended to be viewed largely from a health perspective.

In 1982 President José López-Portillo (1976–1982) issued the second environmental law, the Federal Law of Environmental Protection. This law included specific provisions regarding animal, plant, land, and ocean protection, as well as several preventive measures to protect the environment, such as an environmental impact evaluation of public and private work projects.

In 1983, President de la Madrid-Hurtado created the Secretariat of Urban Development and Ecology (SEDUE) to demonstrate the environmental concerns of his administration. Henceforth, all environmental policymaking responsibilities were transferred from the health sector to SEDUE. For the first time in Mexican history, environmental policy was accorded cabinet level status, and environmental issues were explicitly incorporated into de la Madrid's National Development Plan 1983–1988. In 1984 an amendment to the Federal Law of Environmental Protection introduced the ecological ordering of the national territory as one of the more important aspects of environmental policy. In March 1988, the General Law of Ecological Balance and Environmental Protection (GLEBEP) replaced the previous law. Since its approval, the GLEBEP has been the main force in the national environmental policy.

By the time Carlos Salinas de Gortari assumed the presidency in 1988, Mexico was faced with unprecedented economic and social crises. A huge foreign debt was threatening to erode not only Mexico's international image and credibility but also its domestic stability. The Salinas administration realized that a new economic and trade relationship with the United States and Canada was crucial in order to revitalize Mexico's ailing economy. Such a relationship appeared unlikely without Mexican environmental reform.[5] Indeed, Salinas was fully aware that no American administration could override the environmentally conscious American public opinion unless Mexico demonstrated a strong commitment to reverse its ecological degradation. The future of the North American Free Trade Agreement (NAFTA) was tied to such a commitment.

As a result of this situation, Salinas introduced an accelerated modernization process in government and economy.[6] A crucial aspect of his modernization and development strategy is the National Policy on Ecology and the Environment. Salinas has adopted a leading role in the reversal of environmental degradation. His increased environmental sensitivity is due not only to pressure from abroad but also to domestic pressure. Environmental protection has become a real political issue. In Mexico City, voters placed the environment second or third on a list of "public concerns" in a 1987 poll.[7] The National Policy on Ecology and the Environment spells out Salinas's strategy of modernization and ecological development. The following section briefly outlines the more salient features of this policy.

THE NATIONAL POLICY ON ECOLOGY
AND THE ENVIRONMENT

Policy Principles

The National Policy on Ecology and the Environment is based on the principle that ecosystems are the common property of all Mexicans.[8] The policy stresses that environmental protection must be based on the concerted efforts of individuals, groups, social organizations, and government. It also emphasizes that the relationship between society and nature must be redefined so that the common good of the environment dominates any alleged right of private property. Thus, the "polluters pay" principle should be applied. In the international context, it is argued that activities carried out on Mexican territory should not affect the ecological balance of other nations and vice versa. Finally, the policy reaffirms the Mexican government's commitment to the reestablishment and preservation of the ecological balance in regional and global ecosystems.

Policy Objectives

Based on these principles, the National Policy on Ecology and the Environment aims to achieve the general objective: The planning and execution of government actions and of all new projects shall require that natural resources are a strategic asset for national sovereignty and an essential reserve for future generations.

The National Program for the Protection of the Environment aims to harmonize economic growth with the preservation of environmental quality while advocating the conservation and rational use of natural resources. It is recognized, however, that because ecological problems are of a structural nature, their solutions cannot be immediate. Consequently, the initial goals of the environmental policy are corrective actions to reverse the most critical areas of environmental impairment in the main cities and ecological areas. It is hoped that these long-term preventive activities will be environmentally compatible and contribute to socioeconomic growth.[9]

Legal Framework

The Political Constitution of Mexico provides the constitutional basis for the GLEBEP. Article 25 includes provisions regarding the productive use and care of natural resources and the environment. Article 27 provides for the conservation of natural resources, and Article 73 establishes norms for the prevention and control of environmental pollution. The GLEBEP has a wide perspective on environmental protection and ecological balance and defines the criteria for decentralization by establishing a mechanism for the active involvement of the three levels of government (federal, state, and municipal) on environmental matters. It is an important legal basis for the national policy on the environment that provides guidance and authority to government structures for the planning, execution, and coordination of policy design and implementation in this matter. The law clearly delineates areas of responsibility and the attributes of each of the government agencies involved in the policy.

The GLEBEP promotes the decentralization of functions and resources for the management of the national environmental policy. It endows states and municipalities with the authority to prevent and control environmental and water pollution (especially the water used for human consumption in local communities); to prevent and control pollution caused by noise, thermal energy, vibrations, smells, and lights; to create state or municipal ecological reserves; to introduce, and make mandatory, environmental impact evaluation systems; and to impose fines and sanctions when local regulations are violated. All these regulations provide local government with the means to become proactive agents in the formulation, implementation, and evaluation of environmental policy at the local level.

As discussed earlier, the guiding principle of the GLEBEP is to achieve sustainable development through the use of immediate instruments, such as ecological ordering of the territory and environmental impact evaluations. It also sets technical ecological standards as instruments of environmental policy. By 1990 there were already 50 technical standards in operation, clearly specifying the maximum permissible limits for emission and discharge of pollutants and procedures and specifications regarding water, air, and land pollution. In 1988 regulations pertaining to environmental impact, prevention, and control of atmospheric pollution generated by motor vehicles in Mexico City and its vicinity were implemented.

In brief, the GLEBEP represents a conceptual shift in environmental policy. It implies the substitution of a sectoral perspective of government actions for better defined and more efficient forms of coordination of government initiatives. It also implies the substitution of highly centralized decision making and implementation processes for decentralized mechanisms of cooperation among federal, state, and municipal governments, as well as the introduction of the principle of coresponsibility between government and society in the solution of the environmental problems facing the nation.

Public participation in environmental policy is another aspect stressed by the law. The GLEBEP includes special provisions to induce public participation and makes it mandatory for government organizations to seek and reach consensus and concerted initiatives between government and society.

Despite the efforts of the GLEBEP, much has yet to be done. It is necessary to consolidate the legal framework on ecological balance and environmental protection by issuing additional regulations specifying all subjects covered by GLEBEP. In addition, more technical standards are needed to enhance control over activities that could damage the environment. Similarly, all ecology-related legal dispositions should be analyzed. For example, the new Forest Law and the Federal Fishing Law contain norms aimed at the protection, preservation, and rational use of those same natural resources. In addition, the Hunting Law, the Federal Oceans Law, the General Human Settlements Law, the Rural Development Law, and the Public Works Law, among others, have been reviewed to include ecological aspects in their provisions.

As of 1993, 29 of the 31 states and the Federal District have already passed their own environmental laws.[10] To further decentralize environmental policy, all municipalities must also have legislation on environmental matters and direct sufficient funds for their application. The inclusion of explicit environmental criteria within municipal development programs is imperative, as well as the precise definition of environmental actions that each entity—municipalities, states, and federations—must undertake to consolidate a municipal environmental management system (MEMS). This system will provide municipalities with the necessary elements to efficiently manage and operate their own environmental protection and natural resources preservation programs, as an important part of their municipal urban development plans.

A MEMS attempts to tackle municipal environmental problems and again attaches great importance to private-, social-, and public-sector partnership initiatives. The system operates at three functional levels: establishment of norms, implementation, and vigilance and control. Municipal environmental management is a new responsibility of the municipalities that complements the general process of municipal empowerment initiated by the municipal reform of 1983. To meet their new responsibilities and thereby become active agents of change in the promotion of an environmentally planned development in their communities, the municipalities require sufficient political and economic resources.

A MEMS allows local public officials to identify the most critical environmental problems facing a local community. Local commissions scrutinize the implications of federal and state legislation for local environmental management and attempt to define the policy areas of exclusive competence of municipal governments. The implementation of this system at the local level requires an administrative reorganization of the municipal governments, as well as the training of public personnel at the local level and the reform and updating of municipal legislation.

To operationalize this municipal system, municipalities have three main options: (1) to establish a commission headed by the members of the municipal council, which reports to the full municipal council on progress made in the implementation of the system; (2) to establish a municipal commission chaired by one municipal counselor or the municipal president (equivalent to a mayor) and composed of the relevant public officials of the municipal government; (3) to establish an administrative commission composed of the relevant public officials of the municipal government, presided over by one of these officials or the municipal president and supervised by one counselor. It is worth noting that the proceedings of these commissions are open to the public, encouraging the participation of ordinary citizens. Furthermore, the system establishes "ecological councils of citizens' participation," which are civil associations independent of both the municipal government and the commissions. The councils are composed of diverse members of the local community and provide for greater public participation.

To implement their policies regarding environmental protection, municipalities have the right to choose the institutional design best suited to meet their needs. However, a common organizational scheme proposed by the MEMS stipulates the following:

1. Decision making should be conducted by a municipal environmental commission or council presided over by the municipal president and composed of all relevant municipal public officials involved in areas such as the utilization of natural resources or in activities that may have an impact on the environment. The municipal directors of public works and rural and urban development are normally part of this commission.

2. At the policy formulation level, a technical secretariat, which is integrated in a multidisciplinary fashion, formulates municipal environmental programs and projects; reviews federal and state legislation to delineate distinct areas of responsibility; updates and designs municipal legislation concerning the environment; coordinates municipal activities; and when necessary, formally requests federal and state assistance.

3. At the implementation level, all operative units of the municipal government that were assigned particular functions by the technical secretariat participate in implementation. At this level there is an "environmental protection unit" that executes specific functions, such as surveillance, inspection, and processing of complaints made by individuals and organized social groups.

4. Vigilance and control are performed by the counselor who is responsible for all ecology-related functions. This member of the municipal council is capable of initiating and proposing new legislation based on the analysis of performance made by the technical secretariat.

A MEMS allows municipal governments to identify the environmental problems of the local communities; to design and formulate a municipal environmental protection program; to determine the instruments for municipal environmental management (which may include ecological ordering, environmental impact evaluation, inspection and surveillance, integral administration of resources, and protection measures for natural regions and wild flora and fauna); to reach consensus with different social groups; to reform and update municipal legislation to include environmental issues; to design intermunicipal programs with neighboring municipalities facing similar environmental problems; to collaborate with federal and state governments for the implementation of policies at the local level; and finally, to attend to environmental emergencies or contingencies, such as industrial accidents and forest fires.[11]

Institutional Design

The Secretariat of Social Development (SEDESOL), Mexico's equivalent of the U.S. Environmental Protection Agency, is the federal secretariat responsible for the design, implementation, and evaluation of national environmental policy. Created in 1992 by President Salinas, it replaced SEDUE. SEDESOL is composed of the undersecretaries of regional development, urban development and infrastructure, and housing and public properties.[12] To implement its policies, SEDESOL has created two agencies with a substantial degree of technical and operative autonomy: the National Institute of Ecology (NIE), with the authority for the planning and issuing of norms and research, and the Federal Attorney's Office for Environmental Protection (FAOEP), with special powers to ensure that environmental laws are enforced for surveillance and for public participation.[13]

Headed by a president chosen by the president of the republic in consultation with the secretary of SEDESOL, NIE has four general directorates: ecological planning, environmental norms, ecological use of natural resources, and research and technological development. NIE has the authority to formulate, propose, direct, and evaluate the national policy on ecology and the environment. It dictates the norms and criteria for the general ecological ordering of the territory; promotes the decentralization of ecological management to states and municipal governments; formulates programs, technical norms, measures, criteria, and technical procedures to preserve and protect the environment; elaborates and updates a national inventory of sources of pollution; operates a monitoring network of air pollution in Mexico City's metropolitan area; implements, reviews, and considers decisions on environmental impact evaluations made of public and private work projects; issues permits, concessions, and licenses regarding prevention and control of environmental pollution; establishes ecological technical norms and criteria to regulate high-risk activities; evaluates and considers decisions on environmental-risk studies; formulates, implements, and evaluates programs and norms regarding the conservation and rational use of natural resources; performs and promotes research projects and technological development applicable to the ecological use of natural resources; and proposes to the Secretariat of Education the inclusion of ecological issues in the curriculum of schools, especially at the basic levels.

Headed by a federal attorney nominated by the president of the republic in consultation with the secretary of SEDESOL, FAOEP is composed of three underattorney units: social participation and complaints, environmental auditing, and norms and verification. FAOEP is further divided into eight administrative units, in addition to field offices in all the federal states. Among other responsibilities, FAOEP formulates the criteria for social participation and coresponsibility in environmental initiatives; promotes citizen participation; promotes the creation of an ecological awareness in society; promotes consensual and concerted actions among the private, social, and public sectors; provides advisory services to organized social groups; designs and operates a system of public complaints; runs and updates a directory of private professionals and firms dedicated to environmental auditing; provides fiscal incentives for the prevention and control of environmental pollution; designs and practices environmental auditing and surveillance activities; and evaluates damages made by violators of the environmental laws. FAOEP acts as an ecological ombudsman open to the demands, complaints, and suggestions of the general public and organized social groups.

It is widely accepted, even by radical environmental groups, that the general legal framework for environmental protection is one of the most advanced and developed in the world. However, the general public, as well as government officials, are concerned with the practical implementation of the legal framework. Both administrative units, the National Institute of Ecology and the Federal Attorney's Office for Environmental Protection, were especially designed to put the legal framework into practice.[14]

POLICY ACTIONS

Several policy actions taken by the Mexican government cover the whole range of areas related to ecological balance and environmental protection. They include natural resources (land, water, forest, oceans, islands and their resources, nonrenewable natural resources, wild fauna and flora, and protected natural areas), environmental quality, environmental promotion and public participation, and international cooperation on ecology and environment, among others.[15]

The following discussion focuses on the policies concerning biodiversity, air quality (with special attention given to Mexico City's metropolitan area), forestry, public participation, international cooperation, and the likely impact on the environment of the North American Free Trade Agreement.

Biodiversity

Mexico's geographical position—between two biogeographical regions—provides the country with vast biological diversity.[16] The different ecosystems of the land are home to one of the largest inventories of biological diversity in the world. Mexico and Brazil combined have between 60 percent and 70 percent of the world's biodiversity. In addition, Mexico is rich in endemic plant and animal species. The main threats to this biodiversity come from changes in land use (40 percent of the country may still be considered a natural habitat), pollution of the ecosystem, and illegal traffic in species.

Mexico's preservation strategy includes the strengthening of the present legal framework; consolidation of the National System for Protected Natural Areas; creation of the National Zoo and Breeding House Network and the Botanical Garden and Nursery Network; support of private organizations in the diffusion of knowledge and public awareness on coresponsibility for the protection of biodiversity; publication of the list of endangered species in the official journal of the federation; administrative coordination between the general attorney's office and SEDESOL for the prosecution and prevention of ecological crimes; support of scientific research; and finally, greater inspection and surveillance.[17]

An innovative instrument of the conservationist policy is the exchange of public debt for ecology investment (i.e., "ecological swaps"). This has included the creation of information centers and databases at the National Autonomous University of Mexico (UNAM), the Natural History Institute of Chiapas, and the Research Center of Guaymas, Sonora, as well as specific activities that support research projects on biological diversity of the Lacandon Rain Forest and the islands of the Gulf of California. The sponsors of these projects include Conservation International.

Air Quality

An analysis of environmental problems in Mexico shows a distinct relation between pollution, mountain geography, the size and dynamics of human settlements, and economic growth. Pressure generated by demographic and industrial concentration, combined with the previous lacunae in integral planning for the use of land and its resources, have produced an environmentally unbalanced development. Atmospheric pollution is one consequence of this development although it should be stated that over 60 percent of the country's population reside in places located at more than 500 meters above sea level, where environmental conditions are less favorable anyhow. It is worth noting that three sections of the country produce 40 percent of the atmospheric emissions—the metropolitan areas of the cities of Mexico, Guadalajara, and Monterrey.

Mexico City's Metropolitan Area (MCMA)

Air pollution in this zone is mainly caused by the high demographic, urban, and industrial concentration (the largest in the country), the growing use of motor vehicles, and the existence of large eroded areas and seasonal farmlands, as well as excessive energy demand. It is important to consider that the MCMA extends for more than 1,200 kilometers, houses more than 16 million people (18 percent of the total population) who generate over 36 percent of the country's gross national product and consume 17 percent of the nation's production of energy. An estimated 12,000 service establishments that use combustion and incineration processes operate in the MCMA, and there are 3.3 million motor vehicles in the streets, as well as 30,000 industries. In addition to an estimated 43 million liters of fuel consumed daily, 12,000 tons of pollutants are emitted.[18]

The thermoelectric plants of Jorge Luque and Valle de Mexico combined produce more than 9 percent of the total industrial, commercial, and service-related emission of pollutants. Production, storage, and distribution of fuels generate around 14 percent of the pollution from stationary sources, while motor vehicle pollution represents 76 percent of the total atmospheric emissions in Mexico City (see Table 9.1).

Thermal inversion is one of the elements that most directly contributes to the accumulation of atmospheric pollutants. Thermal inversions occur almost every day throughout the winter in the MCMA. Moreover, during the winter, meteorological phenomena further increase the concentration of pollutants. The presence of high pressure systems limits pollution dispersion.[19] The main pollutants in the MCMA are carbon monoxide, sulphur dioxide, nitrogen oxides, ozone, suspended particles, and lead. The standards by which these pollutants are measured were established by the health sector through a decree published on November 29, 1992.

In order to evaluate air quality in the MCMA, a system of monitoring stations has been implemented: the Automatic Network for Atmospheric Monitoring (ANAM) and the Manual Atmospheric Monitoring Network (MAMN). ANAM's 32 stations evaluate seven pollutants and four meteorological parameters. MAMN's 19 stations evaluate total suspended particles, breathable suspended particles, SO_4, NO_3, and heavy metals (lead, cadmium, copper, zinc, and nickel).

Since 1986, SEDESOL has published the Metropolitan Index of the Quality of Air (IMECA) daily to provide information on the levels of pollution in the five metropolitan zones of the MCMA (Northeast, Northwest, Central, Southeast, and Southwest). An environmental contingency program has also been applied on several occasions since 1987. This program foresees critical situations for all pollutants and seeks to reduce the emission from sources of ozone, thus reducing these pollutants' concentration in the short term (see Figure 9.1).

On the basis of information gathered on the main causes and processes that affect atmospheric conditions, several programs have been implemented at sectoral and interinstitutional levels. These include the creation of a regulatory framework for the motor vehicle emission verification programs, implementation of the no driving program in the MCMA, compulsory use of the most advanced and accessible

Table 9.1
Inventory of Emissions, 1989 (Percentages)

Sector	Sources	SO_2	NO_x
Energy	PEMEX	7.2	1.8
	Thermoelectric Plants	28.3	3.7
Industry and Services	Industry	32.0	16.3
	Trade	10.7	2.2
Transport	Automobiles:		
	Private	1.7	23.7
	Taxis	0.4	5.4
	Minivans and Minibuses	0.4	5.7
	R-100	2.5	4.5
	Cargo trucks:		
	State of Mexico	6.3	10.3
	Gasoline Trucks	0.5	9.6
	Diesel Trucks	9.8	14.7
	Others	0.1	1.5
Ecological Impairment	Eroded Areas	0.0	0.0
	Fires and Other Processes	0.1	0.5
	Total	100.0	100.0
	Total (Tons/Year)	205,725	177,339

Source: Mexico Technical Intergovernmental Secretary, *Integral Program against Atmospheric Pollution*, October 1990.

HC	CO	TSP	Total
5.5	1.8	0.3	2.4
0.0	0.0	0.8	1.6
7.0	0.5	2.3	3.7
0.0	0.0	0.5	0.7
24.7	45.0	1.0	34.9
5.6	10.2	0.2	7.9
7.5	13.7	0.2	10.5
0.4	0.2	0.1	0.5
0.9	0.4	0.1	1.1
11.9	26.4	0.3	19.9
1.3	0.6	0.2	1.6
0.3	0.2	0.0	0.2
0.0	0.0	93.1	9.6
34.9	0.9	0.9	5.3
100.0	100.0	100.0	100.0
572,101	2,950,627	450,599	4,356,391

Figure 9.1
Environmental Contingencies Plan

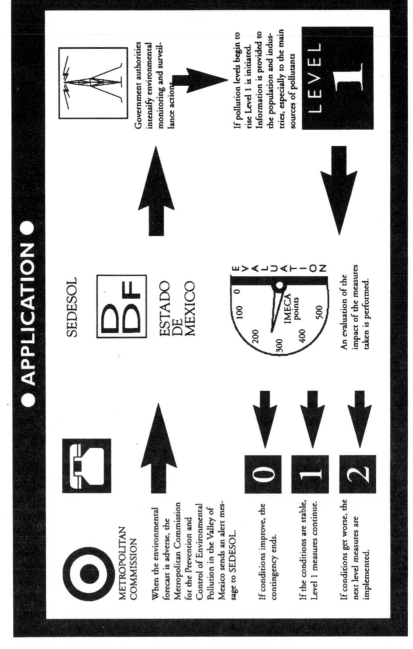

● APPLICATION ●

METROPOLITAN COMMISSION

When the environmental forecast is adverse, the Metropolitan Commission for the Prevention and Control of Environmental Pollution in the Valley of Mexico sends an alert message to SEDESOL.

If conditions improve, the contingency ends.

If the conditions are stable, Level 1 measures continue.

If conditions get worse, the next level measures are implemented.

0
1
2

SEDESOL

DF

ESTADO DE MEXICO

EVALUATION

IMECA points

An evaluation of the impact of the measures taken is performed.

Government authorities intensify environmental monitoring and surveillance actions

If pollution levels begin to rise Level 1 is initiated. Information is provided to the population and industries, especially to the main sources of pollutants

LEVEL 1

Source: Mexico, Comisión Metropolitana para la Prevención y Control de la Contaminación Ambiental en el Valle de México: *¿ Qué estamos haciendo para combatir la contaminación en al Valle de México?* Mexico City, The Commission, 1992, pp. 18–19.

technology for the control of emissions by new automobiles, improvement of gasoline and its combustion by adding oxygenated compounds like methyl-therbutylic ether, total substitution of natural gas for heavy fuels in the two main thermoelectric plants, implementation of the program for the control of vapor emission in PEMEX storage tanks and distribution vehicles, the signing of 118 agreements with industry for the installation of control devices for nitrogen oxide emission, and the investment of $4 billion for the improvement of air quality.[20]

Forestry

Mexico's geography provides favorable conditions for the existence of a great deal of plant diversity, considered to be one of the richest in the world. One of the most critical environmental problems facing the country is deforestation. Lacking reliable data, it is difficult to evaluate the magnitude of the problem. However, figures given by the Secretariat of Agriculture and Water Resources (SARH) indicate that 9.1 percent of the national territory has been damaged. In an effort to solve this problem, there are nationwide reforestation programs going on; and at the same time, there is better regulation and surveillance of forest resources. However, reforestation is currently proceeding at a rate between 25,000 and 99,000 hectares per year, while deforestation proceeds at 1.5 million hectares per year.[21]

PUBLIC PARTICIPATION

Whether environmental concerns are expressed by private citizens or NGOs, awareness, sensitivity, and general public participation in environmental issues are vital elements of genuine and successful environmental reform. Peter M. Emerson, senior economist of the Environmental Defense Fund, and Justine Ward, senior resource specialist of the Natural Resources Defense Council, both testified at the congressional hearing before the subcommittee on international trade of the Committee on Finance that public participation is a way in which to improve the enforcement of environmental laws in Mexico, which has in the past been viewed as lax.[22] President Salinas remarked that "there is no way to solve the environmental challenges without social participation. It is not only a government responsibility, which it is, but it also requires a very strong social participation."[23] Furthermore, Salinas stated that he considered a citizen's role in monitoring environmental laws a "must."

A positive interaction between society and the environment is one of the fundamentals in facing the national challenges related to environmental protection. Such interaction emphasizes adequate utilization of natural resources, improvement of the quality of education by including environmental topics in the curriculum of the national education system, and involving society in activities for the protection and fostering of natural resources. In addition, several projects to promote public participation have been devised: ecological fostering, the improvement of ecosystems, public complaints, and environmental education.

The Role of Nongovernmental Organizations

Essential to the enforcement of environmental laws are NGOs. Since the 1980s, a significant number of NGOs have emerged. Nongovernmental actors have become involved in, among others, citizen initiatives, self-help groups, and private research and consultancy institutes. These groups seek to exert substantial pressure on the federal government to initiate or intensify actions related to environmental protection, to design and execute their own projects, and to contribute—through information dissemination and public denunciations and scrutiny—to the development and fostering of an environmentally sensitive public awareness.[24]

In 1991, the Secretariat of Urban Development and Ecology (now SEDESOL) published a directory of 216 NGOs. In 1992, the National Institute of Ecology published an updated version of that directory, called the "green directory." A total of 510 NGOs are recorded there covering all 31 federal states and the Federal District.[25]

The potential role of these volunteer organizations was recognized during the devastating 1985 earthquake in Mexico City. Though the government handled the crisis in an inept fashion, several NGOs responded quickly and efficiently in aiding quake victims. This effort raised their credibility and profile in the eyes of the general public. The rapid development and multiplication of environmental NGOs in the last few years resulted mainly from the growing national awareness of environmental issues and increasing social participation in environmental protection initiatives. These NGOs cover a wide variety of areas, including ecological promotion, conservation activities, environmental education and research, surveillance of polluting industries, promotion and diffusion of environmental education, advisory services, protection of animal and plant species in danger of extinction, protection of biological diversity, environmental protection training, training in the use of ecology-friendly technologies, and promotion of community participation.

The nature, composition, and scope of Mexico's NGOs are quite diverse. A few of them have received national recognition and influence and have even established contacts with international NGOs. However, most of the Mexican NGOs are small groups with few resources and little training, and their influence is limited to their local communities. Many lack maturity, sound internal organization, financing, and adequately trained personnel. In addition, many are unstable in the sense that their work and existence depends upon the efforts and presence of a few leaders, and their success in promoting public participation is still limited. They have not been able to promote wide and extensive participation of even those social groups that are directly affected by environmental deterioration, neither have they been able to train these people to resolve their problems independently. However, they have achieved media coverage for some of their activities and thereby gained the attention of public opinion. Their professionalization, specialization, and self-financing are essential prerequisites to increasing their political and social importance.[26]

It is noted earlier that environmental degradation has become a potent domestic political issue in Mexico. Nowhere is this more evident than in the recent appearance of official Mexican environmental groups like the Movimiento Ecologista Mexicano, the Pacto de Ecologistas, and the Alianza Ecologista. Equally significant has been the creation of the Partido Ecologista de México, Mexico's green party. Although these fledgling organizations are relatively weak, they perform the important functions of keeping the environmental movement a public concern and holding government organizations responsible for actions that affect the environment.

INTERNATIONAL COOPERATION ON ECOLOGY AND THE ENVIRONMENT

Mexico has been an active international player in environmental issues. It accepts its international responsibility for environmental protection in the international arena to achieve sustainable development. The government asserts that the solution to environmental problems requires international cooperation based on the principles of sovereignty, equity, and equal responsibility among nations. Mexico has signed several international agreements with different agencies of the United Nations, as well as other international organizations. By November 1991, Mexico had signed 48 international environment agreements, including the Vienna Convention for the Protection of the Ozone Layer, the Montreal Protocol on Substances that Diminish the Ozone Layer, and the Intergovernmental Panel for Climate Change. In addition to these international activities, Mexico has signed several bilateral agreements for scientific and technological cooperation.

Financially, Mexico has benefited from several international credits specifically dedicated to the protection of the environment, such as those provided by the Inter-American Development Bank. In addition to the credits from banks for international development, there are several private transactions involving international commercial banks and coinvestment between Mexican and foreign private firms for the development of nonpolluting technology. In the case of Mexico City, there have been agreements with both the Japanese Overseas Fund and the World Bank. The latter has authorized credits to fund several environmental projects, such as the improvement of solid waste disposal in several cities of the country, the sustainable use of forest resources in various states, the implementation of projects to produce drinkable water and sewage-disposal projects at the "Lazaro Cardenas" Industrial Port, and the improvement of urban transport.

Mexico's Position in the Earth Summit

Mexico actively participated in the United Nations Conference on the Environment and Development held in Rio de Janeiro in June 1992. In Rio, President Salinas pledged Mexico's support of sustainable development as an approach to providing a better quality of life to present and future generations. He described sustainable development as a kind of development that is open to financial, technological, and commercial interchange between nations. Salinas warned that ecological issues and concerns should not be used as an excuse for protectionist practices and interventionist policies, mainly by developed countries, to harm the national sovereignty of states. Mexico expressed its will to protect the environment and, at the same time, to promote respect of national sovereignty and international cooperation.[27]

On behalf of the Latin American and Caribbean countries, Salinas demanded free access, in a competitive environment, for the products of these nations to the markets of other countries, to renegotiate their foreign debt, to have open access to green and clean technologies, and to accelerate the integration of this region. He further emphasized that it is not only foreign aid that these nations need. What they needed was a more open access to the great markets of the industrialized countries, as well as free trade practices and a just distribution of the flow of financial resources.[28] Mexico warned that although international awareness of global environmental issues had increased, it was important to concentrate international attention on the implementation of policies at the global, regional, and national levels to achieve sustainable development.

Three other factors were stressed by the Mexican delegation to the summit: that global environmental problems must be linked to the discussion and analysis of poverty and development, that adequate levels of environmental quality should be accompanied by fair levels of resource and wealth distribution between North and South, and that the concept of sustainable development must be complemented by the concept of global development.[29]

THE ENVIRONMENTAL IMPACT OF NAFTA

The North American Free Trade Agreement is a key element of the national strategy for the economic modernization of Mexico. It is hoped that NAFTA will create more permanent, well-paid jobs in the United States, Canada, and Mexico. As a vital element of the social and economic policy of the Salinas administration, NAFTA is also expected to contribute to the achievement of sustainable economic development, the main priority of the National Development Plan 1989–1994, and to facilitate Mexico's ultimate transition to democracy.[30]

NAFTA went into effect on January 1, 1994, despite considerable opposition in the United States—most notably from trade unions, consumer groups, the right wing, and environmental groups—and its seemingly fatal stalling in the summer of 1993 by a U.S. federal court ruling requiring an environmental impact assessment to be completed before Congress decided its fate.[31]

NAFTA was approved by the U.S. House of Representatives on November 17, 1993, by a vote of 234 to 200, an unexpectedly wide margin, making most of North America the world's largest free trade zone.[32] The House's decision paved the way for its subsequent approval in the U.S. Senate and its unreserved approval in the Mexican Senate.[33]

The Parallel Agreements

The conclusion of the negotiations of the parallel agreements has been viewed as an instrumental step toward the final approval of NAFTA. Following the election of Bill Clinton as president of the United States of America, Mexico, the United States, and Canada began negotiations concerning supplementary agreements on labor and environmental issues. Two North American commissions were created to deal with these issues. Negotiations started on March 17, 1993, in Washington, D.C.; and several other meetings were held among the commercial representatives of the three countries.

In Mexico City on August 13, 1993, representatives of the three countries announced the conclusion of these negotiations. In an address to the Mexican Senate, the Mexican minister of commerce and industrial promotion, Jaime Serra-Puche, stressed that there were five fundamental points achieved in the negotiation of the parallel agreements: There will not be any supranational authority with crossboundary powers; Mexican legislation concerning the environment and labor relations will not be modified; there will not be "traditional" commercial sanctions, such as those imposed by both the U.S. and Mexican governments in the case of steel; there will be no foreign intervention in the judicial process of Mexico; and finally, economic sanctions will be limited.[34]

Serra-Puche spelled out the details of the mechanism for the solution of environmental controversies agreed upon by the three parties. In the initial phase, there will be three-party consultations which will attempt to guarantee the implementation of environmental laws. If, in a sixty-day period, there is no solution to the controversy, the case will be submitted to a council, which will have twenty days within which to meet and a further sixty days to reach a decision. If the council is incapable of solving the controversy, the case will be submitted to an arbitrary panel which will make the necessary recommendations. If this panel proves the violation of the law by any of the three countries, it can impose monetary sanctions up to $20 million. The sanction will have to be paid by that country, in addition to complying with the law. If the country does not obey the decisions of the arbitrary panel, there are two different ways to seek compliance. In the case of Canada, the complaining party can sue the Canadian government in its courts of justice, while in the cases of Mexico and the United States, where intervention in the judicial system was not agreed upon, the benefits of NAFTA will be suspended temporarily for a total amount of no more than $20 million. It is believed that this system will avoid unilateral decisions in the solution of controversies among the three countries.[35]

In the short term, NAFTA'S impact in Mexico, and in the United States for that matter, has thus far (spring 1994) been political. Indeed, both presidents Clinton and Salinas banked a considerable amount of personal prestige on the passing of the trade agreement—the latter much more so.[36]

NAFTA has been criticized and praised on interrelated grounds, such as industry migration and human rights. For the purposes of this study, however, the following discussion focuses mainly on environmental issues.[37]

NAFTA has been heralded by President Salinas as a "historic window of opportunity for the United States to improve the often uneven relations it has had with its neighbors to the south."[38] William Reilly, administrator of the U.S. Environmental Protection Agency, called it the "greenest" trade agreement ever negotiated.[39] There are some grounds that seem to support these arguments. NAFTA seeks to "contribute to the harmonious development and expansion of world trade . . . in a manner consistent with environmental protection and conservation; . . . promote sustainable development; [and] strengthen the development and enforcement of environmental laws and regulations."[40] In addition, advocates argue, NAFTA is the first commercial treaty of its kind that explicitly includes specific provisions to protect the environment. Four articles are particularly relevant. First, Article 104 makes it clear that where a conflict arises between NAFTA and the commercial provisions of the international environmental treaties signed by any of the three countries, the latter will prevail. Second, Article 1114 states that environmental protection should not be relaxed as an investment incentive. Third, Article 1106 imposes mandatory sanctions if environmentally friendly technologies are not used. Finally, on the intellectual copyright issue, Article 1709 excludes the commercial exploitation of inventions that may harm the environment.[41]

Furthermore, a 1992 study conducted by the office of the U.S. Trade Representative (USTR) found that NAFTA "explicitly" safeguards the environment and promotes the strengthening of existing environmental standards by maintaining "existing US health, safety, and environmental standards by allowing the US to continue to prohibit entry of goods that do not meet US standards; [allowing] the parties, including states and cities, to enact even tougher standards; and [encouraging] the NAFTA parties to harmonize their standards upward to strengthen environmental and health protection."[42]

In a related study published by the U.S. Office of Public Affairs, the USTR[43] concluded that (1) completing and implementing a NAFTA will enhance cross-border environmental cooperation and provide Mexico with the resources and revenues to fund environmental protection and infrastructure development initiatives;[44] (2) it is reasonable to expect that NAFTA would encourage industry to shift away from the maquiladora section (assembly plants benefiting from Mexican government incentives) and thus reduce stress on the border environment; and (3) NAFTA will not turn Mexico into a pollution haven for firms seeking to escape U.S. environmental standards.[45]

In addition, proponents of NAFTA argue that environmental protection will be further enhanced by the following NAFTA provisions: (1) parties are permitted to require environmental impact assessments to be carried out on new projects; (2) parties are permitted to increase environmental standards on new projects, while rejecting the reduction of environmental standards to draw investment; (3) a reduction of border congestion by allowing trucks to haul their cargoes directly through the border to their destinations in both countries; and (4) a process by which trade disputes creating environmental concerns are resolved.

Environmentally sensitive critics of NAFTA have based their criticism primarily on the agreement's failure to address the perceived laxness of enforcement of environmental laws and regulations in Mexico. Despite the assurances of President Salinas and the USTR that Mexico will not become a pollution haven, many fear that many U.S. industries will relocate to Mexico to avoid the more stringent and generally enforced environmental protection laws and regulations of the United States.[46] Not only might the pressure to compete under a free trade agreement compel U.S. industries to relocate south and abuse the environment, Mexican industries may also feel pressured to ignore environmental standards in order to stay in business.[47] Despite the impressive provisions of Mexico's environmental laws, lacunae in the administrative structure, combined with lack of resources, lead critics to question the Mexican government's ability to enforce environmental protection.[48]

The political situation in Mexico also raises some concerns among opponents of NAFTA. Despite recent political reforms intended to foster democracy, Mexico is still governed by a one-party system that may be considered authoritarian. In such a system the incumbent president, along with the ruling party (PRI), holds a significant degree of discretionary power, with which he dominates the executive and maintains the subservience of the judicial branch.[49] Environmental groups opposed to NAFTA fear that if the Salinas administration opts to disregard the environmental provisions now that the agreement has been approved by the three countries, it can do so with relative ease. Moreover, as Salinas serves a nonrenewable term of six years until August 1994, those groups fear that his environmental initiatives may be suspended by the next president.[50] In addition, NAFTA's parallel agreements provide limited legislation in the way of enforcement, not to mention foreign intervention by the United States or Canada, of Mexican domestic environmental abuses.

An armed insurgency led by the Zapatista National Liberation Army in the southern state of Chiapas has further complicated the political arena in Mexico. Despite a truce and a rapprochement between the Zapatistas and the government, the situation remains tense. Zapatista supporters have increased, especially among peasants and farmers, and inspired protests and uprisings throughout Mexico. The insurgents demand democratic political reforms (as do Mexico's opposition parties), economic aid, land redistribution, and better treatment of the nation's Indians.[51] Though the rebellion remains limited in both scope and scale, it may pose a challenge to the dominant position in the Mexican government enjoyed and perpetuated by the PRI. The uprising also threatens to impede or extinguish NAFTA's momentum.

Critics of NAFTA maintain that the trade accord specifically benefits Mexico's upper classes and provides little for the majority of the populace. Echoing this criticism and resenting both American interference in Mexican affairs and the PRI's seeming passivity to that interference, many rebels and opposition leaders alike have denounced the trade agreement (as it now stands) as an exploitation of Mexico by the North and as a means of perpetuating Mexican subservience to the North (especially to the United States). If the opposition or the insurgents are able to apply serious enough pressure on the PRI or gain access to the decision-making apparatus of the Mexican government, the future of NAFTA is indeed highly questionable. Admittedly, in the near future, prospects for such a development appear weak; but nevertheless, they should not be dismissed lightly. The assassination of the PRI presidential candidate, Luis Donaldo Colosio, on March 23, 1994, and the kidnapping of the president of Mexico's largest bank leaves Mexican politics at crossroads. The nomination of a new presidential candidate, Ernesto Zedillo Ponce de Leon, has not been greeted with great enthusiasm by the party's old guard; and that may divide the party and weaken its 65-year-old domination of Mexican politics.[52] Economic and political observers, however, believe that the assassination will not have a great immediate impact on NAFTA.

As previously mentioned, opponents of NAFTA still question whether the Mexican government is sincerely committed to environmental protection and reform. A brief review of Mexico's most recent environmental achievements and shortcomings may offer part of the answer.

In addition to investing $4 billion in an effort to clean the air in Mexico City, President Salinas, in cooperation with the U.S. EPA, has pledged $460 million to a border environmental plan (see Figure 9.2).[53] To address the problem of enforcement, President Salinas has raised the enforcement budget from $6.6 million to $77 million, increased the number of environmental inspectors along

Figure 9.2
Mexico Is Devoting $460 Million to Border Environmental Protection in 1992–1994

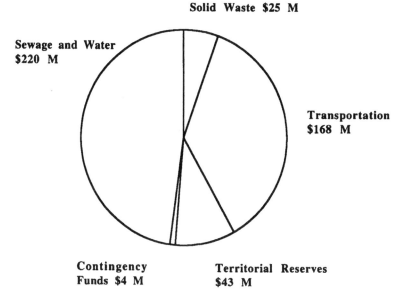

Solid Waste $25 M

Sewage and Water
$220 M

Transportation
$168 M

Contingency
Funds $4 M

Territorial Reserves
$43 M

Source: Office of the U.S. Trade Representative, *Environment*, 1992.

the border from 50 to 200, and permanently or temporarily closed over 1,000 firms violating environmental standards. One of those firms was Mexico City's "18 of March Refinery," which was responsible for 4 percent of Mexico's air pollution.[54] The closing of the plant meant an estimated loss of $500 million and 6,000 jobs, and is considered a noteworthy example of Salinas's commitment to the environment.[55] Mexico has also created 8 reserves, 44 national parks, and 14 biosphere reserves; attempted to end dolphin mortality in the harvest of tuna; and banned the commercial harvest of sea turtles.[56] For these environmental efforts, along with numerous others, President Salinas was awarded the Green Nobel Prize by United Earth in 1991.

Opponents of NAFTA see Mexican environmentalism in a substantially less favorable light. In 1992 a U.S. General Accounting Office (GAO) study "found that none of six U.S. majority–owned maquiladoras sampled had prepared an environmental impact asessment for new plants established in Mexico as required under Mexico's 1988 General Law of Ecological Balance and Environmental Protection."[57] As of the summer of 1992, Mexico also lacked regulations in three significant areas, areas subject to regulation in the United States. These areas in the United States include the cleanup of deserted hazardous waste sites; the underground storage tanks; and the land disposal of hazardous wastes.[58] Finally, as previously noted, limited resources pose an obstacle to environmental reform. Despite Salinas's increased allocation of resources toward the betterment of the environment, funding is still inadequate to meet many pressing matters—most notably the enforcement of environmental rules and regulations—which further impedes serious environmental reform (Figure 9.3).

CONCLUSION

Mexico faces a growing number of challenges related to solving its environmental problems. One of the most important of these is the fact that it did not recognize these problems until very recently and hence faces a

Figure 9.3
The Resource Gap: Per Capita Spending on Environmental Protection in the United States and Mexico (U.S. Dollars)

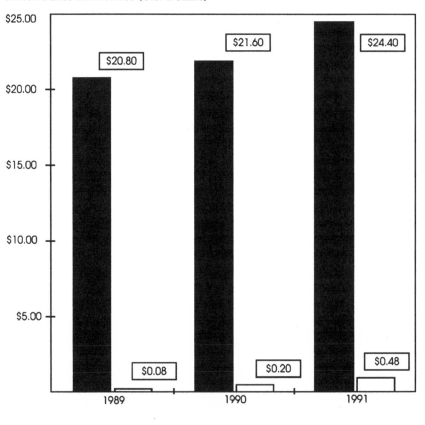

□ SECUE (Mexico) Budget per person
■ EPA (U.S.) Budget per Person

Source: Data provided by Congressional Research Service, based on information obtained from EPA.

Herculean task to resolve them. The historical lag is especially evident in the case of deforestation, depredation of wild fauna and flora, and solid waste disposal, including industrial waste. Prevention activities must be linked to environmental control and restoration initiatives. All this requires a national effort of shared responsibility between the individuals and the institutions that constitute Mexican society. This effort will demand considerable funding. The Mexican government has stated that resource allocation for the environment will not be postponed because of economic problems or other limitations. New productive projects and new public initiatives will inevitably have to include the required costs for an adequate environmental protection policy.

At the international level, globalization of ecological problems will become more evident in the immediate future as these problems breach national borders with increasing frequency. Mexico will promote international cooperation so that governments and societies think globally, build regionally, and act locally with regards to ecological balance. For the foreseeable future, Mexican policy will continue to fight the protectionist tendency of some countries to link trade barriers to ecological balance and environmental preservation.[59]

Finally, and perhaps most important, there is the problem of enforcement. Undoubtedly, Mexico, under the leadership of President Salinas, has initiated an impressive and progressive environmental protection plan. However, the government's record on enforcement has been rated by many environmentalists, Mexican and American alike, as somewhere between mixed and lax. Enforcement is but one of the many obstacles threatening to impede or eliminate environmental reform in both Mexico and other developing countries. It remains to be seen whether the Salinas government (or that of his successor) possesses the ability and the political will to overcome these obstacles. What is certain, however, is that the environmental reforms initiated by Salinas, whatever their impetus or overall objectives may be, are a substantial improvement on the past.

NOTES

1. Stephen P. Mumme, "Clearing the Air: Environmental Reform in Mexico," *Environment* 33.1 (1991): 7.

2. For a discussion of significant institutional developments with the United Nations related to sustainable development, see Mark Imber, "Too Many Cooks? The Post-Rio Reform Reform of the United Nations," *International Affairs* 68.1 (1993): 55–70; United Nations Organization, *The Brundtland Report* (Rio de Janeiro: United Nations, 1987), p. 43.

3. Mumme, "Clearing the Air," p. 8.

4. Ibid., p. 10.

5. Alvin L. Alm, "The Mexican Environmental Revolution," *Environmental Science and Technology* 26.4 (1992): 664.

6. In 1992, gross domestic product registered an annual real growth rate of 2.6 percent, which for the fourth consecutive year was higher than the population growth rate. In 1992, for the first time in modern Mexican economic history, the government obtained a budgetary surplus. High rates of inflation have been reduced to 11.9 percent. Public debt has also been reduced from 75 percent of gross domestic product in 1991 to 10 percent in 1993. Agreements with Columbia, Venezuela, and the Central American countries have further opened the economy. *Plan Nacional de Desarrollo 1989–1994: Informe de Ejecucion 1992* (Mexico City: Poder Ejecutivo Federal, 1993).

7. Mumme, "Clearing the Air," p. 10.

8. For further information, see Secretariat of Social Development, *National Program for Environmental Protection 1990–1994 Mexico* (Mexico City: The Secretariat, 1989).

9. Ibid.

10. The two federal states that have not yet passed environmental laws are Campeche and Tlaxcala.

11. For more information, see the series of seven documents on this topic: *Sistema Municipal de Gestión Ambiental* (Mexico City: Secretariat of Urban Development and Ecology, 1991).

12. Mexico, Secretaría de Desarrollo Social: Reglamento Interno, *Diario Oficial de la Federación*, 17 July 1992, pp. 53–76.

13. Luis Donaldo Colosio, Mexican secretary of social development, speech, working meeting with the director of the U.S. environmental agency to evaluate advances of the integral border plan, Mexico–United States, Santa Fe, New Mexico, 25 June 1992.

14. Mexico, "Acuerdo que Regula la Organización y Funcionamiento Interno del Instituto Nacional de Ecología y de la Procuraduría Federal de Protección al Medio Ambiente," *Diario Oficial de la Federación*, 17 July 1992, pp. 31–50.

15. Colosio, speech, 25 June 1992.

16. For a synthesized account of Mexico's biodiversity richness, "Instituto Nacional de Recursos Bióticos and Conservation International," *Mexico's Living Endowment: An Overview of Biological Diversity*, Mexico City, April 1989.

17. Secretariat of Social Development, "National Report on the Environment (1989–1991)," United Nations Conference on Environment and Development, Mexico City, July 1992.

18. Ibid., p. 22.

19. "Comisión Metropolitana para la Prevención y Control de la Contaminación Ambiental en el Valle de México," *Programa Integral Contra la Contaminación Atmosférica. Medidas de Invierno 1992–1993: Informe de Actividades*, 15 April 1993, p. 120.

20. Ibid., p. 23.

21. SEDUE, *Informe sobre el estado del medio ambiente en México*, Mexico City, 1986, pp. 11–12.

22. The enforcement of environmental regulations in Mexico is debated in "Environmental Impact of the Proposed North American Free Trade Agreement," hearing before the Subcommittee on International Trade of the Committee on Finance, United States Senate, 102nd Congress, 16 September 1992, Washington, D.C., U.S. Government Printing Office, 1993, pp. 43, 47.

23. Jonathan Fisher, "We Are Talking about Our Children," *International Wildlife* Sept./Oct. 1992, p. 50.

24. For an account on Mexican NGOs, see E. Kuurzinger et al., *Política Ambiental en México: El Papel de las Organizaciones No Gubernamentales* (Mexico City: Friedrich Ebert Stittung, 1991).

25. SEDESOL, Instituto Nacional de Ecología, *Directorio Verde: Organismos No Gubernamentales*, Mexico, 1992, p. 116.

26. Mumme, "Clearing the Air," pp. 28–29.

27. President Carlos Salinas de Gortari, speech during the meeting of heads of state and of government, II United Nations Conference on Environment and Development, Rio de Janeiro, Brazil, 12 June 1993.

28. President Carlos Salinas de Gortari, speech on behalf of the Latin American and Caribbean countries, II United Nations Conference on Environment and Development, Rio de Janeiro, Brazil, 13 June 1992.

29. President Carlos Salinas de Gortari, on behalf of the Latin American and Caribbean countries, II United Nations Conference on Environment and Development, Rio de Janeiro, Brazil, 12 June 1992.

30. For an overview of Mexico's recent domestic economic and political situation, in addition to a discussion of NAFTA's economic, political, and environmental impact on Mexico, see Jorge G. Castañeda, "Can NAFTA Change Mexico?" *Foreign Affairs* 72.4 (1993): 66–80.

31. "U.S. Congressional Approval," *Keesing's Record of World Events*, November 1993, p. 39728.

32. David E. Rosenbaum, "House Backs Free Trade Pact in Major Victory for Clinton after a Long Hunt for Votes," *The New York Times* 18 November 1993. Also, seen as paving the way for NAFTA'S ultimate congressional approval, is the November 9 televised debate between Ross Perot and Vice President Al Gore. For a concise account, see "U.S. Congressional Approval."

33. On the Mexican Senate's vote on NAFTA, see Tim Golden, "South of the Border, the Trade Deal Was a Breeze," *The New York Times* 24 November 1993, p. A4.

34. Jaime Serra-Puche, secretary of commerce and industrial promotion, report on the address to the Senate of the Mexican Republic, *El Nacional* 18 August 1993, p. 13. For a critical review, see Castañeda, "Can NAFTA Change?"; Golden, "U.S. and Mexico Spar."

35. For more information, see the articles on the end of the negotiations of the parallel agreements in the Mexican newspaper *El Financiero*, 18 August 1993, pp. 14, 18, 19.

36. According to Castañeda in "Can NAFTA Change Mexico?" not only was Salinas's political career threatened but also threatened was the dominance of the Mexican government by the ruling Institutional Revolutionary Party (PRI). Failing to secure the passage of the trade act could seriously jeopardize the successful assumption of the presidency by the PRI's candidate in the August 1994 presidential elections. Tim Golden, "Mexican Leader a Big Winner as the Trade Pact Advances," *The New York Times* 19 November 1993, p. A26; David E. Rosenbaum, "House Backs Free Trade Pact."

37. A concise review of NAFTA is provided by Linda M. Aguilar, "NAFTA: A Review of the Issues," *Economic Perspectives* (Federal Reserve Bank of Chicago) 16 (Jan./Feb. 1993): 12–20. For a more critical analysis of NAFTA, see Robin Broad and John Cavanagh, "Beyond the Myths of Río," *World Policy Journal* 10.1 (1993): 65–72; George E. Brown, Jr., J. William Goold, and John Cavanagh, "Making Trade Fair," *World Policy Journal* 9.2 (1992): 309–327; Jorge G. Castañeda and Carlos Heredia, "Another NAFTA: What a Good Agreement Should Offer," *World Policy Journal* 9.4 (1992): 675–685.

38. Todd Robberson, "A Cloud Drifting over Trade and Texas," *The Washington Post* 28 June–4 July 1993, p. 16.

39. "Environmental Impact of the Proposed North American Free Trade Agreement," p. 16.

40. "The North American Free Trade Agreement," *Environment*, Washington, D.C., Office of the U.S. Trade Representative, August 1992.

41. The Salinas administration made it clear that the regional cooperation initiatives among Mexico, the United States, and Canada to protect the environment do not start or end with NAFTA. There is a long tradition of pre–NAFTA cooperation that will continue in the future. For a synthesized account of these pre–NAFTA bilaterial and regional cooperation initiatives, see Herminio Blanco-Mendoza, "Avances en los Acuerdos Complementarios del TLC," *Mercado de Valores*, Mexico, 15 June 1993, pp. 33–34.

42. "The North American Free Trade Agreement," *Environment*.

43. "Special Environmental Issues," *Environmental Review*, Washington, D.C., Office of Public Affairs, 1992, pp. 4–5.

44. The first conclusion has been based, in part, on an analysis conducted by two Princeton University professors, Gene M. Grossman and Alan B. Krueger, assessing the environmental impacts of NAFTA. They found that "economic growth tends to alleviate pollution problems once a country's per capita income reaches about $4,000 to $5,000." They conclude that "Mexico, with a per capita GDP of $5,000 is now at the critical juncture." The findings of this study have been challenged by Robin Broad and John Cavanagh (Broad and Cavanagh, "Beyond the Myths," pp. 67–68).

45. Based on the USTR's belief that NAFTA will not encourage the relocation of U.S. firms to Mexico because of Mexico's commitment to the protection of the environment and because the costs of pollution reduction represent a minor proportion of total production costs in most industries. See, "The North American Free Trade Agreement," *Environment*, p. 2.

46. Fisher, "We Are Talking," p. 51.

47. *Los Angeles Times* 17 July 1991.

48. "The North American Free Trade Agreement," *Environment*, pp. 17, 19.

49. Castañeda discusses some of the authoritarian aspects of Mexican politics.

50. On November 28, the ruling PRI selected Luis Donaldo Colosio, the minister for social development, as its candidate for the presidential election scheduled in August 1994. Considering the past electoral practices of Mexico's presidential succession process, the PRI candidate's election to the presidency is virtually assured. See Castañeda, "Can NAFTA Change Mexico?"; Golden, "U.S. and Mexico Spar," p. A3.

51. Tim Golden, "'Awakened' Peasant Farmers Overrunning Mexican Towns," *The New York Times* 9 February 1994.

52. Timothy Golden, "Mexican Leader Picks Successor to Slain Nominee," *The New York Times* 30 March 1994, pp. A1, A6.

53. "The North American Free Trade Agreement," *Environment*.

54. Mumme, "Clearing the Air," p. 26.

55. Fisher, "We Are Talking," p. 51.

56. "The North American Free Trade Agreement," *Environment*.

57. "Environmental Impact of the Proposed North American Free Trade Agreement," p. 73.

58. Sheldon Friedman, "NAFTA as Social Dumping," *Challenge*, Sept./Oct. 1992, p. 29.

59. Seymour J. Rubin and Thomas R. Graham, eds., *Environment and Trade: The Relation of International Trade and Environmental Policy* (Totowa, N.J.: Allanheld and Osmun, 1982).

Selected Bibliography

"Acid Pollution Threatens Much of Third World." *International Wildlife* January/February 1986.

Adams, J. S., and T. McShane. *The Myth of Wild Africa: Conservation without Illusion.* New York: Norton, 1992.

Adams, Patricia. "All in the Name of Aid." *Sierra* January/February 1987.

African Population and Capitalism. Cordell, D., and J. Gregory, editors. Boulder, Colo.: Westview, 1987.

Agarwal, Anil, and Sunita Narain. *The State of India's Environment, 1984–85: The Second Citizen's Report.* New Delhi: Center for Science and Environment, 1985.

Akuffo, S. *Pollution Control in a Developing Country: A Study of the Situation in Ghana.* Accra: Ghana University Press, 1989.

Alm, Alvin L. "The Mexican Environmental Revolution." *Environmental Science and Technology* 1992.

Alvares, Claude, and Ramesh Billorey. "Damning the Narmada: The Politics behind the Destruction." *The Ecologist* 17.2-3 (1987).

Amte, Baba. "Narmada Project: The Case against and the Alternative Perspective." *Economic and Political Weekly* 21 April 1990.

Anderson, Christopher, and Peter Aldhous. "Global Warming: Third World Muscles on Climate Treaty." *Nature* February 1991.

Anderson, Fredrick R., et al. *Environmental Improvement through Economic Incentives.* Baltimore: Johns Hopkins University Press, 1977.

Anderson, Robert S., and Walter Huber. *The Hour of the Fox.* New Delhi: Vistar, 1988.

Aufderheide, Pat, and Bruce Rich. "Environmental Reform and the Multilateral Banks." *World Policy Journal* Spring 1988.

Bachleti, N. *Social Forestry in India: Problems and Prospects.* New York: Advent, 1987.

Badaracco, Joseph L., Jr. *Loading the Dice: A Five-Country Study of Vinyl Chloride Regulation.* Cambridge: Harvard University Press, 1985.

Baden, John, and Richard L. Stroup. *Bureaucracy vs. Environment*. Ann Arbor: University of Michigan Press, 1981.

Bairoch, Paul. *The Economic Development of the Third World since 1900*. Berkeley: University of California Press, 1975.

Baker, Randall. "Institutional Innovation, Development and Environmental Management: An 'Administrative Trap' Revisited." *Public Administration and Development* 9, 1989.

Bandopadhyay, J., N. D. Jayal, U. Schoettli, and C. Singh. *India's Environment: Crises and Responses*. Dehradun: Natraj, 1985.

Barbier, Edward B. "Sustaining Agriculture on Marginal Land: A Policy Framework." *Environment* November 1989.

Barfield, Seymor. "Garbage Bags for Boat Dwellers." *Journal of Environmental Health* July/August 1987.

Barrett, Richard N. *International Dimensions of the Environmental Crisis*. Boulder, Colo.: Westview, 1982.

Bartelmus, Peter. "Sustainable Development—A Conceptual Framework." Working Paper No. 13. New York, United Nations Department of International Economic and Social Affairs.

Bartelmus, Peter, E. Lutz, and S. Schweinfest. *Integrated Environmental and Economic Accounting: A Case Study for Papua New Guinea*. Washington, D.C.: World Bank. Environment Working Paper #54, 1992.

Bassow, W. "The Third World: Changing Attitudes toward Environmental Planning." *Annals* 444, 1979.

Baumol, William, and Wallace Oates. *Economics, Environmental Policy and the Quality of Life*. Englewood Cliffs, N.J.: Prentice-Hall, 1979.

Beardsley, Tim. "Business at Rio: An Industrial Agenda for the Environmental Convention." *Scientific American* May 1992.

Beecroft, Niyi, et al. *Report of the Kaduna River Pollution Study*. Zaria: Department of Chemical Engineering, Ahmadu Bello University, 1986.

Bell, M. *Contemporary Africa: Development, Culture and the State*. New York: Longman, 1986.

Bellow, Walden, David Kinley, and Elaine Elinson. *Development Debacle: The World Bank in the Philippines*. San Francisco: Institute for Food and Development Policy, 1982.

Berle, Peter A. "Charting a Sustainable Course (Worldwide)." *Audubon* January 1991.

Bhartari, Rajiv, Ashish Kothari, and Pallava Bagla. "The Narmada Valley Project: Development or Destruction?" *The Ecologist* 15.5-6, 1985. *Discussion* 15.5-6, 1985.

Bhatia, J. "India Finds Green Gold in Its Social Forests." *Far Eastern Economic Review* 113, 1986.

Bhatt, S. *Environmental Laws and Water Resources Management*. New Delhi: Radiant, 1986.

Boardman, Robert. *International Organization and the Conservation of Nature* Bloomington: Indiana University Press, 1981.

Bonalume, Ricardo. "Debt Swaps: The Greening of Collor." *Nature* July 1991.

Bordering on Trouble: Resources and Politics in Latin America. Maguire, Andrew, and Janet Welsh Brown, editors. Bethesda, Md.: Adler and Adler, 1986.

Boserup, Ester. "Environment, Population and Technology in Primitive Societies." *Population and Development Review* 2, 1976.

Boxer, Baruch. "China's Environmental Prospects." *Asian Survey* 29.7, July 1989.

Brown, Janet Welsh. "Developing Nations: Four Environmental Profiles." *EPA Journal* July/August 1990.

Brown, L. *State of the World*. New York: Norton, 1992.

Bunyard, Peter. "Brazil and the Amazonian Pact." *The Ecologist* 19, 1989.

Bunyard, Peter. "Colombia—Hydorelectric Schemes on the Rio Sinu." *The Ecologist* 16, 1986.

Burley, J. *Obstacles to Tree Planting in Arid and Semi-arid Lands: Comparative Case Studies from India and Kenya*. Lanham, Md.: Berman-UNIPUB, 1983.

Burns, Bradford. *Latin America: A Concise Interpretative History*. Englewood Cliffs, N.J.: Prentice-Hall, 1986.

Cairns, John. "Ecosystem Peril vs. Perceived, Personal Risk." *Chemtech* February 1992.

Caldwell, Lynton. *In Defense of the Earth: International Protection of the Biosphere*. Bloomington: Indiana University Press, 1972.

Caldwell, Lynton K. *Between Two Worlds, Science, Environment Movement and Policy Choice*. New York: Cambridge University Press, 1990.

Caldwell, Lynton K. *International Environment Policy*. Durham, N.C.: Duke University Press, 1984.

Campbell, J. "Land or Peasants? The Dilemma Confronting Ethiopian Resource Conservation." *African Affairs* 90.358, 1991.

Canadian International Development Agency (CIDA). *Marine and Coastal Sector Development in Indonesia, 1; A Strategy for Assistance*. Ottawa: The Agency, 1987.

Cantley, Mark F. "World Bank Series on Integrated Resource Recovery." *Environment* October 1986.

Carey, John. "Will Saving People Save Our Planet?" *International Wildlife* May/June 1992.

Carpenter, Richard A. "Foreign Assistance for China's Environment?" *Environmental Science and Technology* June 1990.

Carpenter, Richard A. "The Ganges: An Example of Environmental Incongruity." *Environment* October 1986.

Carson, Rachel. *The Silent Spring*. Boston: Houghton Mifflin, 1987.

Cater, Nick. "Rich Countries Fail to Support Third World Wetlands Fund." *New Scientist* July 1990.

Chatterji, Manas. *Energy and Environment in the Developing Countries*. New York: Wiley, 1981.

China Facts and Figures. Scherer, J. L., editor. Gulf Breeze, Fla.: Academic International Press, 1991.

Cigler, B. A. "Environmental Policy and Management: A New Era." *Policy Studies Journal* 16, 1987.

Cleaves, Peter. *Bureaucratic Politics and Administration in Chile*. Berkeley: University of California Press, 1974.

Cohen, Norman. "AID's Dolars: Reaching for a Better Environment." *EPA Journal* September 1987.

Conflict over Natural Resources in South-east Asia and the Pacific. Ghee, Lim Teck, and Mark J. Valencia, editors. Manila: Manila University Press, 1990.

Cooper, Charles. *Policy Intervention for Technological Innovation in Developing Countries*. Washington, D.C.: World Bank, 1980.

Cooper, C. M., and R. Otto. *Social and Economic Evaluation of Environmental Impacts*

in Third World Countries: A Methodical Discussion. Brighton, Sussex: Institute
  of Development Studies, 1977.

*Cooperation for International Development: The United States and the Third World in the
  1990s.* Berg, Robert J., and David F. Gordon, editors. Boulder, Colo.: Lynne
  Reinner, 1989.

Cronon, William. *Changes in the Land.* New York: Hill and Wang, 1983.

Cross, N. *The Sahel: The People's Right to Development.* London: Minority Rights
  Group, 1990.

Cultural Transformations and Ethnicity in Modern Ecuador. Whitten, N. E., Jr., editor.
  Urbana: University of Illinois Press, 1981.

Dankelman, I., and J. Davidson. *Women and Environment in the Third World: Alliance
  for the Future.* London: Earthscan, in association with Alliance Mondial pour
  la Nature (IUCN).

Davies, K. "What Is Eco-feminism?" *Women Environment* 10, 1988: 4–6.

Davis, Shelton H. *Victims of the Miracle: Development and the Indians of Brazil.* New
  York: Cambridge University Press, 1977.

de Jongh, Hans H., et al. *Environmental Profile: West Java.* The Hague: Ministry of
  Foreign Affairs, 1988.

Dejene, A., and J. Olivares. "Integrating Environmental Issues into a Strategy for
  Sustainable Agricultural Development." *World Bank Technical Paper No. 146.*
  Washington, D.C., World Bank, 1991.

Desai, Arijana. *Environmental Perception: The Human Factor in Urban Planning.* New
  Delhi: Ashish, 1985.

"Developing Countries Urged to Conserve Natural Resources." *Journal of Environmental Health* May/June 1988.

Development Adminstration in Papua New Guinea. Dwivedi, O. P., and Pitil P., editors. Boroko: Administrative College of Papua New Guinea, 1991.

Dhawan, B. D. "Mounting Antagonism towards Big Dams." *Economic and Political
  Weekly* 20 May 1989.

Dickinson, Robert E. *The Geophysiology of Amazonia—Vegetation and Climate Interactions.* New York: Wiley–United Nations University Press, 1987.

Dilemma of Amazonian Development, The. Moran, Emilo F., editor. Boulder, Colo.:
  Westview, 1983.

Donner, Wolf. *Land Use and Environment in Indonesia.* Honolulu: University of Hawaii Press, 1987.

Downing, T. "Vulnerability to Hunger in Africa: A Climate Change Perspective."
  Global Environmental Change 1.5, 1991.

Downs, Anthony. "Up and Down with Ecology: The Issue-Attention Cycle." *Public
  Interest* 28, 1972.

Dwivedi, O. P. "An Ethical Approach to Environmental Protection: A Code of Conduct and Guiding Principles." *Canadian Public Administration* 35.3, 1992.

Dwivedi, O. P. "India: Pollution Control Policy and Programmes." *International
  Review of Administrative Science* 43, 1977.

Dwivedi, O. P., and Brij Kishore. "Protecting the Environment from Pollution:
  A Review of India's Legal and Institutional Mechanism." *Asian Survey*
  22, 1982.

Ecological Change: Environment, Development and Poverty Linkages. Kirdar, Uner, editor. New York: United Nations Publications, 1992.

Ecology, Economics, Ethics: The Broken Circle. Bormann, Herbert F., and Stephen R. Kellert, editors. New Haven: Yale University Press, 1991.

Economy of Indonesia, The. Glassburner, Bruce, editor. Ithaca: Cornell University Press, 1971.

Ehret, C. "On the Antiquity of Agriculture in Ethiopia." *Journal of African History* 20, 1979.

Emmel, Thomas C. *Global Perspectives on Ecology.* Palo Alto, Calif.: Mayfield Publishing, 1977.

Enloe, Cynthia. *The Politics of Pollution in a Comparative Perspective: Ecology and Power in Four Nations.* New York: David McKay, 1975.

Environment and Trade: The Relation of International Trade and Environmental Policy. Rubin, Seymour, and Thomas R. Graham, editors. Totowa, N.J.: Allanheld and Osmun, 1982.

Environment Impact Analysis: Emerging Issues in Planning. Jain, R. K., and B. Hutchings, editors. Urbana: University of Illinois Press, 1978.

Environmental Accounting for Sustainable Income. Ahmad, Yusef J., Salah El Serafy, and Ernst Lutz, editors. Washington, D.C.: World Bank, 1989.

"Environmental Impact of the Proposed North American Free Trade Agreement." *Hearing Before the Subcommittee on International Trade of the Committee on Finance,* U.S. Senate, 102nd Congress, 16 September 1992. Washington, D.C.: U.S. Government Printing Office, 1993.

Environmental Law in Indonesia and Canada: Present Approaches and Future Trends. VanderZwaag, David, Stephen Mills, and Barbara Patton, editors. Halifax, N.S.: Dalhousie University, School for Resource and Environmental Studies, 1987.

Environmental Policy Formation: The Impact of Values, Ideology and Standards. Mann, Dean E., editor. Lexington: Lexington Books, 1981.

Environmental Policy in China. Bloomington: Indiana University Press, 1988. "Environmental Protection: A View from Brazil." *Environmental Science and Technology* June 1992.

Environmental Politics and Policies: An International Perspective. Knoepfel, P., and N. Watts, editors. Frankfurt: Campus Verlag, 1983.

Environmental Profile of Indonesia 1990. Jakarta: University of Indonesia, Centre for Research of Human Resources and the Environment, 1990.

Environmentally Sound Technology for Sustainable Development. Pilari, Dirk, editor. ATAS Bulletin No. 7. New York: United Nations Publications, 1992.

Ethics of Environment and Development: Global Challenge, International Response. Engel, Roland J., and Joan Gibb Engel, editors. Tucson: University of Arizona Press, 1990.

Fairness to Future Generations: International Law, Common Patrimony and Intergenerational Equity, In. Weiss, Edith Brown, editor. New York: Transnational Publishers, United Nations University Press, 1988.

Fearnside, Philip M. "A Prescription for Slowing Deforestation in Amazonia." *Discussion* 31, 1989.

Fearnside, Philip M., and Gabriel de Lima Ferreira. "Amazonian Forest Reserves, Fact or Fiction?" *The Ecologist* 15.5-6, 1985.

Ferguson, Yale. *Developing in the Periphery: External Factors in Latin American Policies.* Englewood Cliffs, N.J.: Prentice-Hall, 1972.

Fisher, Anthony. *Resource and Environmental Economics.* Cambridge: Cambridge University Press, 1981.

Forging Identities and Patterns of Development in Latin America and the Caribbean. Díaz, Harry P., et al., editors. Toronto: Canadian Scholars' Press, 1991.

Franke, R. W., and B. Chasin. *Seeds of Famine: Ecological Destruction and the Development Dilemma in the West African Sahel.* Montclair: Allanheld and Osmun, 1980.

Frederick, Buttel, and William Flinn. "The Politics of Environmental Concern." *Environment and Behavior* 10, 1978.

Fritsch, Albert J. *Science Action Coalition, Environmental Ethics: Choices for Concerned Citizens.* New York: Anchor Press, 1980.

Fuller, Kathryn S. "Debt-for-Nature Swaps." *Environmental Science and Technology* December 1989.

Further Look at the Environment as a Political Issue, A. *International Journal of Environmental Studies* 12, 1978.

Garreton, Manuel Antonio. "The Feasibility of Democracy in Chile: Conditions and Challenges." *Canadian Journal of Latin American and Caribbean Studies* 15.30, 1990.

Glaeser, Bernhard. *Learning from China? Development and Environment in Third World Countries.* London: Allen & Unwin, 1987.

Glantz, Michael H. *Drought and Hunger in Africa: Denying Famine a Future.* Cambridge: Cambridge University Press, 1987.

Glantz, Michael H. *Societal Responses to Regional Climatic Changes: Forecasting by Analogy.* Boulder, Colo.: Westview, 1988.

Global Environmental Change: New Dimensions in International Law and Institutions. Weiss, E. Brown, editor. Tokyo: United Nations University Press, 1993.

Global Partnership for Environment and Development: A Guide to Agenda 21, The. New York: United Nations Publications, 1992.

Goodin, Paul. *Global Studies, Latin America.* Sluice Dock, Guilford, Conn.: Dushkin Publishing Co., 1992.

Gore, Al. *Earth in the Balance—Ecology and the Human Spirit.* Boston: Houghton Mifflin, 1992.

Gorze, A. *Ecology as Politics.* Trans. P. Vigderman and J. Cloud. Montreal: Black Rose, 1980.

Gray, Paul E. "The Paradox of Technological Development." *Technology and Environment.* Ausubel, Jesse H., and Hedy E. Sladovic, editors. Washington, D.C.: National Academy Press, 1989.

Greening of Aid: Sustainable Livelihoods in Practice, The. Conroy, C., and M. Lituinoff, editors. London: Earthscan, 1988.

Greenwar: Environment and Conflict in the Sahel. Bennett, O., editor. Washington, D.C.: Panos, 1991.

Hainsworth, Geoffrey B. "Economic Growth, Basic Needs and Environment in Indonesia." In *Southeast Asian Affairs 1985.* Singapore: Institute of Southeast Asian Studies, 1985.

Hardjasoemantri, Koesnadi. *Environmental Legislation in Indonesia.* Yogyakarta: Gadjah Mada University Press, 1987.

Hassan, Shaukat. *Environmental Issues and Security in South Asia.* London: Brassey's, for the International Institute for Strategic Studies, 1991.

Heaton, George, Robert Repetto, and Rodney Sobin. *Transforming Technology: An Agenda for Environmentally Sound Technology in the 21st Century.* Washington, D.C.: World Resources Institute, 1991.

Hirji, R., and L. Ortolano. "Strategies for Managing Uncertainties Imposed by Environmental Impact Assessment: Analysis of the Kenyan River Development Authority." *Environmental Impact Assessment Review* 11.3, 1991.

"How a Monkey Saved the Jungle." *International Wildlife* 22.1, 1992.

Hughes, Sylvia. "North–South Split Kills Hopes of Forest Treaty." *New Scientist* September 1991.

Hugo, Graeme J., Terence H. Hull, Valerie J. Hull, and Gavin W. Jones. *The Demographic Dimension in Indonesian Development.* Singapore: Oxford University Press, 1987.

"Implementation of Environmental Policy in China: A Comparative Perspective, The." *Administration and Society* 15, 1984.

Independent Commission on International Development Issues. *Common Crisis North–South: Cooperation for World Recovery.* Cambridge: MIT Press, 1983.

Independent Commisssion on International Development Issues. *North–South: A Programme for Survival.* London: Pan Books, 1980.

Industrial Pollution in Japan. Ui, Jun, editor. Tokyo: United Nations University Press, 1992.

International Monetary Fund in a Multipolar World: Pulling Together, The. Gwin, Catherine, and Richard E. Feinberg, editors. New Brunswick, N.J.: Transaction Books, 1989.

Jain, Vinod. "Disposing of Pesticides in the Third World." *Environmental Technology and Science* February 1992.

James, Jeffrey. "Growth, Technology and the Environment in Less Developed Countries: A Survey." *World Development* 6, 1978.

Jasanoff, Sheila. "Managing India's Environment: New Opportunities, New Perspectives." *Environment* October 1986.

Jhaveri, Nayna. "The Three Gorges Debacle." *The Ecologist* 18.2-3, 1988.

Johnson, D. "Political Ecology in the Upper Nile." *Journal of African History* 30, 1989.

Johnson D., and D. Anderson. *The Ecology of Survival: Case Studies from Northeast African History.* Boulder, Colo.: Westview, 1988.

Jones, Charles O. *Clean Air: The Policies and Politics of Pollution Control.* Pittsburgh: University of Pittsburgh Press, 1975.

Joshi, Gopa. "Forests and Forest Policy in India." *Social Scientist* 11, 1983.

Kaufman, Herbert. *The Forest Ranger: A Study in Administrative Behavior.* Baltimore: Johns Hopkins University Press, 1970.

Kay, David A., and Harold K. Jacobson. *Environmental Protection: The International Dimension.* Totowa, N.J.: Allenheld and Osmun, 1983.

Khanna, Gopesh Nath. *Environment Problems and the United Nations.* New Delhi: Ashish, 1990.

Khator, R. *Environment, Development and Politics in India.* Lanham, Md.: University Press of America, 1991.

Kimmage, Kevin. "Nigeria's Home-Grown Dust Bowl. " *New Scientist* July 1990.

Krueger, A., et al. *Aid and Development.* Baltimore: Johns Hopkins University Press, 1989.

Kuurzinger, E. *Política Ambiental en México: El Papel de las Organizaciones No Gubernamentales.* Mexico City: Friedrich Ebert Stittung, 1991.

Land, People, and Planning in Contemporary Amazonian. Barbira-Scazzocchio, F., editor. Cambridge: Cambridge University Center for Latin American Studies Occasional Publications 3, 1980.

Lasswell, Harold D. *Politics: Who Gets What When and How*. New York: McGraw Hill, 1950.

Latin America to the Year 2000: Reactivating Growth, Improving Equity, Sustaining Democracy. Ritter, Archibald, Maxwell Cameron, and David Pollock, editors. New York: Praeger, 1992.

Latin American Prospects for the 1980s: Equity, Democratization and Development. Ritter, Archibald, and David Pollock, editors. New York: Praeger, 1983.

Lee, J., and R. Goodland. "Economic Development and the Environment." *Finance Development* 23, 1986.

Leonard, Jeffrey H., et al. *Environment and the Poor: Development Strategies for a Common Agenda*. New Brunswick, N.J.: Transaction Books, 1989.

Leonard, J. H., and D. Morell. "Emergence of Environmental Concern in Developing Countries: A Political Perspective." *Stanford Journal of International Law* 17, 1981.

Lesser, Stan. "A Reporter at Large: Logging the Rain Forest." *The New Yorker* 27 May 1991.

Lewis, L., and L. Berry. *African Environments and Resources*. London: Unwin Hyman, 1988.

Lohmann, Larry. "Who Defends Biological Diversity? Conservation Strategies and the Case of Thailand." *The Ecologist* 21.1, 1991.

Lovejoy, T., and H. O. R. Schubart. "The Ecology of Amazonian Development." In *Land, People, and Planning in Contemporary Amazonian*, edited by F. Barbira-Scazzocchio. Cambridge: Cambridge University Center for Latin American Studies, Occasional Publications 3, 1980.

Lovejoy, Thomas E. "The Third World's Environment: A Global Dilemma." *EPA Journal* July/August 1989.

Lovelock, James. "Geophysiology: A New Look at Earth Science." *The Geophysiology of Amozonia: Vegetation and Climate Interactions*. Dickinson, Robert E., editor. New York: Wiley, United Nations University Press, 1987.

Lowe, Philip, and Jane Goyder. *Environmental Groups in Politics*. London: Allen and Unwin, 1983.

Lundquist, Lennart J. "Political Structures Matter in Environmental Politics?" *American Behavioral Scientist* 17, 1974.

Lundquist, Lennart J. "The Comparative Study of Environmental Policy." *Policy Studies Journal* 1, 1973.

Lyman, Francesca, et al. *The Greenhouse Trap: What We're Doing to the Atmosphere and How We Can Slow Global Warming*. Boston: Beacon Press, 1989.

Macgregor, J. "The Paradoxes of Wildlife Conservation in Africa." *Africa Insight* 19.4, 1989.

Macintyre, Andrew. *Business and Politics in Indonesia*. North Sydney: Allen and Unwin for ASAA, 1991.

MacKenzie, Debora, and James Mpinga. "Africa Wages War on Dumpers of Poisonous Waste." *New Scientist* June 1988.

MacNeill, Jim, Pieter Winsemius, and Taizo Yakushiji. *Beyond Interdependence*. Oxford: Oxford University Press, 1991.

Makinwa, P. K., and A. O. Ozo. "Introduction." In *The Urban Poor in Nigeria*, edited by P. K. Makinwa and O. A. Ozo. Ibadan: Evans Brothers, 1987.

Mayda, Jaro. "Environmental Legislation in Developing Countries: Some Parameters and Constraints." *Ecological Law Quarterly* 12, 1985.

Mayur, Rashmi. "Environmental Problems of Developing Countries." *American Academy of Political and Social Science Annals* 444, 1979.

McCormick, John. *Acid Earth: The Global Warming*. Washington, D.C.: Earthscan and International Institute for Environment and Development, 1985.

McCormick, John. *Reclaiming Paradise: The Global Environmental Movement*. Bloomington: Indiana University Press, 1989.

Meadows, Donella H., Dennis L. Meadows, and Jorgen Randers. *Beyond the Limits*. Post Mills, Vt.: Chelsea Green, 1992.

Meadows, Donella H., et al. *The Limits to Growth*. New York: Universe Books, 1992.

Mellor, John W. "The Intertwining of Environmental Problems and Poverty." *Environment* November 1988.

Miller, G. Tyler. *Environmental Science, Sustaining the Earth*. Belmont, Calif.: Wadsworth, 1991.

Miller, J. C. "Demographic History Revisited." *Journal of African History* 25, 1984.

Miller, Kenton, and Laura Tangley. *Trees of Life: Saving Tropical Forests and Their Biological Wealth*. Boston: Beacon Press, 1991.

Montgomery, J. D. "Environmental Management as a Third World Problem." *Policy Sciences* 23, 1990.

Mumme, Stephen P. "Clearing the Air: Environmental Reform in Mexico." *Environment* 33.10, 1991.

Munslow, B., et. al. *The Fuelwood Trap: A Study of the SADCC Region*. London: Earthscan, 1988.

Ngau, Harrison, Thomas Jalong Apoi, and Chee Yoke Ling. "Malaysian Timber: Exploitation for Whom." *The Ecologist* 17.4-5, 1987.

Nicholson, S. "The Methodology of Historical Climate Reconstruction and Its Application to Africa." *Journal of African History* 20, 1979.

Nijkamp, Peter. *Environmental Policy Analysis: Operational Methods and Models*. New York: Wiley, 1980.

"Nile Crocodiles Cut Brazil's Cayman Down to Size." *New Scientist* August 1991.

Obeng, Letita E. "Some Environmental Issues in Water for Development." *Water Supply and Management* 4, 1980.

O'Connor, James. "Uneven and Combined Development and Ecological Crisis: A Theoretical Introduction." *Race and Class: A Journal for Black and Third World Liberation* 30.3, 1989.

Oil Boom and After: Indonesian Economic Policy and Performance in the Soeharto Era, The. Booth, Anne, and Peter McCawley, editors. Singapore: Oxford University Press, 1981.

Okello-Oleng, C. "National Environmental Issues and Strategies in Uganda." *Integrated Management of Resources of Africa: A Reader*. Nairobi: UNEP, 1989.

Orr, David W., and Marvin S. Soroos. *The Global Predicament: Ecological Perspectives on World Order*. Chapel Hill: University of North Carolina Press, 1979.

Pal, B. P. *Environmental Conservation and Development*. New Delhi: Indian Environmental Society, 1981.

Payer, Cheryl. *The World Bank: A Critical Analysis*. New York: Monthly Review, 1982.

Pearce, David W. *Sustainable Development Economics and Environment in the Third World*. Brookfield, Vt.: Grower, 1991.

Pearce, Fred. "Hit and Run in Sarawak." *New Scientist* May 1990.

Pearce, Fred. "Why It's Cheaper to Poison the Poor." *New Scientist* February 1992.

Pearson, Charles S., and Anthony Pryor. *Environment, North and South: An Economic Interpretation.* New York: Wiley, 1978.

Pilari, Dirk. *Environmentally Sound Technology for Sustained Development.* New York: U.N. Department of Social and Economic Development, 1992.

Pilat, J. F. *Ecological Politics: The Rise of the Green Movement.* Beverly Hills, Calif.: Sage, 1980.

Planting for the Future: Forestry for Human Needs. Washington, D.C.: Worldwatch Institute, 1979.

Please, Stanley. *The Hobbled Giant: Essays on the World Bank.* Boulder, Colo.: Westview, 1984.

Polak, Jacques. *The Changing Nature of IMP Conditionality.* Princeton: Princeton University Press, 1991.

Porter, Gareth, and Janet W. Brown. *Global Environmental Politics.* Boulder, Colo.: Westview, 1991.

Pradervand, Pierre. *Listening to Africa: Developing Africa from the Grassroots.* New York: Praeger, 1989.

"Price of Amazonian Gold, The." *Environment* April 1990.

Protest Movements in South and South-east Asia: Traditional and Modern Idioms of Expression. Ghose, Rajeshwari, editor. Hong Kong: Center of Asian Studies, University of Hong Kong, 1987.

Rao, U. R. "Energy, Environment and Ethics." *Society and Science* 2, 1979.

Redclift, M. *Development and the Environmental Crisis: Red or Green Alternatives?* New York: Methuen, 1984.

Reid, Walter V. C. "Sustainable Development: Lessons from Success." *Environment* May 1989.

Reilly, Conor. "Environmental Action in Zambia." *Environment* 17, 1975.

Repetto, Robert. *Promoting Environmentally Sound Economic Progress: What the North Can Do.* Washington, D.C.: World Resources Institute, 1990.

Rich, Bruce M. "The 'Greening' of the Development Banks: Rhetoric and Reality." *The Ecologist* 19, 1989.

Rich, Bruce M. "The Multilateral Development Banks, Environmental Policy and the United States." *Ecology Law Quarterly* 12.4, 1985.

Riddel, Robert. *Ecodevelopment.* London: Gower, 1981.

Rohrschneider, Robert. "Citizen's Attitudes toward Environmental Issues: Selfish or Selfless?" *Comparative Political Studies* 21, 1988.

Rondinelli, Dennis A. *Development Administration and U.S. Foreign Aid Policy.* Boulder, Colo.: Lynne Reinner, 1987.

Rondinelli, Dennis A. *Development Projects as Policy Experiments: An Adaptive Approach to Development Administration.* New York: Methuen, 1983.

Rosenbaum, Walter A. *The Politics of Environmental Concern.* New York: Praeger, 1973.

Rosenblum, M., and D. Williamson. *Squandering Eden: Africa at the Edge.* New York: Harcourt, 1987.

Ross, Lester. *Environmental Policy in China.* Bloomington: Indiana University Press, 1988.

Ross, Lester. "Environmental Policy in Post-Mao China." *Environment* 29 May 1987.

Ross, Lester, and Mitchell A. Silk. *Environmental Law and Policy in the People's Republic of China.* New York: Quorum, 1987.

Sachs, I., and Donna Silk. *Food and Energy—Strategies for Sustainable Development.* Tokyo: United Nations University Press, 1990.

Said, Salim. *Genesis of Power: General Sudirman and the Indonesian Military in Politics, 1945–49.* Singapore: Institute of Southeast Asian Studies, 1991.

Sandbach, F. *Environment, Ideology and Policy.* Oxford: Basil Blackwell, 1980.

"Saudi Experience, A." *Journal of Environmental Health* May/June 1989.

Schmidheiny, Stephan. *Changing Course—A Global Perspective on Development and the Environment.* Cambridge: MIT, 1992.

Scudder, Thayer. "Conservation vs. Development: River Basin Projects in Africa." *Environment* March 1989.

Secrett, Charles. "The Environmental Impact of Transmigration." *The Ecologist* 16.2-3, 1986.

Sen, G., and C. Grown. *Development, Crises, and Alternative Visions: Third World Women's Perspectives.* New York: Monthly Review, 1987.

Shaw, R. P. "The Impact of Population Growth on Environment: The Debate Heats Up." *Environmental Impact Assessment Review* 12.44, 1992.

Sheahan, John. *Patterns of Development in Latin America: Poverty, Repression, and Economic Strategy.* Princeton: Princeton University Press, 1987.

Shiva, Vandana. *Staying Alive: Women, Ecology and Development.* London: Zed, 1988.

Shuaib, Hamid A. "Oil, Development, and the Environment in Kuwait." *Environment* July/August 1988.

Sigurdson, John. "Water Policies in India and China." *Ambio* 6, 1977.

Silk, Donna, and I. Sachs. *Food and Energy: Strategies for Sustainable Development.* Tokyo: United Nations University Press, 1990.

Silvertown, Jonathan. "A Silent Spring in China." *New Scientist* July 1989.

Simandjuntak, Djisman S. "The Process of Deregulation and Privatization: The Indonesian Experience." *Asian Quarterly* 19.4, 1991.

Singh, Digvijay Pratap. *The Eco-vote: People's Representatives and Global Environment.* New Delhi: Prentice-Hall, 1985.

Sjahrir. *Basic Needs in Indonesia: Economics, Politics and Public Policy.* Singapore: Institute of Southeast Asian Studies, 1986.

Smicock, B. L. "Environmental Pollution and the Citizen's Movement: The Social Sciences Are the Significance of Anti-pollution Protest in Japan." *Area Development in Japan* 5, 1972.

Smil, Vaclav. *The Bad Earth: Environmental Degradation in China.* Armonk, N.Y.: M. E. Sharpe, 1984.

Social and Environmental Effects of Large Dams, The. Goldsmith, E., and N. Hildyard, editors. San Francisco: Sierra Club, 1984.

Soerjani, Mohamad. *Environmental Problems and Management in Indonesia.* Jakarta: University of Indonesia, Centre for Research of Human Resources and the Environment, 1982.

Southeast Asia, an Emerging Center of World Influence? Raymand, Wayne, and K. Mulliner, editors. Athens: Ohio University Center for International Studies, 1976.

Southeast Asian Affairs 1991. Singapore: Institute of Southeast Asian Studies, 1991.

Stallings, Barbara. *Class Conflicts and Economic Development in Chile, 1958–1973.* Stanford: Stanford University Press, 1978.

Starke, Linda. *Signs of Hope: Working towards Our Common Future.* Oxford: Oxford University Press, 1990.

State of the Environment in Mauritius. Dwivedi, O. P., and V. Venkatasamy, editors. Port Louis: Ministry of Environment and Quality of Life, Government of Mauritius, 1991.

Stein, Robert, and Brian Johnson. *Banking on the Biosphere? Environmental Procedures and Practices of Nine Multi-lateral Development Agencies.* Toronto: Lexington Books, 1979.

Steinhart, E. "Hunters, Poachers, and Gamekeepers: Towards a Social History of Hunting in Colonial Kenya." *Journal of African History* 30, 1989.

Stone, Roger D., and Eva Hamilton. *Global Economy and the Environment: Toward Sustainable Rural Development in the Third World.* New York: Council of Foreign Relations Press, 1991.

Sustaining Earth. Angell, David J. R., et al., editors. New York: St. Martin's, 1991.

Tangsubkul, Phiphat. *ASEAN and the Law of the Sea.* Singapore: Institute of Southeast Asian Studies, 1982.

Technology and Environment. Ausubel, Jesse H., and Hedy E. Sladovic, editors. Washington, D.C.: National Academy Press, 1989.

Thomas, Caroline. *The Environment in International Relations.* London: Royal Institute of International Affairs, 1992.

Timberlake, Lloyd. *Africa in Crisis: The Causes, The Cures of Environmental Bankruptcy.* Philadelphia: New Society Publishers, 1986.

Timberlake, Lloyd. "From Washington to Panama: Buying Destruction." In *Only One Earth: Living for the Future.* New York: Sterling Publishing, 1987.

Tolba, M. *Sustainable Development: Constraints and Opportunities.* Toronto: Butterworths, 1987.

Toward Inter-Governmental and Inter-Agencies Cooperation on Indonesian Eco-Development. Haeruman, Herman, editor. Jakarta: Ministry of State for Population and Environment, 1979.

Tripathi, Salil, and N. K. Singh. "A Flood of Controversies: Narmada Valley Project." *India Today* October 1988.

Tucker, William. "Environmentalism and the Leisure Class." *Harper's* February 1978.

Tuntawiroon, Nart. "The Environmental Impact of Industrialization in Thailand." *The Ecologist* 15.4, 1985.

Turnham, David. "Multilateral Development Banks and Environmental Management." *Public Administration and Development* July-August 1991.

Turshen, M. *The Political Ecology of Disease in Tanzania.* New Brunswick: Rutgers University Press, 1984.

Tyner, Wallace E. *Energy Resources and Economic Development in India.* Leiden, Netherlands: Martinus Nijhoff, 1978.

U.S. Interest: Resources, Growth, and Security in the Developing World, In the. Brown, Janet Welsh, editor. Boulder, Colo.: Westview, 1990.

Vir, Arti K. "Toxic Trade with Africa." *Environmental Science and Technology* January 1989.

Vogel, D. *National Styles of Regulation: Environmental Policy in Great Britain and the United States.* Ithaca: Cornell University Press, 1986.

vonWeizsaecker, Ernst Ulrich. "Sustainability: A Task for the North." *Journal of International Affairs* 2.44, 1991.

Wagley, Charles. *Welcome of Tears: The Tapirape Indians of Central Brazil.* New York: Oxford University Press, 1977.

Walter, Ingo. *International Economics of Pollution*. New York: Wiley, 1975.

Weber, T. "Is There Still a Chipko Aandolan?" *Pacific Affairs* 60, 1988.

White, Allen L. "Venezuela's Organic Law: Regulating Pollution in an Industrializing Country." *Environment* September 1991.

"Will Saving People Save Our Planet?" *International Wildlife* 22.3, 1992.

Witte, J. "Deforestation in Zaire: Logging and Landlessness." *The Ecologist* 22.2, 1992.

Wood, W. "Tropical Deforestation: Balancing Regional Development Demands and Global Environmental Concerns." In *Global Environmental Change*. Tokyo: United Nations University, 1990.

World Bank. *Sub-Saharan Africa: From Crisis to Sustainable Growth*. Washington, D.C.: International Bank for Reconstruction and Development, 1989.

World Bank. *The World Bank and the Environment: Annual Report*. Washington, D.C.: The Bank, 1990.

World Bank. *World Development Report*. New York: Oxford University Press, 1983.

World Bank. *World Development Report 1992: Development and the Environment*. New York: Oxford University Press, 1992.

World Commission on Environment and Development. *Our Common Future*. New York: Oxford University Press, 1987.

World Development Report 1991: The Challenge of Development. New York: Oxford University Press, 1991.

World Resources Institute. *Environmental Almanac*. Boston: Houghton Mifflin, 1992.

World Resources Institute. *World Resources 1992–1993—A Guide to the Global Environment*. Oxford: Oxford University Press, 1992.

World-Watch Reader on Global Environmental Issues, The. Brown, L., editor. New York: Norton, 1991.

Wrigley, C. C. "Population in African History." *Journal of African History* 20, 1979.

Yishai, Y. "Environment and Development: The Case of Israel." *International Journal of Environmental Studies* 14, 1979.

Young, John. "Mining the Earth." *State of the World: 1992*. Brown, L., editor. New York: Norton, 1992.

Zeitlin, Maurice, and Richard Earl Ratcliff. *Landlords and Capitalists: The Dominant Class of Chile*. Princeton: Princeton University Press, 1988.

Zhonggong Nianbao (Yearbook on Chinese Communism). Taipei, Taiwan: Zhonggong Yanjiu Zazhi She (Institute for the Study of Chinese Communist Problems), 1991.

Zijin, Wu. "The Origins of Environmental Management in China." In *Learning from China? Development and Environment in Third World Countries*. Glaeser, Bernhard, editor. London: Allen and Unwin, 1987.

Index

About the Editors and Contributors

O. P. DWIVEDI is Professor of Public and Environmental Administration, Department of Political Studies, University of Guelph, Guelph, Canada. He has been policy consultant to the governments of India, Nepal, Papua New Guinea, Mauritius, and Canada. He has authored and edited twenty books, thirteen conference proceedings, and over sixty articles in professional journals. He was president of the Canadian Political Science Association in 1986–1987 and at present is vice president of the International Association of Schools and Institutes of Administration, Brussels, Belgium.

DHIRENDRA K. VAJPEYI is Professor of Political Science at the University of Northern Iowa, Cedar Falls, Iowa. He has authored, coauthored, and edited eight books, including *Technology and Development* and *Local Government and Politics in the Third World*; further, he has contributed numerous articles in professional journals.

PITA OGABA AGBESE is Associate Professor in the Department of Political Science at the University of Northern Iowa, Cedar Falls, Iowa. He has published articles on the state and private accumulation in Nigeria and military coups in the Third World.

ROBERT BOARDMAN is Professor of Political Science and Environmental Studies, Dalhousie University, Halifax, Canada. He is author and editor of several books, most recently *Canadian Environmental Policy: Ecosystems, Politics, and Process*.

CHADWICK BENJAMIN DeWAARD is a graduate student in the Political Science Department of the University of Northern Iowa, Cedar Falls, Iowa. His studies and research have focused on international relations and comparative politics.

MARÍA EMILIA JANETTI-DÍAZ is a Professor of Public Administration and Director of the National Institute of Public Administration, Mexico City, and has written several papers and chapters on issues related to bureaucracy and administration issues of Mexico.

JOSÉ MARIO HERNÁNDEZ-QUEZADA is a public administrator who has held several positions in the Mexican government. He was recently deputy director of International Relations at the National Institute of Public Administration and is currently a political analyst for the largest political party of Mexico.

GEORGE P. JAN is Professor of Political Science, and Director of the Asian Studies Program at the University of Toledo in Toledo, Ohio. He is author and editor of ten books including *Government of Communist China, International Politics of Asia,* and *The Chinese Commune Experiment.* He has contributed numerous articles to professional journals.

RENU KHATOR is Associate Professor of Government and International Affairs at the University of South Florida, Tampa, Florida. She has authored several books including *Environment, Development and Politics in India.*

DIETER KOENIG is a Scientific Affairs Officer in the Division for Science and Technology at the United Nations Conference on Trade and Development, Geneva. Previously, he was with the United Nations University in Tokyo as Academic Officer for Environment, Science, and Technology.

JORGE NEF is Professor of Political Studies (specializing in Latin American Studies), University of Guelph, Guelph, Canada. He has published over sixty articles and several books on comparative administration, international development, and international relations. At present, he is editor of the *Canadian Journal of Latin American and Caribbean Studies.*

TIMOTHY M. SHAW is Professor of Political Science and International Development Studies, Dalhousie University, Halifax, Canada. His latest monograph is *Reformism and Revisionism in Africa's Political Economy in the 1990s: The Dialectics of Adjustment.* He is editor of the Macmillan/St. Martin's Press Series in International Political Economy, and Director of the Center for Foreign Policy Studies at Dalhousie University.

PETER J. STOETT has published articles on environmental politics and policy, and is author of a forthcoming publication, *Global Environmental Security and International Organization*. He teaches at the University of British Columbia, Vancouver, Canada.

ISBN 0-313-29397-X

90000>

EAN

9 780313 293979

HARDCOVER BAR CODE